"Many have noted the pact of such changes Chapell takes—which is so helpful. The crisis is real, as generations struggle to relate to one another, and Chapell offers a wealth of statistical information and spiritual encouragement to face the challenges of today. This book will help you and your team to navigate our cultural moment."

Ed Stetzer, dean of Talbot School of Theology

"All across the country you can see a generational crisis in our churches. Older and younger Christians often don't understand each other and their differing priorities and perspectives. In this book Bryan Chapell demonstrates remarkable breadth and depth of understanding of these issues. Even better, he sketches a way forward that will keep the church on mission during our turbulent times."

Collin Hansen, vice president of content for The Gospel Coalition;
author of Timothy Keller: His Spiritual and Intellectual Formation

"In *The Multigenerational Church Crisis*, Bryan Chapell has done two very important things: He has perceptively described the generational differences affecting how the church engages our challenging culture, and he has given us helpful warnings and guidelines for how best to navigate the moment we are facing. If evangelical church leaders would study, discuss, and apply Bryan's insights, the church would be richly blessed and also be a greater blessing."

Sandy Willson, interim president for The Gospel Coalition; pastor
emeritus at Second Presbyterian Church, Memphis, Tennessee

"As church leaders, we lament the present decline in church attendance, the continuing secularization of our culture, and the divisions among Christians that have emerged in response to these challenges. You don't have to agree with every point of Chapell's assessment and proposals to find him a helpful guide in identifying the various pressure points that have created a crisis for the evangelical church. In *The Multigenerational Church Crisis*, he aims to prepare the church to make a way for the gospel that transforms individuals and unites the church to gain a hearing in our day. That is our mission. And that is our only hope."

Juan R. Sanchez, senior pastor at High Pointe
Baptist Church, Austin, Texas

"Bryan Chapell's *The Multigenerational Church Crisis* offers timely and crucial insights for churches seeking to bridge the gap between generations. With a clear focus on fostering unity and mission, Chapell helps leaders and congregations understand the challenges of today while offering hope and strategies for nurturing faith across all ages."

Ryan Burge, author of *The Nones*

"*The Multigenerational Church Crisis* is a must-read for pastors, church leaders, and anyone seeking to navigate intergenerational challenges within the church. With a clearly hopeful tone, Chapell doesn't frame the generational divide as a problem to be fixed but rather an opportunity to speak Christ's healing, vision, and restoration to a lost and hurting world. It's an invitation not to talk across one another but to build bridges that unite believers of all ages in a shared calling to do the hard work of discipleship in a world that has forgotten God."

Andrea Minichiello Williams, chief executive at Christian Concern and Christian Legal Centre

"In this well-researched and comprehensive doctrinal manifesto, Dr. Bryan Chapell gives the church a road map to reclaiming and stewarding intergenerational faith through biblical principles. His engaging prose coupled with irrefutable evidence compels readers to enter the battlefield for the Lord clothed with knowledge and truth, shod with the gospel of peace, and encouraged by the wisdom of history. This work is pivotal for the future of the church willing to seek God's face."

Dr. Robert Smith Jr., Distinguished Professor of Divinity at Beeson Divinity School, Samford University

"For those who have followed—or been part of—American evangelicalism over the past few decades, *The Multigenerational Church Crisis* is an ambitious attempt to explain the change that is happening. Chock full of trend lines and statistics, it offers plenty of food for thought for evangelical churchgoers of any generation. Serious about the challenges but also bright with hope, Chapell's work is not only a great read individually but would spark good discussions in book clubs or Sunday school classes."

Sarah Eekhoff Zylstra, senior writer for The Gospel Coalition; coauthor of *Gospelbound*

"I have long appreciated Dr. Chapell for his theological acumen, pastoral precision, and thorough research and wisdom. In *The Multigenerational Church Crisis*, he delivers all those things to us again but with an added bonus: extraordinary timeliness. This book comes to God's people at the perfect time as we are indeed facing a multigenerational crisis in the American church. What many in the church have recently felt and experienced along generational lines, Dr. Chapell supports with clear data, statistics, and personal stories that help us embrace the challenge we face . . . but not without hope! True to fashion, he helps us see the great hope that still lies ahead for God's church as we grow in our understanding of one another and unite together around God's mission. This is a must-read for every Christian!"

Jeff Norris, senior pastor at Perimeter Church, Johns Creek, Georgia

"*The Multigenerational Church Crisis* is Bryan Chapell's pastoral rallying cry to deploy generational bridge builders dedicated to cultivating rich multigenerational discipleship cultures in their churches. Its compelling content urges us to forsake the anxiety and fear surrounding our current cultural challenges and instead to step compassionately and boldly toward the next generation in faith, clinging to God's covenant promises to build his church."

Karen Hodge, coordinator of women's ministries for the Presbyterian Church in America (PCA); author of *Transformed* and *Life-Giving Leadership*

"'Any church that does not become multigenerational dies.' This simple yet profound statement from Bryan Chapell makes this book worth our full attention. In this age where we are experiencing new challenges to the current generation embracing faith in Christ, Dr. Chapell helps us understand where the challenges are coming from. And, more importantly, he has done us a service in demonstrating how to non-anxiously move forward in hope."

Dr. Irwyn L. Ince Jr., adjunct professor of pastoral theology at Reformed Theological Seminary, Washington, DC; coordinator of PCA Mission to North America; author of *The Beautiful Community* and *Hope Ain't a Hustle*

THE MULTIGENERATIONAL CHURCH CRISIS

Why We Don't Understand Each Other
and How to Unite in Mission

BRYAN CHAPELL

BakerBooks
a division of Baker Publishing Group
Grand Rapids, Michigan

© 2025 by Bryan Chapell

Published by Baker Books
a division of Baker Publishing Group
Grand Rapids, Michigan
BakerBooks.com

Printed in the United States of America

All rights reserved. No part of this publication may be reproduced, stored in a retrieval system, or transmitted in any form or by any means—for example, electronic, photocopy, recording—without the prior written permission of the publisher. The only exception is brief quotations in printed reviews.

Library of Congress Cataloging-in-Publication Data
Names: Chapell, Bryan, author.
Title: The multigenerational church crisis : why we don't understand each other and how to unite in mission / Bryan Chapell.
Description: Grand Rapids, Michigan : Baker Books, a division of Baker Publishing Group, [2025] | Includes bibliographical references.
Identifiers: LCCN 2024036378 | ISBN 9781540904850 (paperback) | ISBN 9781540904997 (casebound) | ISBN 9781493450466 (ebook)
Subjects: LCSH: Church growth—United States. | Church renewal—United States. | Christian leadership—United States. | Pastoral theology—United States.
Classification: LCC BV652.25 .C46 2025 | DDC 262.001/7—dc23/eng/20241115
LC record available at https://lccn.loc.gov/2024036378

Scripture quotations are from The Holy Bible, English Standard Version® (ESV®). Copyright © 2001 by Crossway, a publishing ministry of Good News Publishers. Used by permission. All rights reserved. ESV Text Edition: 2016

Italics added to direct Bible quotations reflect the author's emphasis.

Cover design by Greg Jackson.

Baker Publishing Group publications use paper produced from sustainable forestry practices and postconsumer waste whenever possible.

25 26 27 28 29 30 31   7 6 5 4 3 2 1

*To the children and grandchildren
of Bryan and Kathy Chapell,
the generations we celebrate by
God's blessing and for Christ's sake*

CONTENTS

Organizations, Studies, Reports, and Surveys Consulted 11

Introduction: Celebrating the Faith of Generations 15

1. Our Generational Challenges: *Loss of Truth and Youth* 25
2. Our Church Challenges: *Loss of the Mature* 41
3. Our Cultural Challenges: *Loss of a Majority* 55
4. The Mature Uniform 73
5. The Minority Mission 93
6. The Zeal of Loss 113
7. Hope for the Future: *Leveraging Gospel Opportunities* 133
8. Hope for the Nations 157

Questions for Review and Discussion 169

Notes 177

ORGANIZATIONS, STUDIES, REPORTS, AND SURVEYS CONSULTED

The following is a list of research organizations, studies, reports, and surveys consulted for this book. Lest readers become lost in the blizzard of statistics that many formal reports or primary surveys necessarily contain, please note that the author also frequently cites those who analyze or synthesize the material in these sources.

AddictionHelp.com
Addictions.com
American Enterprise Institute
American Gaming Institute
American Religious Benchmark Survey
The Apollos Project
Autism Research Institute
Baylor Religion Survey
Bowling Green State University National Center for Family & Marriage Research
Bureau of Economic Analysis
The Catholic World Report
The Census of Religious Bodies (conducted every ten years, 1906–1946)

Centers for Disease Control and Prevention

Church Answers Research

ChurchTrac

Cooperative Election Study (formerly the Cooperative Congressional Election Study)

Covenant Eyes

Drug Enforcement Administration

Faith Communities Today (FACT) series of national surveys by Hartford Institute for Religion Research

Focus on the Family

Fuller Youth Institute

Gallup, Inc.

General Social Survey

George Barna and the Barna Group

Graphs About Religion by Ryan Burge

Grey Matter Research & Consulting

Incarceration Statistics of the Vera Institute of Justice

Institute for Family Studies

Lausanne Global Analysis

Lausanne Movement, *State of the Great Commission: Report Prepared for Lausanne Global Congress Seoul 2024* (available as a free pdf download at https://lausanne.org/report)

Lifeway Research

Ligonier Ministries

Massachusetts Uniform Citation Data Analysis Report

National Center for Family and Marriage

National Center for Health Statistics' National Vital Statistics System

National Congregations Study

National Study of Youth and Religion, University of Notre Dame (funded by Lilly Endowment Inc.)

Office of the US Surgeon General

Organizations, Studies, Reports, and Surveys Consulted

Peter G. Peterson Foundation
Pew Research Center
Public Religion Research Institute
"Religious Landscape Study" of the Pew Research Center
SermonSearch.com
Statista
Survey Center on American Life
US Census Bureau
US Centers for Disease Control and Prevention
US Religion Census: Religious Congregations & Membership Study

INTRODUCTION

Celebrating the Faith of Generations

Multigenerational Faith

On a New Year's Day, our adult daughter posted the following thoughts on her social media page:

> Today, release last year to God with a thankful heart of worship. Dedicate the coming year into his hands and prayerfully place all of your desires and needs for this New Year underneath His Lordship. He will never fail you.

I don't think all the words are original to her, but the source is not as important to me as the content. The words express our daughter's desire to embrace and share the faith of her parents. No one forced her to post these words. Our daughter now lives far from us and has her own family and friends that are much more present than our influence.

So, when she posts her faith to share it with others, dear biblical truths burst upon our hearts like New Year's Eve fireworks. We first feel the echoes of gratitude expressed long ago by the apostle John: "I have no greater joy than to hear that my children are walking in the truth" (3 John 1:4). When faith becomes intergenerational, there is profound joy and thanksgiving in the church—and in the hearts of Christian parents. With the spiritual opposition of our world so intense and growing (as we shall see later in this book), we know there are no guarantees that our faith will be our children's. We give thanks to God for claiming our children from the evils of the world and the threats of hell.

The gratitude that swells our hearts also humbles us. We remember with tears our many faults and shortcomings as Christian parents. The imperfections of our parenting force us to confess that our children's faith is not simply the product of our merits. So, we celebrate the work that God has done through the church to supplement and repair our efforts.

When our children were small and we were learning what it meant to raise eternal souls in little bodies to love Jesus, we needed the experience and wisdom of other Christian parents. We had little understanding of how precious, powerful, and necessary the care and example of so many others in the church would be. As new parents, we went from times of certainty that we would never repeat our parents' errors to days of doubting that we should be trusted to raise pets, much less children. We and our children needed the collective wisdom and love of our church family.

In the church, we were blessed to have peer parents who shared our doubts about our capabilities, more seasoned parents with boots-on-the-ground and diapers-in-the-hamper experience to advise and console us, and spiritual grandparents who gave unconditional love to the children we were sometimes too frazzled to discipline or hug. The Lord worked beyond our innocence, ignorance, and exhaustion through the many days and ways those in the church showered our children with attentive love, examples of faith, and caring discipline that built memories for a lifetime and faith for eternity.

Years later, I would find the studies that confirm how caring adults in the church help instill faith in children that is likely to last the rest of their lives. I will share some of these studies later in this book. But when our children were small, we simply experienced the blessing of others' faithfulness and love. We did not fully understand then how powerful and needed these influences in our children's hearts would be.

In their preschool and elementary school years, God worked beyond our distractions, frustrations, and ambitions by using the example of others to teach us the formative routines of family and faith. No one had to teach us to cheer at soccer games or to endure music recitals, but we did need to learn how to pray as a family at mealtimes, bedtimes, and before travel.

We learned to make memories and form faith beyond church walls by following the patterns of Christian parents who loved family hikes, fishing trips, and frequent hugs.

Through peers and older parents, we learned the books and videos that helped to teach biblical truths at reading times, mealtimes, and family events. When we saw others' children memorizing Scripture and catechisms, we realized that it was possible and even fun for our children—as long as our pride was not what drove their absorption of God's Word and truth.

Sometimes those who made us better parents were older parents and sometimes they were peers. The peers were going through the consternations and questions of child-rearing with us. Through them, we learned that we weren't strange or alone or dumb because we had similar struggles. The older parents were sometimes our cheerleaders, sometimes our guides, and sometimes our cautionary tales. Some we learned to follow, and others—without always intending it—became our brake signals or detour signs.

We were also blessed by spiritual and teaching professionals in the church who knew how different children have different ways of maturing, different patterns of learning, and different stages of understanding. We learned through some humbling experiences that children are not just adults in little bodies. When we tried to discipline all our children the same way, despite their differences in personality, learning style, or activity level, church elders and educational professionals steered us beyond the child-rearing patterns of our own parents. Sometimes we were amazed at how people as smart as we thought we were could be so slow to understand or adapt to each individual child's spiritual needs. The church helped us without blaming us—or at least without the spiritually mature blaming us.

The help that we needed from the church in our children's earliest years was only increased in their teen years. Then we had to learn, as do all parents, that the children who worshiped our fire-making skills on family camping trips can become the adolescents convinced that we are totally ignorant about high school trauma and that for some reason we are determined to embarrass them in front of their friends.

In those years when parental credibility erodes and peer approval controls, we learned to treasure Sunday school teachers, youth leaders, and

Introduction

adult volunteers who lived for Jesus and loved our children. We worked hard to surround our teens with adult Christians they admired during the normal (yet painful) processes of separating from parents in order to prepare for adulthood.

To keep our teens near and safe, we opened our lovely home to the ravaging antics and activities of our children's peers and teams. We also leaned on Christian parents who were consistent in their discipline and insistent on practices that would ensure our children's physical and spiritual safety in their homes. Too often, we discovered, there were adults so dependent upon their children's approval, that the parents were willing to compromise their own children's safety or souls to get it. So, when we found Christian parents in our church who would join us in unpopular decisions about church attendance or what was available at parties, appropriate for social media, allowed at concerts, or acceptable in clothing, we supported those parents and arranged activities with them.

We included Christian teachers and leaders that our children respected in our family activities. We encouraged our children to play sports, practice music, hike, camp, and socialize with peers, parents, grandparents, preachers, teachers, neighbors, and friends who loved Jesus. The reason was not so much that we believed "it takes a village" to raise a child; we believed that it takes a church.

This belief was driven not by Christian prejudice or the church version of helicopter parenting but by instruction in Scripture about how God works to preserve his church and transfer Christ's love from one generation to the next. Understanding of Scripture's patterns is important not only so that we will recruit peers, parents, and preachers to the cause of our children's spiritual nurture, but so that we will depend upon the designs of the Holy Spirit that work beyond our wisdom and weaknesses to create multiple generations of faith.

Multigenerational Mission

The reason that churches ought to celebrate faith that passes from one generation to the next should be obvious: Any church that does not become multigenerational dies. God requires churches to honor the contributions of legacy generations and to care for the needs of the present generation, but his Word also instructs us to "tell to the coming generation the glorious deeds of the Lord" (Ps. 78:4). Disregarding the needs, contexts, and pressures of future generations is ultimately to sign the death warrant of a church. Monogenerational churches die with the generation that dominates them. This book is designed to help churches fulfill their biblical responsibilities to each generation so that churches maintain faithfulness for many generations.

We do not need to guess how churches become multigenerational. The Bible carefully describes the patterns and practices that maintain the mission of God across generations. The principles are repeated in many passages. One key text is the first chapter of 2 Timothy, where the aging apostle Paul addresses what is probably the last letter of his ministry on earth to a young pastor named Timothy. How will Paul pass the baton of faith to a younger man?

The apostle begins his instruction by identifying himself as the spiritual father of Timothy. He addresses Timothy as "my beloved child" (2 Tim. 1:2), and in doing so identifies his care with that of "God the Father" from whom we learn in this same verse come "grace, mercy, and peace." Though he is not Timothy's biological father, Paul uses fathering language to describe his spiritual responsibility to a young leader of the next generation in the church.

Paul's cross-generational care is not a new feature of church life. In this same passage, he says his own service to God is built on the foundation of the faithfulness of his "ancestors" (v. 3). Faith has been passed to him by other spiritual fathers in the ancient family of faith. In passing the principles of faith to Timothy, the apostle is following a pattern established long before either of these servants of God was in the church.

Paul recognizes, however, that he is not solely responsible for nurturing the faith of Timothy—and that fathers are not the only ones responsible for spiritual parenting. He reminds Timothy that the faith that now dwells in the young pastor "dwelt first in your grandmother Lois and your mother Eunice and now, I am sure, dwells in you as well" (v. 5). Multiple generations of mothers have passed the message of God's care to this child who now prepares future generations to honor the Lord.

Introduction

Many generations, genders, and leaders contribute to the multigenerational mission and ministry of the church. So, in this passage, Paul also encourages Timothy "to fan into flame the gift of God, which is in you through the laying on of my hands" (v. 6). That "gift of God" was the enabling of Timothy to pastor his church. The gift was confirmed by the church as hands were laid on Timothy to commission him for this ministry. But Paul's hands were not the only ones laid on Timothy. We learn from Paul's earlier letter to Timothy that the older apostle was only one of a "council of elders" that laid hands on the young man to set him apart for the church's leadership (1 Tim. 4:14).

There is a picture being drawn through the pattern of intergenerational faith detailed by the apostle in these letters. The picture is one of human figures and families being coordinated with instruction from God's Word and the power of the Holy Spirit (2 Tim. 1:13–14) to create a church that will remain faithful to God's purposes for many generations. The implied caption under that picture is clear: The continuous health of the church requires celebration of all generations for the preservation and propagation of the gospel.

No single generation can do all the work of the church. For the church to remain strong and for the witness of Christ to remain powerful, each generation must consider what is necessary to pass faith to the next one. This is not always easy. Generational contexts, cultures, and preferences change. Unless a church makes the nurture of the next generation a high priority of its mission, the preferences and priorities of the dominant generation will limit that church's witness to the lifespan of those presently in charge.

For churches to continue to participate in the mission of the gospel that has been Christ's priority since his Great Commission, we must seek to understand the peculiar pressures, differences, and contributions of each generation. The goal of this book is to help different generations grasp why they may have trouble understanding each other, and at the same time to help them treasure and steward the contribution each can make to Christ's mission in their particular time and context.

When we learn enough about one another that we can celebrate the generations, then we will rejoice in the gifts God gives to each so that the gospel of Jesus Christ can be spread by all believers in all times and contexts. I know the joy of such intergenerational influences because of the care others have taken to contribute to my own life and ministry. In the account that follows, I rejoice to tell about a man of such influence, and I do so with the prayer that this book will equip many such spiritual fathers and mothers for the multigenerational ministry Christ himself supports and celebrates.

Multigenerational Influence

Gene Mintz will have a forever impact on my life. When I was a shrimp of a third grader, this mountain of a man, whose hand could have enveloped about ten of mine, closed his heart around my life. At the time, I did not know that my family would be one that pastors talk about behind closed doors as "troubled."

My father was a lay minister, responsible for preaching on a three-state circuit of minuscule, one-room churches in an equally minuscule Baptist association. No church in the association had a sufficient number of people, or a sufficiently available preacher, to justify weekly services. So, each church met once a month, allowing my father (who daily worked as a farm manager) to preach to his far-flung flocks as regularly as his long drives would allow.

So that our family would have a stable church experience, the children and my mother attended a local independent church while my father made his circuit. As a child, it all seemed normal, but I learned in my adolescence that the reason for the pattern was more than church consistency for the children. My mother and father had significant problems that presented themselves as denominational differences, but these were only the visible symptoms of deeper marital struggles. My father going his way to church and my mother going her way with the kids was their way of keeping the peace—most of the time.

Gene Mintz inserted himself into my life without invitation and without ever hinting that he was aware of the way our family foundations were shaking. He was simply a mountain of calm and tenderness for a child who did not know that the occasional upheavals in my family were the early signs of deep relational fissures—cracks in a marriage that were already apparent to pastors and would eventually become the earthquake reality that would shake my life and faith.

Introduction

All I knew, as a third grader in his Sunday school class, was that this huge man was kind to me. He asked me questions about what I was reading; he commended my answers and encouraged my love of books; and he asked me how I was growing spiritually.

Even after I left that class, when I would pass Mr. Mintz and his wife, Betty, in the hallways of the large church my mother attended with her children, he would always stop, bend to me, extend that gigantic hand of his, and greet me: "Bryan, how are you doing? How is your walk with the Lord? I am praying for you."

He continued to greet me that way long after I was out of his class—no longer his official responsibility. Several years later, after more numerous hallway greetings from Mr. Mintz than I can recall, my family moved away from that town and church. My father's company transferred him. He continued to drive to his circuit of churches, but my mother gathered us children in another church in the new town as her relationship with my father continued to crumble.

While I was out of the sight of Gene Mintz, I was not out of his mind— nor far from his heart. Though I was no longer his responsibility nor in his region, he would write me during my high school years: "Bryan, how are you doing? How is your walk with the Lord? I am praying for you."

When I went to college, the letters slowed down, but still—maybe once a year—the letter would come: "Bryan, how are you doing? How is your walk with the Lord? I am praying for you."

When I entered seminary, another letter: "Bryan, how are you doing? How is your walk with the Lord? I am praying for you."

And when, after years of pastoring, I eventually became the president of that same seminary, another letter: "Bryan, how are you doing? How is your walk with the Lord? Betty and I have been praying for you all of these years."

There came a day when I learned that time and age had claimed the life of Mr. Mintz, the mountain of a man in my life who had so often reached toward heaven on my behalf. The ministry for which he had prayed had taken me temporarily out of the country, so I could only write to those who gathered to memorialize the one who had so faithfully shepherded my soul.

Introduction

I wrote this:

One day in heaven I believe that I will have the privilege of seeing how much Mr. Mintz's outstretched hand really held me in God's plan, and how much his heart taught me of God's heart, and how much his prayers strengthened me for God's calling. But, until that day, I simply have the privilege of telling you that there was a man named Mr. Gene Mintz who befriended a child named Bryan, by greeting him, writing him, and praying for him for many years.

There have been more able scholars and more powerful preachers along my course, but no one has been more influential for my eternity than the man who really taught me, "The effectual, fervent prayer of a righteous man availeth much" (James 5:16 KJV). Thank you for so teaching me this truth, Mr. Mintz, and thank you, Jesus, for Mr. Mintz.

1

OUR GENERATIONAL CHALLENGES

Loss of Truth and Youth

Any church that aspires to become multigenerational must face contemporary cultural realities that make faith commitments particularly difficult for our children. A general decline in the faith commitments of adult Americans combined with the temptations of youth culture create pressures for young people that are unlike—and more intense than—anything their parents and grandparents faced. Without understanding these realities and sympathizing with the generation that must deal with them, any church will have little hope of becoming multigenerational.

Loss of Truth

Understanding

Educational approaches of the last fifty years have created a consensus in Western culture that makes it exceedingly difficult for young people to accept a worldview governed by Scripture. The perspective that dominates virtually every field of study involving art, history, literature, and philosophy is that there is no transcendent truth that should or can guide our thoughts, values, and practices.

Writers, philosophers, religious leaders, educators, and pop culture influencers concur that all truth is relative. All propositions must be tentative; all values need to be contextualized and seen as subject to the changing moral standards of the dominant culture. As a consequence, presidents of our nation's leading colleges have recently testified before Congress that they are uncertain if their institutions' policies make it wrong to advocate Jewish genocide.[1] Writer, missionary, and musician Ben Pierce well characterizes the effects of our uncertainty consensus upon university culture:

> There is one thing a professor can be absolutely certain of: almost every student entering the university believes, or says he believes, that truth is relative. If this belief is put to the test, one can count on the students' reaction—they will be uncomprehending. That anyone should regard the proposition as not self-evident astonishes them, as though he were calling into question 2+2=4.[2]

The notion that there are truth principles for morals and values that transcend time and culture because they are given by God is viewed as not only out-of-date but also ignorant and bigoted. In the place of transcendent truth (once characterized by Christian philosopher Francis Schaeffer with a capital *T*) that should govern all morals and ethics, our society tends only to recognize the validity of personal truth (lowercase *t*) to guide one's individual choices. The movement from a capital-T to a lowercase-t consensus in Western culture in the late twentieth century was directly contrary to the ideals of previous centuries. Previous claims to truth that were "self-evident" were formed on the presumption that science, faith, natural law, or some combination of them could establish universal truths for human conduct that would provide for the common good of "life, liberty, and the pursuit of happiness."

Now the "Oprah ethic" of needing to speak "your truth" is presumed to be not only a mark of courage but a necessity resulting from the recognition that there is no other standard that makes sense because there is no other truth that can have universal application or shared meaning. The radical relativism of our day argues that the only truth on which anyone can operate is that which is derived from their own experience.

For example, if my only experience with cats is my spotted tabby, and your only experience with cats is your yellow Persian, then—even though we are using the same word "cat" to describe our pets—we are thinking of different meanings. So, modern philosophies conclude that our experience governs the definitions that we give to our terms. Consequently, conventions of language and science do not override the effects of personal experiences that are the only way we can give meaning to the truths we express.

Communication theorists say that we may come close to shared understanding to the extent that we share experiences, but they argue that because no two life experiences are the same, there is never a totally shared understanding of the truths that we express. So, truth remains personal, fluid, and evolving.

In fact, according to modern educators, it would not matter if there were a transcendent truth given by God, or any other authority, to guide our lives because meaning can only be assigned to any concept through personal experience that is constantly changing. Just as a person cannot put their foot in the same stream twice, so also the meaning of words—even for the individual using them—is changing as life progresses and one's experiences widen or narrow the understanding behind one's terms. So, since truths can only be known and expressed by terms whose meanings are always changing according to the advancing days and events of each life's experience, truth is ever-changing and indeterminate, with final meaning always deferred and never certain.

Celebrating

Such logic is difficult to refute except by the lives we actually must live—and Scripture's own claims. Real life does not allow the impossibility of Truth, except in the ivory towers of academic sophistication or the darkest corridors of morality vacuums. The engineer still requires a math that works and the mother still knows the meaning of a child's cry. If there were no absolute truths to guide us, then there would be no building safe to enter and no child safe from abuse. As much as people may choose to follow the logic of experiential relativism, few consistently live by its principles. To do so would be to live in a world where no horror could be defined or outlawed.

Knowing that the core temptation of humanity is always to make an idol of its own judgment, the Bible gives us a clear counter to the claim that transcendent truth can neither be expressed or known. Anticipating the modern philosophies that deny the possibility of knowing God's truth, the apostle Paul wrote against such sophisticated denials in his own age:

> The natural person does not accept the things of the Spirit of God, for they are folly to him, and he is not able to understand them because they are spiritually discerned. The spiritual person judges all things, but is himself to be judged by no one. "For who has understood the mind of the Lord so as to instruct him?" But we have the mind of Christ. (1 Cor. 2:14–16)

Paul first agrees that God's truth cannot be known by persons who only have natural capacities to understand his ways. So, the modern relativists may be ready to start their victory dance. Even an apostle seems to concede that the things of the Spirit of God (even if they are transcendent truths) cannot be understood through ordinary experience. But Paul does not end his argument there. He goes on to say that "the things of the Spirit of God . . . are spiritually discerned."

We *can* know and understand the transcendent truths of God because the same Spirit that gave those truths in God's Word (2 Pet. 1:21) now indwells us to receive and explain God's Word to our hearts and minds (Rom. 8:5–9). We are not limited to personal experience to discern the truths of God. We have spiritual discernment because the Holy Spirit opens the eyes of our hearts to the meanings that he intends (Eph. 1:18).

The result is that we are not limited to the experiences of our flesh to know transcendent truth. We have God's Spirit within us to interpret and apply God's Word so that we are operating with "the mind of Christ." Residual effects of the fall and our own sin bar us from perfect understanding and behavior, but Scripture and the Spirit allow us to celebrate that we can know God's will and conduct our lives according to the standards of his truth.

Responding

Bible-believing Christians may readily affirm these statements about our ability to know transcendent truth and still not recognize how much we have all been affected by the relativism of our age. Who has not faced someone in the church with a different theological point of view or an immoral lifestyle choice who denied the need for correction with a reflexive, "That's just your interpretation." The assumption is that no one has special access to God's mind. We are presumed only to have our personal interpretations to determine how God wants us to apply his truths.

Our relativistic tendencies do not only apply to theological matters. As much as devout Christians may deny the validity of the idea that no one can know transcendent truth and we should only trust our personal experience, we tend to live quite differently. We often act as though we trust no one to have transcendent truth.

Want proof? Ask yourself whether it is biblical to wear masks during a pandemic or to host church services when a secular governor issues health standards that limit them. Is climate change real? Should COVID vaccines be taken? Should Christian children be homeschooled or go to public schools or classical schools or Christian schools?

In our present realities, we trust almost no authority but our own to determine what is true or what we should do.[3] We do not trust science because it is supposedly "in the pocket" of whoever is paying for the research. Many do not trust medical professionals because of claims that they are the puppets of "Big Pharma." Others do not trust the business community because it is driven by profits. Huge swaths of society do not trust the law, assuming it is controlled by whoever has the most power. More and more people do not trust government officials because so many of them appear to govern by political pragmatics rather than by principled leadership. And, as the conflicts in our churches proved during the COVID pandemic, we do not necessarily trust church leaders when they make decisions that don't align with what we think is right.[4]

We may give the pastor his thirty minutes of say on Sunday, but we actually form our perspectives based on whatever news channel or internet commentators we consume for many more hours each week.[5] Very often the basis for choices and conduct even among Christians is our own personal truth (t) informed by any number of personal choices because we presume there is no applicable transcendent truth (T).

The consequence of living in a culture where almost everyone believes personal truth should determine personal values and conduct is that there is little patience for anyone or anything that seems to limit personal freedoms.

In particular, there is disdain for any church that claims it knows what biblical truths should govern all persons in matters regarding marriage, sex, gender, and choice. Morals once considered traditional and universal are now considered both outdated and intolerant. Churches that insist upon them are seen as not just obsolete but bigoted and hateful.[6]

Al Mohler, long-term Southern Baptist Theological Seminary president, says that traditional Christian values have made us the new "moral outlaws" in an anything-goes society where love means never having to say "no."[7] The impact upon the church is staggering. As Jim Davis and Michael Graham report in their much-cited book *The Great Dechurching*, "In the last twenty-five years . . . about 40 million people have stopped attending church. More people have left the church in the last twenty-five years than all the new people who became Christians from the First Great Awakening, Second Great Awakening, and Billy Graham crusades *combined*."[8]

All of these truth realities indicate how critical it is for our churches' future that contemporary church leaders recognize that no group has been more challenged by the consequences of this dechurching than our young people. If we do not address their plight and pressures, there is little hope that our churches will experience multigenerational health.

Loss of Youth

Understanding

Church leaders today regularly recite the assessment of the Lifeway Research organization that two-thirds of young people will cease attending church regularly after high school.[9] About one-third of these (31 percent) will return when they have children of their own, but the majority will remain disconnected from regular church involvement.[10]

Quantifying these assessments among different faith communities is extremely difficult and can be affected by the organizational or political perspectives of those measuring. Still, a clear picture is emerging. Echoing the Lifeway study cited above, the Barna Group indicated more than a decade ago that three out of five young people (60 percent) disconnect from the church for an extended time.[11] A much older Barna study more disturbingly reported, "Only one-fifth of twentysomethings (20%) have maintained a level of spiritual activity consistent with their high school experiences."[12]

Researcher Ryan Burge believes that the disconnect is not as complete as some earlier studies suggest—that given enough time more may come back or maintain basic Christian values.[13] Still, it is undeniable that the trend lines are discouraging. Only 31 percent of Americans now *say* they attend services weekly or nearly weekly, but 67 percent reported they attended weekly when they were growing up.[14] Current trend lines for high school seniors show that the percentage never attending religious services is roughly three times what it was in 1976, and those rarely or never attending now comprise almost two-thirds of the total.[15]

In 1975 only about 8 percent of America's young adults (ages 18–34) claimed no religious affiliation. By 2021, research based on the General Social Survey indicates those entirely unaffiliated with any religion were approximately 42 percent of this same youth contingent.[16] Relating these statistics to those in the immediately preceding and following paragraphs means that young adults with no religious affiliation now total almost a third more than those active in any religion, and they outnumber their actively involved Evangelical church peers by more than four to one.

Gallup indicates a third of Gen Z and Millennials (those in their teens to early forties) have no religious affiliation,[17] and less than 20 percent of those ages 18–25 regularly attend religious services of any sort.[18] Factoring this reality with the awareness that Evangelicals are less than a third of the overall American population means that faithful (i.e., regularly attending church) Evangelical youth probably total no more than 7 percent of their peers—and, as we will soon see, that estimate is far too high based on the experience of many.[19]

Subsequent studies have attributed youth disenchantment with our churches to the convergence of a number of factors, including:

- Reaction to the Evangelical courting/coalescing of conservative politics[20]
- The destructive influences of social media on young psyches[21]
- The materialistic nominalism of many Christian parents

- The drivenness of some "helicopter parents" whose egos (or fears) demand the success or control of their children[22]
- The moral erosion of the American landscape influenced by Mainline churches (that is, Protestant denominations that are theologically/politically liberal) and post-Catholic urban centers
- Clergy sex scandals
- Liberal university philosophies moving steadily downward into childhood education
- Church hypocrisy, racism, intolerance regarding sexuality and gender, along with the perceived irrelevance of church teaching
- Combinations of all of the above integrated with a young person's personal experience[23]

The COVID-19 pandemic clearly accelerated the exodus of young people from the church. While most adult Americans reported no difference in their church attendance prior to and after COVID, one-third of those ages 18–29 who were attending church have now stopped entirely.[24] In contrast, the attendance rate of seniors (age 65 and older) was only slightly different before and after the pandemic.[25] COVID cannot take all of the blame. Those with more comprehensive perspectives recognize that neither COVID nor imperfect parenting could account for the immensity of the challenges to faith that our children and grandchildren are facing. Why have so many of them not seen faith as comfort or strength for the challenges of a dangerous and depressing world?

Stephen Bullivant, a Roman Catholic theologian and sociologist, sees the accelerating religious discontent as the fallout of key developments around the end of the twentieth century. In his book *Nonverts* he writes, "The most dramatic historical examples of religious growth or decline tend to occur over many generations," but in the United States something gave way in our religiosity in the early 2000s.[26] He identifies the accelerants of religious change as the fallout of Cold War perspectives, 9/11 uncertainties, and the internet.[27]

Bullivant thinks these three factors, combined with the cultural tumult of the 1960s and '70s, opened up a nonreligious space in the American consciousness. This gap in the application or appreciation of religion was later supported and normalized (or made socially acceptable) by the secular media's celebration of a New Atheism ably represented and popularized by spokespeople such as Sam Harris, Richard Dawkins, and Christopher Hitchens.

Bullivant reasons that this nonreligious space allowed people—and especially young people who were not habituated to religious norms—to consider matters of divorce, abortion, women's roles, sexual mores, and a host of other social, familial, or justice issues without church guidance. The result is subsequent generations that do not see the church as necessary or right in addressing issues of human dignity, justice, or sexuality.[28]

We may debate whether Bullivant's selection of recent causes adequately explains how noncommitment to church reached a tipping point among America's youth at and since the century's turn. Some have argued that the seeds of our present religious quandaries are rooted in a myriad of other factors that converged to reach critical mass after World War II, including the malleable Deism of America's founders failing to provide social stability or personal comfort in the face of multiple wars and a Great Depression; the profound reverberations of Darwin and Freud; the corrosive influences of liberal theologies and secular philosophies; industrial affluence untethering the necessity of traditional faith in Western culture; the World War II insertion of women into the workplace; the development of the Pill; and the transportation, technology, and information revolutions that have collapsed boundaries of nations, cultures, and privacy.[29]

Celebrating

Whatever the explanations, including the compromises of the church itself, it's unquestionable that the status of faith in our culture has changed rapidly for our nation's youth. Few persons over age fifty can truly fathom the pressures that children and teens daily face in seeking to live for Christ.[30] Faithful youth in today's culture should be the heroes of the modern American church and deserve to be celebrated. They are sailing upwind against secularizing influences and moral confusion such as their parents and grandparents did not face and could not have imagined at their age.

As a multidecade leader of an institution training church leaders, I would echo the claim of many that our secularizing society increasingly affects the biblical knowledge and Christian lives of rising generations. At the same time, I would argue that these young people who have committed themselves to Christian leadership, and those who join them in worship, are the best evangelists Americans have known for many generations. Yes, they often experience the relational and sexual challenges of coming from fractured families. And, yes, it is true that they must be trained to recognize and resist the influences of secular education and pop culture in which they have been immersed since childhood.

Still, by being surrounded all their lives by a majority of friends and family who are not Christian or are nominally Christian, young people who are committed followers of Jesus have become immune to previous generations' reticence or fears about sharing their faith. Unlike the many Christian leaders of my generation who would be put off by the entertainments, language, and lifestyles of those we were supposed to be evangelizing, our children have been unable to function at school or work without befriending those who do not share their values or habits. As a consequence, our young adults are more ready and able to invite unbelieving friends to conversations about Jesus than their parents or grandparents ever were.

Our faithful children are typically turned off by canned evangelism methods in this age of "authenticity," but they don't have to be coaxed, prodded, or guilted into relationships that enable them to tell others about Jesus. To honor their Savior, they have made heroic choices to live contrary to the values of their culture, and actually desire to let others they genuinely care about know why.

Almost all of our children have faced the dilemma of diving into social media to medicate feeling misfit and alone only to experience increased isolation as a consequence.[31] None are better equipped to explain what a difference Jesus can make to friends who are dealing with loneliness, depression, self-harm, and suicidal thoughts in unprecedented numbers.[32] And no generation has been more willing to offer such care to non-Christian friends, family, and neighbors in the ordinary courses of work and play. Such care has remarkable potential for the revival of faith that we desire for our culture because the majority of young people from a variety of faiths, or no formal faith, still report that they are grateful for connections with the sacred aspects of life.[33]

Responding

Failure to recognize the faith challenges and spiritual potential of our youth has too often led those responsible for their spiritual nurture to look past the ordinary practices that have powerful spiritual impact in young lives. Virtually all studies of what makes faith last a lifetime ("sticky faith" in the current vernacular) prioritize parental care and example.[34]

Models of Hope

Church youth programs are great, and Christian teachers, coaches, and peers are invaluable, but nothing more powerfully engenders lifetime faithfulness than consistent and caring Christian parenting. Parents instill the faith they model. While studies previously cited indicate that as many as two-thirds of young people will leave the church after high school (at least for a time), these figures are based upon those who *call* themselves "Christian," not necessarily upon those who have been raised in homes where life patterns and relationships consistently honor Christ. The children of such homes are twice as likely to retain their parents' faith as those with contradictory or insincere parental examples.[35]

The truth that counters despair over the large exodus of youth is the fact that the vast majority (60 to 87 percent, depending on the study) of children continue to embrace their parents' faith, if their parents live it.[36] Such parental faithfulness is not simply about insisting on our children's good behavior (requiring children to put on their "Jesus Jacket" with its crushing restrictions and expectations). Instead, parents exert their greatest influence on their children's future faith when demonstrating a loving and trusting relationship with Christ that is reflected in gracious attitudes and biblically consistent actions toward those in and outside the home.[37]

When such attitudes and actions are reinforced by models of faith in church and school, then the likelihood of instilling lifetime faith in children soars even higher—even into the 90 percent range.[38] Of course, there are no guarantees, but when home and church partner in providing models of sincere faith (among adults and peers), then it is more than fair to say that two-thirds of the children of such backgrounds do not leave the church after high school; rather, at least two-thirds remain engaged.

These observations and studies affirm that nothing nurtures lifetime faith more than simple, non-heroic, non-legalistic, but consistent Christian practices in everyday family life.[39] These include:

- Prayer—at meals, bedtimes, and family events
- Family worship—regularly reading Scripture or Bible stories at meals and bedtimes, joyfully memorizing verses or catechisms, and singing age-appropriate songs together
- Loving discipline with regular praise
- Forgiveness of wrong and repentance for wrongs
- Sacrifice for the sake of one another
- Generosity toward the needy inside and outside the home
- Prioritizing church worship and relationships
- Making decisions for schooling that prioritize faith more than success
- An involved mother of sincere faith
- A believing father who has strong relationships with his children (true for both sons and daughters)
- And, most especially, a loving relationship between a mom and dad[40]

The old cliché has never been more true: The best gift you can give your child is to love your spouse. Nothing more promotes a child's sense of security and love with the ability to navigate relationships in both childhood and adulthood than the example and experience of Christian parents loving one another through hurts, decisions, and trials.

I know that I cannot keep the prior few paragraphs from sounding like a sermon or insist strongly enough that these are *not* magic methods that will ward off all family ills. Persons who approach prayer, Bible reading, and church attendance as ritualistic bribes to stay on God's nice side or to keep their children in control will almost inevitably become legalistic Pharisees. Children of such parenting will tend to flee the faith as soon as they are able—or, worse, may inflict the same painful strictures on their own children.

My best way to encourage both grace and consistency is to encourage parental conscientiousness through citing the studies of what creates sticky faith.[41] These are wonderful and encouraging reminders of the biblical truth: "Train up a child in the way he should go; even when he is old he will not depart from it" (Prov. 22:6). We need to remember, however, that these words are a proverb of what tends to be true, not God's promise of what will always result. No parenting is so perfect or determinative that children will never wander or make mistakes (Luke 15:11–32). God does not guarantee perfect children to faithful parents. He also leaves no mystery as to the most effective tools for nurturing the faith of a child who must ultimately make his or her own commitment to Christ.

Parents are ordinarily the most important provision of God for shaping the soul commitments of children.[42] Sociologist Christian Smith writes, "All the empirical data tells us that for intergenerational religious transmission today, the key agents are parents. Not clergy or other religious professionals . . . not programs, preaching, or formal rites of passage."[43] Parents cannot outsource the spiritual nurture of their children without putting them in spiritual jeopardy.[44]

Partners in Hope

In addition to the influence of parents, studies that have sought to discover the source of lifelong faith have made two key discoveries that can aid parental care and decision-making: (1) the faith that children hold between ages 14 and 18 is the faith that will usually shape their thinking for the rest of their lives; and (2) if five adults in the church significantly invest in a child between ages 15 and 18, that child is likely to remain loyal to the faith of those adults through life.[45]

Even if only one adult outside the family gives care and attention to a teen in church settings, then that influence is likely to have a significant effect on that young person's lifetime faith.[46] This means that teens (at the ages their parents may seem to have the least credibility) need to rub shoulders with believers of all ages. Good parenting includes involving our children in communities of faith with extended family (especially grandparents), friends, and trusted exemplars.[47]

The significance of such interactions is underscored by surveys indicating that nearly 70 percent of those ages 13–25 say they have three or fewer meaningful interactions per day with anyone. Nearly 40 percent say they feel they have no one to talk to and that no one really knows them.[48] This includes a large proportion of young people who say they are Christians but have no one in the church who relates to them.[49]

Such reports indicate how important are those in the church who give of themselves to act as parent or grandparent figures for young people. My experience also teaches that teens are often most profoundly influenced by role models a half generation older (reflecting similar mentor dynamics in sports, arts, and the business world).[50] Parents who team with young adults in the church that their children respect (especially in teen years) are employing powerful instruments for present guidance and lifetime faith.

Patterns of Hope

Yet, though the late teen years are typically the most influential in determining the faith that will stick for a lifetime, these are the very years when parents often de-emphasize youth involvement in church. While it is true that two-thirds of young people will leave church after high school, many will have left prior to that time due to well-intended but naive decisions of their parents.

Pastors often learn of such a decision after it is made, and will pull down their polite, window-shade smiles listening to parents share "good news" that the pastor doubts will be good for children. One of those "happy" announcements occurs in affluent congregations, when parents have reached an occupational stature that allows them to say, "Pastor, I have great news. Our family just purchased a lake home."

The pastors smile politely but know that they have probably just listened to an exodus announcement from an active church family. The parents look at the lake house as a way to bless their family on weekends freed from work stresses (and many blessings are likely to occur). Yet, the family's level of affluence usually indicates they are at an age and career stage when their children need the influence of other Christian adults to nurture lifelong faith.

Lake houses and mountain retreats are not the only things that tend to take teens out of regular involvement with the life of the church. So do other seemingly happy announcements from well-intentioned parents. "Pastor, I've got great news. My child just made the travel team." Whether the travel is for sports, dance, or scholarship competitions, the pastors know they just heard another exodus announcement at a time that is crucial for eternal commitments in the heart of a child.

In less affluent communities, teens' spiritual nurture may be compromised by Sunday work. Sometimes family support may require teens to take positions not desired by adults on weekends. Yet, parents may also encourage such work to teach financial responsibility, or to enable a teen to have pocket money, afford a car, save for college, or enjoy expensive entertainments. Each may have value in the teen's life but must be weighed by spiritually responsible parents against the absence from church at such a critical time in a child's faith development. Never are the choices more apparent than when the waiter, waitress, or caddy serving a church group on Sunday is the teen now regularly absent from the church.

Depending on the part of the country, the educational aspirations of a family, or the hobbies of a child, families may have wonderful extracurricular activities for their children to pursue on Sundays. We are far from the days when most communities and schools reserved Sundays and Wednesday evenings for church activities. As our culture secularizes, Sunday becomes an "open day" for any activity that will advance a child's college or career opportunities.[51] Again, the consequence is that Christian worship and nurture get sacrificed at a time that is frequently critical for our teens' eternity.

Not only have communities and schools largely ceased protecting Sundays for worship, so have many employers. While Christians may praise Chick-fil-A for its Sunday closings, such commitments may be considered increasingly unrealistic by employers in a 24/7 economy. More and more Christians are finding themselves required to work or travel during the time that their family needs church nurture. These pressures will increasingly mean that Christian employers and employees will need to make hard decisions weighing spiritual and material values.

Churches also may find themselves needing to offer services according to the pattern of first-century Christians who worshiped before daybreak and late at night so those without choices about when they worked could still participate in church life. Such decisions will require truly celebrating the influence that parents and churches can have on future generations, and weighing the factors that make that influence most effective. Yet, finding mature leadership to understand these dynamics and make decisions according to present realities rather than traditional practices is also becoming increasingly difficult.

So, while the overall goal of this book is to help churches understand how our changing culture is affecting generations of faith, helping different generations work and worship together will require assessing how different generations are differently affected. This first chapter has been intended to help mature leaders understand the challenges of rising generations who will soon lead our churches. The next chapter intends to ensure that no one simply attributes present challenges to the failures or compromises of the young. In chapter 2 we will consider how a shifting culture has affected the lives and faith of mature believers. Later chapters will delve more deeply into specific challenges all churches must face to minister to multiple generations seeking to live according to our Savior's priorities in a rapidly secularizing society.

2

OUR CHURCH CHALLENGES

Loss of the Mature

There is a temptation for older believers to shrug off the loss of youth from our churches by muttering some version of "Kids these days!" with the presumption that things will turn around when the next generation "grows up." There is little to support that presumption. In fact, if we believe that parents are the primary influencers of the next generation's faith commitments, then the loss of so many young people indicates related concerns for mature members.

The loss of today's youth is but one factor in the general decline of faith in American culture. A recent Pew Research Center study reports, "Starting in the mid-1990s, it became more common for adults in middle age and beyond to discard Christian identity. Before that, changing religions after 30 was rare."[1] Without the departures of the mature, we could not account for the assessment that less than half of Americans now consider themselves "religious and spiritual."[2]

Only 39 percent of Americans report that religion is very important to them—a decline from 68 percent in 1998.[3] Such attitudes were being reflected, even before the pandemic, as 1.2 million were walking away from the American church every year.[4] These are not dynamics solely determined by youth culture but are a consequence of a general decline in the involvement of all ages in their faith commitments. The mature are leaving our churches too. The goal of this chapter is to identify why churches are experiencing an unprecedented loss of mature Christians who used to be churchgoers in this dominantly Christian culture.

In 2008–2010 polling, 73 percent of Americans born before 1945 said they were church members. By 2020 that figure dropped to 66 percent.[5] Of course, much of that drop could be explained simply by age factors, with immobility and incapacity leading to less church involvement. But those born before 1964 (the Baby Boomers) were also becoming less inclined to church involvement. Their membership dropped from 63 percent to 58 percent in the same time period.[6]

Greater drops were occurring in Generation X adults, those born from 1965 to 1980. Their percentages went from 57 percent in 2008–2010 to 50 percent ten years later. By 2021, only 36 percent of Millennials (those now in their thirties and forties) were members of any church—down from 51 percent since 2010.[7] In summary, there is no age category in which church membership has not shrunk over the last four decades.[8]

Magnitude of Loss

Gallup reported in 2021 that less than half of all Americans now claim to be members of a religious organization (church, synagogue, temple, mosque, etc.).[9] This is the first time that those formally affiliated with a religion have been a minority of our population since the research firm began measuring in the 1930s.[10]

We need to be clear that this decline is not simply reflected in the decreased religious activity of people belonging to other faiths as they integrate into American society. In fact, the largest factor in the decline of active religious involvement is changing patterns among Christians. Though the percent of Americans identifying as Christian is now 63 percent, that total is down from 90 percent in 1972, with most of the change occurring in this new century.[11]

The changes in membership have had understandable effects on attendance. Even prior to the COVID pandemic, the majority of those who were religiously affiliated said that they attended religious services a few times a year or less.[12] Of course, this data reflects self-reporting, which is notoriously "optimistic" among those who want to be identified as "faithful."[13]

Approximately 21 percent of Americans now *say* that they attend church weekly (down from a reported 42 percent only twenty years ago).[14] But when a professor at the University of Chicago tracked us by our cell phone data, he found that 21 percent was our monthly—not weekly—attendance, and that "only about five percent of Americans are actually at a religious service on their primary day of worship."[15] Such patterns are strong confirmation of other studies that indicate only 16 percent of us now say that religion is of highest import in our lives.[16]

As I am writing for an Evangelical audience, I recognize my readers may be tempted to think that these declines only apply to Protestant Mainline or Roman Catholic churches. That would be a mistake. It is true that Mainline and Catholic churches have taken the brunt of Christianity's decline across the United States. Mainline membership is generally down 30 percent since 1987 and 60 percent since the mid-1970s.[17] Additionally, Roman Catholic attendance was seeing a similar decrease even prior to COVID.[18] However, as we will see below, the Evangelical movement has not been exempt from such declines and is experiencing a growing loss in attendance for a variety of reasons.

Contributors to the Losses

COVID

Just as COVID accelerated the exodus of many young people from our churches, it has stimulated a further decline in the involvement of all attenders. While people tend to *say* that their church attendance has not significantly changed since prior to COVID,[19] more objective studies note significant shifts.

Author and researcher Ed Stetzer, now dean of the Talbot School of Theology, initially reported that COVID restrictions and nonattendance choices shrunk most Evangelical churches 20 to 30 percent from their pre-COVID patterns.[20] More recent Lifeway studies indicate that most churches are still experiencing only 85 percent of their pre-COVID attendance.[21]

There are a variety of reasons that COVID has had such a profound effect on all churches among all age groups. As churches moved to streaming services online, some people simply got out of the church habit. Others so strongly objected to their leadership's decision to (or not to) continue meeting during the pandemic that they left church altogether or joined another.[22] The opportunity to change churches or attendance patterns without being noticed by friends or without offending the pastor triggered the "Great American Church Shuffle" that changed familiar faces in many congregations. Nineteen percent of individuals changed their religious identification between pre-pandemic years and the spring of 2022,[23] with almost 40 percent of churchgoers either changing churches or ceasing to attend.[24]

As COVID-induced hybrid office patterns also became common among American employers, churches in the Midwest, North, Northeast, and Far West surrendered newly mobile members to the Sunbelt or to less expensive or less taxed regions—where not all then returned to regular church attendance patterns.[25] And even when churches in those new locations benefited from the influx of new people, congregations still lost longtime members to the "great shuffle."[26] In all these cases, we should note that it was not primarily young people who were making these reaffiliation decisions but their parents and those with enough employment seniority to make such changes without damaging their careers.

In addition to attendance losses due to mature members taking advantage of COVID opportunities, most churches also experienced the loss of those whose attendance was considered "iffy" prior to COVID. We understand those who were iffy in the context of groups likely to be involved in any church across various traditions. Historically healthy churches have always been composed of three groups of people: communicants (mature believers), catechumens (children and new believers), and seekers (those exploring if Christ and his people are for real).

In modern times, these historical categories have been recalibrated as

- *Contributors*—the 40 percent who provide time and resources to train, teach, and reach others; from these ranks we get our officers, teachers, and volunteers.
- *Consumers*—the 40 percent who attend because, for a variety of reasons, they think church is good for them or their children; these are often regular attenders who are not otherwise significantly involved in the life or support of the church.

Seekers—the 20 percent checking in because they are checking out the faith or meeting expectations of a family member, neighbor, or work associate.

It is this last category of people (i.e., the seekers) whose attendance has been most negatively affected by COVID, with adults of the Boomer generation dropping out in greatest numbers.[27] Experts tell us that, with the changing patterns of church attendance and the lowered societal expectation of religious affiliation, this seeker group is likely gone permanently—and the consumers may be on their way out too.[28]

The church that will flourish in the future must find new means of reaching those whose attendance or exploration of the faith can no longer be assumed.[29] And we may find that such outreach efforts are best expressed by the rising generations that are more experienced and gifted in relating to unbelievers who make no pretense of faith.

Denominational Decoupling

While consumers and seekers have been most likely to depart local churches, pastors are also noting the departure of more of their contributors (the mature) than ever before. COVID has stimulated some of these exits, but there are more factors at work.

In my role as a denominational leader, I visit many churches. Often pastors will convene the adult Sunday school classes during my visit so that I can report on denominational vision and health. To make the point of our need for outreach, I always ask how many of these adults (those whose Sunday school attendance indicates that they are among the most active and committed) were raised in our denomination. The total almost never exceeds 15 percent, no matter how historic or established the church.

A few years ago, I recounted this practice while conducting officer training in one of our largest and most historic churches. The pastor scoffed and questioned whether my assessment was true in his church. So, I said, "Let's test it." Seated before me were over a hundred elders and deacons in training—the most committed members that it would be possible to sample in this historic church. I asked my usual question: "How many of you were raised in a Bible-believing Presbyterian church?" Less than 10 percent of the hands went up.

The clear message in this church and many others is that movement in and out of Evangelical churches is *not* primarily driven by denominational loyalties. A generation ago, a Lutheran, Baptist, or Presbyterian moving across the country or across town would look for another church of the same denomination. Today, prior denominational experience may cause a family in transition to give the streaming service of another church of the same denomination a look before determining where next to attend. However, the final decision is not likely to be made on the basis of a denominational label. Other factors are weighing more heavily in our common affiliation decisions.

Ed Stetzer writes, "Our people are being sorted by ideology not theology. . . . People are inflamed by cable news and discipled by social media."[30] They may listen to the pastor for thirty minutes on Sunday, but cable news is the video wallpaper of their homes and offices for more than thirty hours a week. As a consequence, many will adjust their religious affiliations to align with their political views, rather than the reverse.[31]

In fact, some estimate that the proportion of those identifying as Evangelical for political reasons is larger than of those so identifying for theological reasons.[32] I would suggest that the term "political" in this context should be expanded to include those who are cultural traditionalists, wanting simply to maintain a familiar way of life. The result is a large segment of the population (as much as 35 percent in some surveys[33]) identifying as Evangelical, but a much smaller portion (only 6 to 12 percent, depending on the survey) actually embracing Evangelical faith distinctives.[34]

One in five who switch churches will do so because they do not agree with the church's position on social issues or politics.[35] In part, this is because so many more churchgoers are accustomed to worship by streaming and are more likely than ever to be disengaged from any discipleship or community group.[36] Now between 20 and 30 percent of practicing Christians are worshiping online exclusively.[37]

Pastors know that one effect of these relational disconnects is that their people will be more apt to troll fellow parishioners (or the pastor) on social media about political differences, to shift streaming to another church with a more aligned political bent, or to stop worship practices altogether. It will not even occur to many that a face-to-face meeting with church leaders for a better understanding of theological priorities and political explanations would be Christ-honoring and community-building.

More and more evidence is accumulating that our people identify their religious convictions on the basis of their political associations.[38] They simply know their politics better than they know their theology. Various surveys indicate that roughly half of those identifying as Evangelicals believe many religions can lead to eternal life and do not believe the Bible is necessarily true.[39] As a consequence, denominational distinctives mean less and less to many because they do not know their church's basic teachings, much less its nuanced, denominational distinctives.

Nondenominational churches have been clear beneficiaries of these trends. Nondenominational church attendance grew by 6.5 million between 2010 and 2020.[40] Sadly, these increases were not nearly enough to compensate for the overall exodus of 40 million attenders from church membership nationwide in the last twenty-five years.[41]

People go to churches where they are comfortable with general beliefs, worship practices, and the pastor's perceived warmth. Thus, when mature members leave a local church for work or retirement relocation—or to attend a church closer to their children or recreational choices—only the most informed and committed will feel any obligation to attend another church of the same denomination in the new location. The result is a decrease in overall denominational loyalty and attendance among Evangelicals, with very few exceptions.[42]

Post-COVID statistics are still coming in, but one pre-COVID survey had already revealed that one in six American Christians changed their church or religious affiliation in the previous decade.[43] A more recent survey indicated that 53 percent of regular churchgoers have attended more than one church as an adult.[44] While Protestants tended to stay Protestant, about one in four have changed denominational affiliations.

While most non-Catholics who switch churches will do so prompted by a residential move, 40 percent are driven by something else: disapproval of changes in the church, not believing the church is addressing their or their children's needs, becoming disenchanted with the pastor, or combinations of such factors.[45] Half of those who switched said their previous church had a traditional worship style; most of the churches to which they moved had a mix of contemporary and traditional worship.[46]

Roman Catholic researchers have reported a mass exodus from their churches for over a decade. If we were to count ex-Catholics as a separate denomination in the US, it would be the third largest. Instead, about half become unaffiliated, but half become Protestant.[47] This should be a wake-up call for pastors and congregations wanting to reach beyond their traditional constituencies in the wake of their own attendance challenges.

Ex-Catholics tend to be looking for churches that are perceived as traditional in worship, gracious in teaching, and safe for children. Many of the newcomers to my own denomination are ex-Catholics, even though many of our pastors and people are still learning how to speak to them and of them with grace and respect.

Moral and Material Choices

More evidence of the weakening ties between local churches and their people lies in the life choices of contemporary Evangelicals. Despite what our churches teach, most surveys indicate there is little difference between the moral practices, entertainment choices, and personal expenditures of those in our churches and those outside. On issues such as Sabbath observance, abortion, premarital sex, pornography use, alcohol abuse, divorce, sex outside of marriage, and charitable giving, our people's practices little differ from the general population or other faith traditions.[48]

Tim Sansbury, a professor of philosophy and theology at Knox Theological Seminary, explains: "A generation ago, the concern of Evangelicals was to prove the truth of the Bible to those who believed it was historically inaccurate but still thought its moral principles were valid. Now most Evangelicals do not question the facts of the Bible (they believe Jesus died for sin and rose from the dead), they just don't believe those facts are constraining for, or relevant to, their moral choices."[49] We have an Evangelical consensus affirming the facts of Scripture while simultaneously discounting its standards for conduct. We confess that the Bible is true but live as though its truths are inapplicable.

As a consequence, most pastors expect their adult members will struggle to apply Scripture to everyday life, but many will not understand how much more intense is the struggle of their young people. For example, the Centers for Disease Control (CDC) reports that over half of married adults in the US today enter marriage with five or more previous sexual partners.[50] Our churches' young people are not unaffected.

Two-thirds of young Evangelicals will be sexually active prior to marriage, which either makes them think of themselves as spiritual failures or of the church as irrelevant to them (or judgmental of them).[51] Either opinion will jeopardize their future relationship with spiritual leaders, not to mention endangering the spiritual health and future security of their marriages.

Those who engage in premarital sex will have a twofold to threefold (151 percent) greater likelihood of marriage failure, leading to further estrangement from the church.[52] When an unwanted child is the result of sexual activity prior to or within marriage, many with an Evangelical background will have an abortion, causing even more distancing.

Of the 930,000 abortions in 2020—the last year for which we have national religious comparisons—13 percent were performed on those claiming Evangelical backgrounds, compared to 17 percent of those with Mainline church backgrounds. Though these are significantly lower percentages than for those from Roman Catholic or unchurched backgrounds (24 percent and 38 percent, respectively), they still indicate that Evangelicals are responsible for 120,000 to 130,000 of recorded abortions per year.[53]

Due to other changing societal values among America's younger generations, approximately one in every four people ages 30–39 are now cohabitating without marriage (with one in five of those in their twenties and forties also cohabitating).[54] These stats make it apparent that young people are not the only ones choosing to live together. Those who are mature in years, whose marriages have ended with divorce or death of a spouse, may often choose to cohabitate rather than risk loss of a previous spouse's pension or social security benefits. Many say they will not commit to another in marriage "before we know if it will work out."[55] For those from Evangelical backgrounds, these cohabitation choices will strain their relationship with their churches and their Savior.

Couples of all ages are choosing to move in together to test their relationship prior to marriage. Studies indicate that many Americans and most young people consider such a marital "test drive" to be a good idea before making a long-term commitment that may end in the same unhappiness as a previous relationship or of their parents' marriage.[56] Some estimate that among all who now marry, 70 percent will have cohabitated prior.[57]

Sadly, but understandably, the decision not to commit to another unconditionally—based on the model of Christ's love that is the foundation of Christian marriage—only weakens the relationship. Whenever we say to another, "I will love you so long as you measure up to my expectations," we are relating to another person contrary to the grace of our Savior's love and diminishing the comforts and confidence of his love in our own hearts.

So, most cohabitating relationships will not be permanent, and even secular studies indicate those who marry after cohabitating do *not* have a lower incidence of divorce. In fact, their likelihood of marriage dissolution increases by almost 60 percent over those who do not cohabitate prior to marriage,[58] and by more than 100 percent (more than double) over those who are virgins at marriage.[59]

It is worth inserting here that those who are virgins at the time of their marriage stay married almost 90 percent of the time[60] and have greater sexual satisfaction in their marriages,[61] undermining the "test drive" theories and doing much to affirm God's blessing upon faithfulness. While such counterstatistics do much to encourage church leaders in the wisdom of the Bible's instruction, we will need to do more than make virginity a talisman or restart the purity culture movement that failed so badly in recent decades.[62]

God's people (especially young people caught up in the throes of our sexualized culture) lean upon his wisdom and remain faithful to his ways because they understand the character of his grace, not because they are threatened with future marriage consequences or church leaders' frowns. The reality that church leaders and parents need to face is that, despite our teaching, great numbers of both our young and mature people will experience societal temptations and personal failures affecting the stability of their marriages. Many will fail, straining their relationship with any Evangelical church that preaches only about the sanctity and permanence of marriage without equal emphasis upon the gospel of grace.

Divorce

By no means are young people the only ones to have divorce threaten their church associations. The loss of mature believers from the church is frequently precipitated by the dissolution of their marriages. With the so-called "gray divorce revolution," the divorce rate for people over age fifty has more than doubled (and tripled for those over 65) since 1990—and is still rising.[63] Now over one-third of individuals who divorce are over age fifty, and these are not only unchurched people.[64]

The debate continues to rage over whether Evangelicals divorce at roughly the same rate as the general population. Many studies confirm that roughly half of all American marriages will end in divorce, but theologically conservative church leaders still question whether this is true for their people.[65]

Sadly, some research indicates that those who claim to be "born again" (especially if they rarely attend church) divorce at an even greater rate than those of most other faiths or other Christian traditions.[66] These studies are hotly debated and often are driven by political and ideological agendas. Still, even those who argue most strenuously that Evangelical faith is a strong counter to divorce have placed the dissolution rate of our regular attenders at 30 to 38 percent.[67] However, those who merely identify as "Christian" but rarely attend any church have a divorce rate of approximately 60 percent.[68]

Perhaps we will be tempted to question whether those statistics are largely caused by the marriage practices of nominal or non-Evangelical Christians. But even when we consider those who identify as conservative Protestants and regularly attend church, read their Bibles, and pray privately and with their families, the variance from the national, secular norm is not as significant as we would wish.

"Active conservative Protestants" are only 35 percent less likely to divorce than Americans with no church affiliation.[69] That still puts the divorce rate among active Evangelicals in the 30–35 percent range.[70] That's a lot of divorces in churches that place a high value on marriage commitment, leading to the discomfort and exodus of many who divorce—and of their children, who will later be leery of both marriage and the church as a consequence of their parents' experience.

Divorce ramifications for our churches are also increasing as a consequence of marriage breakdown among our most mature and depended-upon members. While the most likely time for a marriage to end in divorce remains in a couple's earliest years, the most rapidly rising rates for divorce are now at the empty nest time ("We only stayed together for the children's sake") and retirement stage ("I don't want to be buried next to that person").[71] In 1990, fewer than one in ten people who got divorced were fifty or older; today, one in every four divorces are senior couples.[72]

Many pastors of midsize and large churches are discovering the need to make major ministry adjustments due to the surprising commonness of divorce that, for the reasons indicated below, leads to the departure of key lay leaders and longtime members. The marriage dissolution and departure of those most likely to be in the officer, teacher, or volunteer ranks can cripple the ministry of a local church and devastate its community life.

Few church leaders want divorced persons to depart the fellowship and healing the church can offer, but we often don't know how to relate to those who are divorced and they don't know how to relate to the church.[73] Those whose marriages have failed may hate facing the pastors or church friends whose relationships were established during the marriage. This is not necessarily because the church's care was inadequate or poorly expressed.

Almost every pastor has had the experience of seeing in public someone in whom many pastoral hours and tears were invested to save a marriage, only to have that person cross the street or leave a store to avoid contact after the marriage failed. Young ministers may wonder what they did wrong to cause such evasion; experienced pastors have learned to accept others' need to avoid painful reminders or embarrassing conversations.

Divorce inevitably causes people to feel some measure of failure and to wonder who in their church will be angry with them, suspicious of them, judgmental of them, or will still welcome them (or their former spouse) to social occasions. Social events or worship services primarily attended by married couples or families create awkwardness for the unattached, along with fresh awareness of relational failure, embarrassment, and pain.

Sadly, we are discovering that divorce leads to church departure not only for those who were married but also for their children, who view their parents' failures as indicative of the church's failures or faith's inadequacy. Almost 70 percent of those now dechurched say that parental tensions were a factor in their own decision to depart.[74]

Singleness

Many of those over fifty who have divorced will remarry (sometimes contrary to their church's teaching or discipline) but will face double or triple the likelihood of their subsequent marriage's future dissolution compared to those in first marriages. Most who have divorced will remain single. Only 38 percent of men will remarry in their senior years; only 23 percent of women.[75] In their singleness, those who are mature believers will find more reasons to leave the church in this era when there is little social pressure to remain religiously active.

We tease that Evangelical pastors are most comfortable preaching 3M sermons that focus on some aspect of *morality*, *marriage*, and *materialism*. Yet, for those who are newly single and still raw from the pain of divorce—most often caused by issues of adultery, sexual frustrations, tensions in family relations, and money—such sermons will only contribute to their feeling out of place in church.

Because the average pastor has been trained to "focus on the family," and the average church is ill-equipped to minister to singles, sheer population dynamics are contributing to the overall decline of the American church. Three times as many adults (38 million) now live alone as compared to 1970, which some correlate to the significant rise in adult depression rates.[76] Government statistics reveal that 46.4 percent of all those over eighteen are single, and more than 50 percent of adult women are not married.[77] As a consequence of these realities, Evangelicals' family focus almost certainly (albeit unintentionally) excludes or creates discomfort for almost half of the adult population—which spells opportunity for insightful congregations and obsolescence for those who cannot or will not change.[78]

Impact of Losses

The factors identified in this chapter that are contributing to the loss of the mature are, of course, not the only reasons that the Evangelical church is struggling. As indicated in the previous chapter, there are many streams flowing into the increasing secularism of our time. The goal of this chapter was narrow: identifying why we are experiencing an unprecedented loss of mature members of our churches in addition to the youth who have been raised in a largely pluralistic and relativistic society.

When multiple generations are increasingly abandoning the church, then internal vitality and future viability are the obvious casualties. Fewer mature people involved today spells fewer mentors, supporters, disciplers, exemplars, and leaders for our children and their children. Additionally, a shrinking national church will have less sway over the attitudes, values, and priorities of present and future generations, society, and government. Still, this is not primarily a book about growing churches, influencing or cursing secular culture, or wringing our hands about our losses.

As indicated earlier, my goal is to help churches understand how our changing culture is affecting different generations within their midst so that we can work together for future health and mission. The first chapter was intended to help mature leaders understand the challenges of rising generations who will soon lead our churches. This second chapter has been intended to make sure that no one simply attributes present challenges to the failures or compromises of the young. Our churches are also being stretched by changes in the practices, perspectives, and patterns of their mature members.

The cultural ground has shifted beneath the feet of all of us—young *and* mature—with remarkable swiftness. Only as we now compare those who can remember when the ground wasn't shaking to those who have been raised with the ground always shaking will we be able to understand and support one another from multiple generations in Christ's present mission.

To prepare us for that united effort, we need to consider one more key loss that has had different effects on different generations. We need to consider how the loss of a majority Christian culture (real or perceived) now affects the perspectives of a generation who lost it and a generation who never knew it.

Assessing the magnitude of that loss is the goal of the next chapter. Identifying the effects of this loss on different generations is the goal of subsequent chapters. Overall, the larger goal is to understand generational differences so that we may celebrate how God has differently gifted his people for the purposes of his church at this critical time and so that we may respond with a unified mission.

3

OUR CULTURAL CHALLENGES

Loss of a Majority

The previous chapter began with a description of the general decline of religion in America to help explain the attendance losses of many of our mature members. Still, no statistic is more likely to help us understand differing generations' perceptions of the character of their society (and their place in it) than Pew research indicating that 90 percent of Americans identified as Christians in 1972 and continued to do so at near the same percentage into the 1990s.[1]

Any adult of that era, and any child coming of age in those decades, would perceive the United States to be a Christian nation. This means that for the vast majority of Evangelical Christians now age fifty and above, their family roots, school experience, and career environments were dominated by those who called themselves Christians.

Everyone was a Christian it seemed. Coworkers, classmates, neighbors, politicians, teachers, and family members—all used the Christian label. There were liberal and conservative Christians, Protestant and Catholic Christians, Republican and Democrat Christians, dedicated and Sunday-only Christians, good and bad Christians, but most everyone in most everyone's common experience identified as a Christian.

Things are different now.

Changes in Practices and Perceptions

The dominance of Christian identification in American society caused the percentage breakdowns of the population's church affiliations to vary little in the decades following World War II until the beginning of the twenty-first century.[2] Until the century's turn, people tended to stay within the faith tradition in which they were raised, maintaining the proportions of faith communities as they had developed from previous immigration patterns and ethnic identities.

For a nonrefined snapshot of the post-WWII American faith landscape, researcher Ed Stetzer once segmented religion in America according to the chart below.[3]

Population Percentages Based on Late Twentieth-Century Religious Affiliations

- Atheist 3–5%
- Other Religions 15%
- Roman Catholic 20%
- Mainline Protestant 30%
- Evangelical 30%

Stetzer readily acknowledges that economic, political, and cultural trends caused the actual statistics to vary somewhat from year to year, but the approximations in this chart were close enough to reality to affect how most thought of religion in America and how many older Americans still perceive our culture.[4] However, more recent studies reflect a very different picture.

The Roman Catholic Picture

As previously noted, Roman Catholic trends have de-anchored reality from traditional perceptions of the significance and size of this largest single branch of American Christianity. In the early 1970s, Catholic church members were about a quarter of the American population according to the General Social Survey.[5] The Cooperative Election Study[6] placed membership at 17.5 percent—lower but still close enough to Stetzer's analysis to maintain the related perceptions.[7]

Today, generally accepted surveys identify 18.7 percent of the American population as Roman Catholic,[8] but active involvement is much less. Regular attendance at Mass has dropped from about 50 percent of members in the 1970s to about 25 percent today.[9] This means that only about 5 percent of the American population is composed of practicing Catholics. The result is a so-called post-Catholic culture in places that used to be Catholic strongholds, such as major cities in the Northeast and Midwest.[10] In such places, people often still think of themselves or their families as Catholic, even if they have not been to confession or Mass in decades.

The Mainline Picture

Americans identifying as members of Mainline denominations have fallen to 10–13 percent of the overall population; in the 1950s they were over half of all Americans (52 percent).[11] Researcher Ryan Burge, a member of a Mainline church, pulls no punches in examining the seven major Mainline denominations that hold the vast majority of Mainline members, and then reporting, "The mainline is just a bloodbath."[12]

For example, since 1987, the Evangelical Lutheran Church membership is down 41 percent. The United Church of Christ is down more than 50 percent. The Presbyterian Church (USA) has decreased in membership roughly 4 percent per year since 1984,[13] going from more than three million members to fewer than one million in thirty-eight years (a decline of more than 62 percent, or an average of 53,000 people per year).[14] In the single decade between 2009 and 2020, the PCUSA lost 40 percent of its membership.[15] The United Methodist Church was already down 30 percent before losing 15 percent of its churches in 2023 over sexuality and gender issues, with some estimating that it will soon shrink another 40 percent.[16]

Plummeting wedding and baptism rates in Mainline churches, combined with the aging membership of these historic denominations, points to a demographic cliff that is likely unavoidable. Church consultant Dwight Zscheile says of the Episcopal Church, "The overall picture is dire—not one of decline as much as demise within the next generation. . . . At this rate, there will be no one in worship by around 2050 in the entire denomination."[17]

Yet, even these stark membership declines do not tell the full story. When attendance figures are also considered, only one-quarter of Mainline members report being in their churches weekly. Danny Olinger's summary is sobering even for those who would disagree with the theology of Mainline churches. He writes, "A generation into the twenty-first century, only 3 percent of the population of the United States are active members of a mainline Protestant church."[18] It is hard to quantify, though not hard to imagine, the coarsening and secularizing effects this exodus of so large a residual Christian influence has had on our society.[19]

Evangelicals may be tempted to think that the demise of the Mainline is purely a consequence of theological erosion. For those who may not be aware, key distinctives of Mainline theological trends emerged with late nineteenth-century movements that were critical of Scripture's truthfulness. In the twentieth century these critiques evolved into new perspectives that were considered consistent with "the Spirit of Jesus" but were detethered from the specifics of the Bible.

One window into the effects is the 1924 Auburn Affirmation, developed by the branch of Presbyterianism that is now known as the Presbyterian Church (USA).[20] This document sought to release church leaders from having to confirm their belief in five specific Christian teachings that were considered outdated:

1. Inerrancy of the Scriptures
2. The virgin birth (and the deity of Jesus)
3. The doctrine of substitutionary atonement
4. The bodily resurrection of Jesus
5. The authenticity of Christ's miracles

Most Christians reading this book will think that these teachings are the very essence of their faith, especially the third item that teaches Jesus died on the cross for our sins. Still, over 1,200 Presbyterian ministers ultimately signed the Auburn Affirmation without losing positions in their churches.

Over time, virtually all of America's largest denominations (Baptist, Methodist, Episcopal, Lutheran, etc.) had similar challenges to historic Christian teaching, and virtually all split into so-called Mainline and Evangelical wings. The Mainline churches initially kept the most people, money, and influence by saying that their pastors were not being forced to reject any of these historic Christian doctrines—but they were not being bound to such teachings either.

Detachment from scriptural truths ultimately led to widespread Mainline teaching that seemed little different from whatever were prevailing philosophies of the age. Then, members of Mainline churches (as demonstrated in the paragraphs above) increasingly wondered what was the point of being part of a church that offered no other guidance than the world around us.

By contrast, Evangelicals expected their pastors and people to hold to the tenets of historic Christianity. The Evangelical wings typically began small, but over time became the dominant Protestant denominations in the United States. Today about 60 percent of all Protestants identify themselves as Evangelical or "born again."[21] Only 40 percent of Protestants are members of Mainline churches,[22] and total attendance figures further favor Evangelicals.[23] So also does the number of pastors, pastors in training, schools, and churches who now consider themselves Evangelical. All might seem to be rosy for the Evangelicals. It's not.

The Evangelical Picture

Those who self-identify as Evangelicals now account for about 24 percent of the American population, according to the Pew Research Center.[24] However, during the 2016–2020 years of the Donald Trump presidency, that segment had again grown to almost 30 percent of the total population. This return to the familiar proportion of the population is largely due to 16 percent of Trump supporters who previously had not identified as Evangelical coming to claim that identity by 2020.[25]

Before any Evangelical leader starts a victory dance, rejoicing at this Evangelical ascendancy in the wake of the demise of liberal denominations and institutions from which we separated in the twentieth century's so-called "Battle for the Bible," a bit more analysis is needed.

Numbers

Yes, almost 30 percent (maybe even up to 35 percent) of the American population has *self-identified* as Evangelical in recent years.[26] But that is not necessarily an indication of Evangelical faith being as significant an influence in American society as some would tout or desire. In the political sphere, white Evangelicals are often courted with the expectation that they will have significant election clout. However, that segment of Evangelicalism is now only 14.5 percent of the population. This is down from 23 percent in 2006, and indicates that there are actually fewer white Evangelicals than white Mainline Protestants.[27] Without the entire Evangelical community united in biblical expression, the numbers indicate that the Evangelical church will continue to lose influence in every sphere of our culture.

Attendance

We also need to remember that for many Americans the term "Evangelical" has become more of a political identifier, or a statement of traditional conservative values, rather than a religious distinction.[28] As a consequence, a certain percentage of Roman Catholics, Jews, Hindus, and even atheists identify themselves as "Evangelical."[29] Perhaps more discouraging, two-thirds of Protestant Republicans who call themselves Evangelical report attending church "yearly" (i.e., only once a year).[30] Further, the proportion of self-identified Evangelicals that never attend church increased from 25 percent prior to COVID to 33 percent today.[31]

These nonattenders are not the only ones whose religious practice seems disconnected from the ideals of their faith. Among all self-identified Evangelicals, over 40 percent report attending church once a year or less.[32] Only half say that they attend weekly or more. The remaining 10 percent say they attend about once a month.[33] So, according to their own reporting, Evangelicals who are consistently engaged in the life and mission of their churches total only about 12 percent of the population—but, as we will see, this *self-reported* number may be a significant overestimate.

Beliefs

The effects of these attendance patterns on the faith commitments of those who claim to be Evangelical are becoming increasingly plain. Lifeway researchers report that less than 50 percent of those who claim to be "born again" agree with standard Evangelical beliefs about the nature of Jesus, salvation, Scripture, and evangelism.[34]

Evangelicals were defined by Lifeway as people who strongly agreed with the following four statements:

- The Bible is the highest authority for what I believe.
- It is very important for me personally to encourage non-Christians to trust Jesus Christ as their Savior.
- Jesus Christ's death on the cross is the only sacrifice that could remove the penalty of my sin.
- Only those who trust in Jesus Christ alone as their Savior receive God's free gift of eternal salvation.

Most informed Evangelicals would think that these statements are such a basic reflection of the historic and orthodox Christian faith that virtually everyone who identifies as a Christian would affirm them—and surely those claiming to be Evangelical would readily affirm these basics. But this is hardly the case.

The picture doesn't get much better, even when we use other standard measures for identifying Evangelical commitments, such as British theologian David Bebbington's "Quadrilateral." His marks of an Evangelical include Biblicism (a high regard for the Bible); Crucicentrism (a focus on the atoning work of Christ on the cross); Conversionism (the belief that human beings need to be converted); and Activism (the belief that the gospel needs to be expressed in effort).[35] George Barna identifies Evangelicals by seven "core convictions" relating to the Trinity, the Bible, faith, Jesus, salvation, evangelism, and discipleship.[36] Tim Keller identified Evangelicals by three "shared theological marks" that included an experience of grace and conversion, the realization of the sufficiency of Christ's sacrifice, and the knowledge of the power of the living Word in Scripture.[37] However, no matter what identifiers are chosen to mark an Evangelical, more and more who go by that title are seeming to miss the mark.

Over and over surveys reveal that a startlingly large percentage of those who call themselves Evangelical do not actually believe what Evangelicals teach as God's truth. In fact, only a quarter to half of adults identifying as Evangelicals believe what Evangelical churches historically teach—an inescapable reality for most of the last decade.[38]

Using such basic criteria for Evangelical belief from earlier studies, Barna and others conclude that the actual percentage of adult Americans who qualify as Evangelical by belief is 8 percent or less.[39] Ligonier studies matched with the percent of the population who presently identify as Evangelicals but yielded a slightly more optimistic result, placing the percent of the US population that is Evangelical by belief closer to 12 percent.[40] That is still remarkably lower than almost any regular attender of an Evangelical church would think.

The Present Picture

What's Real Now

The cumulative effect of the declines in each branch of Christianity identified above is the loss of the majority of Americans in church involvement.

Total Numbers

To be precise, the majority of Americans still *say* that they are Christians. But, as reported in chapter 1, that percentage has gone from 90 to 80 percent in the decades from 1970 to 2010, and currently stands at 60 percent.[41]

What people *say*, however, is not what their collective commitments indicate.[42] As indicated in the previous chapter, Gallup reported in 2021 that, for the first time since the organization began collecting data in the

1930s, less than half of Americans are members of a church, synagogue, or mosque.[43] More arresting is the sharp decline in those who regularly attend church.

Total Attendance

In 2010, roughly 40 percent of Americans said they had attended worship in the last seven days.[44] Today, if we add together the totals of those Roman Catholics, Mainliners, and Evangelicals who are regularly attending their houses of worship, then the total percentage of active Christians in American society is less than 20 percent (5 percent practicing Roman Catholics, 3 percent regularly attending Mainliners, and 12 percent consistently engaged Evangelicals). More than half of Americans (56 percent) now say they seldom or never attend religious services, while the percentage of those never attending church has doubled since the 1990s.[45]

The effect upon the traditional picture of the American religious scene—the picture that reflected the landscape from World War II until the first decade of the twenty-first century, and continued to influence most Christians' perceptions until COVID—is dramatic. The religious ground has shifted beneath our feet, and it has happened so fast that our perceptions, practices, and plans have not kept up.

National Identity

Despite a little more than 60 percent of the American population identifying as Christians, only about 50 percent believe in "God as described in the Bible."[46] For many, the term "Christian" seems to have become a family or ethnic identity rather than a faith distinction. Only 40 percent of Americans say that their religion is "very important" to them.[47] As a consequence, researchers estimate that Christians will be a minority of Americans within the next half century, or even within the next twenty years, depending on immigration, birth rate, and faith-switching trends.[48]

The common faith expressions and affiliations no longer exist that formed the general perception of religion in America in the late twentieth century shown here:

Population Percentages Based on Late Twentieth-Century Religious Affiliations

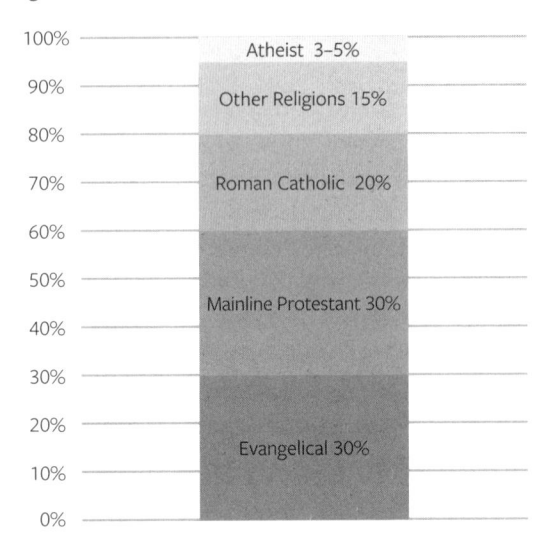

- Atheist 3–5%
- Other Religions 15%
- Roman Catholic 20%
- Mainline Protestant 30%
- Evangelical 30%

If we consider what people currently *say* about their affiliations, then the proportions of Americans in different religious categories look more like the chart below. *(Note: Self-reporting means the numbers will not total 100 percent.)*

Population Percentages as Indicated by Regular, Self-Reported Religious Affiliation

- Atheist 3–7%[49]
- Other Religions 8.8%[50]
- Nones (nonaffiliated but not atheists) 22%
- Roman Catholic 19%
- Mainline Protestant 12%
- Evangelical 24%

Rise of the "Nones"

Obviously, the major difference in the preceding two charts, apart from the percentage changes, is the appearance of an entirely new category of religious association: the much discussed "Nones." Though the technical definition varies by researcher, the Nones are basically those who say they are "spiritual but not religious," meaning they still believe in God or a spiritual dimension of life beyond our material world, but do not wish to be part of organized or institutional religion.[51]

The increasing secularization of our culture and the increasing nominalism of all branches of Christianity evident in membership, attendance, and belief erosion have resulted in many Americans, especially young ones, dropping out of church participation. In a country that until recently identified as 90 percent Christian, there remains enough residual spirituality to make full atheism socially uncouth, but being spiritual and unaffiliated is deemed trendy and authentic.

For informed discussion, we need to understand that in most (not all) studies, being a None is not necessarily the same as being an atheist.[52] Nones typically believe in God but have lost confidence in the church. As late as 2022, sociologists indicated that the proportion of actual atheists in the US has held steady at 4 percent for more than eighty years.[53] Other studies put the proportion slightly higher, but even the New Atheism made popular for the last two decades by Christopher Hitchens, Richard Dawkins, and their allies has largely fallen into disfavor among generations looking for relief from record levels of loneliness, depression, and suicide.[54]

Those seeking solace from the isolation and dehumanization of technology, economic competition, constant war, and the incessant materialistic pursuits that favor the already wealthy have not turned to the religions their parents are abandoning. Understandably, the religiously tentative of all ages are also not rushing to religious institutions immersed in scandals, power struggles, and politics. The more theologically and sexually compromised the Mainline and Catholic churches have become, and the more shrill or culturally adapted the Evangelical church appears, the more all generations are taking a pass on America's cultural religions. The result is the rise of the Nones.[55]

In 2024, the Pew Research Center reported that 28 percent of Americans are religious Nones (but included people who describe themselves as atheists, agnostics, or "nothing in particular" when asked about their religious identity).[56] That percentage is down slightly from earlier Pew studies,[57] but can go as high as 30 or even 35 percent, depending on how individuals are questioned.[58] However, no one questions that a major shift in American religion is underway. Of significance for the future, the percentage of Nones is calibrated as high as 44 percent among young adults ages 18–29.[59]

The total number of Nones has been steadily increasing since the late twentieth century, with periods of significant acceleration in this century. In 1993, Americans who said they were not affiliated with any religion made up 9 percent of the population; the number ticked up slightly to 12 percent in 1996 and 14 percent in 1998, then held steady until 2008 before a sharp increase to 24 percent by 2021.[60] Since 2007, the Nones have grown slightly less than 1 percent per year on average.[61] But that percentage has accelerated to 2 percent per year since 2018.[62] As a result, the Nones have more than doubled in the early decades of this century to roughly a third of American adults, totaling more than 40 million.[63] During that same period, the number of Americans identifying as Christian has fallen from almost 80 percent of the population to 60 percent.[64] By some estimates the Nones are now larger than any other single religious category of Christians (Catholic, Orthodox, Mainline, Evangelical, etc.) in America.

Earthquakes

These percentages blur on the page, but they have real effects on the everyday experience of those who still participate in church life and desire to see the gospel flourish. My own experience during a recent Christmas celebration helped illustrate to me the changing religious landscape. For most of the last decade, I have been pastor of a church in the Midwest. As do many large churches, we used our community's cultural appreciation for Christmas traditions to conduct outreach through a Christmas extravaganza.

For decades, the program brought many thousands through our doors during the holiday season. But more recently the crowds have thinned, and the number of performances has shrunk. When one of our Christmas Eve services, traditionally the largest, did not fill the sanctuary one year, I was met in the center aisle by one of our aging members.

She took both my elbows in her hands, looked earnestly and with a touch of anger into my face, and said, "Pastor, I can remember when we filled this church every night for a week prior to Christmas!" Let me translate what that meant: "Pastor, what are you doing wrong, that even on Christmas Eve we cannot attract crowds that make us look as significant as we once were?"

It did not matter that our discipleship programs were flourishing, that our ethnic diversity was increasing, that our college and family ministries were thriving again in our once aging and dying congregation. What mattered was that our townspeople no longer felt obligated to endorse our church's significance with traditions reflecting a faith that many people in our region no longer affirm.

I have been blessed with ministry opportunities and fruit far beyond my abilities and deserving. Still, I well remember the embarrassment I experienced in that moment and the frustration that dear senior saint expressed in that aisle. I need to remember in order to be prepared to minister in the present age and for future years.

Remembering will help me recognize that the rapid rise of the Nones, the increasing nominalism of all branches of Christianity, and the shrinking role of religion in American society mean that the embarrassment and frustration of that Christmas Eve are the weekly experience and constant bewilderment of thousands of pastors and millions of parishioners across the United States.

To repeat the obvious, the world has shifted beneath our feet more rapidly than anyone could have predicted. The earthquakes are also more significant than almost anyone in the pew can be expected to absorb. The erosion is not merely in the growing numbers of those who do not identify as Christians, but in the changing convictional patterns and practices of those who are Christian, including those who identify as Evangelical.

Ryan Burge summarizes the present situation this way:

> It's hard to fully grasp just how much different Americans' behavior is around church attendance today versus fifty years ago. . . . In the very first administration of the GSS [the General Social Survey conducted in 1972] only 9 percent of respondents said they never attended religious services. Another 8 percent

said their attendance was less than once a year. Compare that to 2021, when 31 percent described their attendance as "never" and another 15 percent said they attended less than yearly. Seventeen percent of people were less than yearly attenders in 1972, but that's [the practice of] nearly half the population today.[65]

Yes, 60 percent of Americans still call themselves Christian. However, if we summarize *their* reports of their attendance along with the self-reporting of those with other religious affiliations discussed above, then the actual practice of America's religions looks like this:

Population Percentages as Indicated by Affiliation and *Self-Reported* Regular Worship Attendance

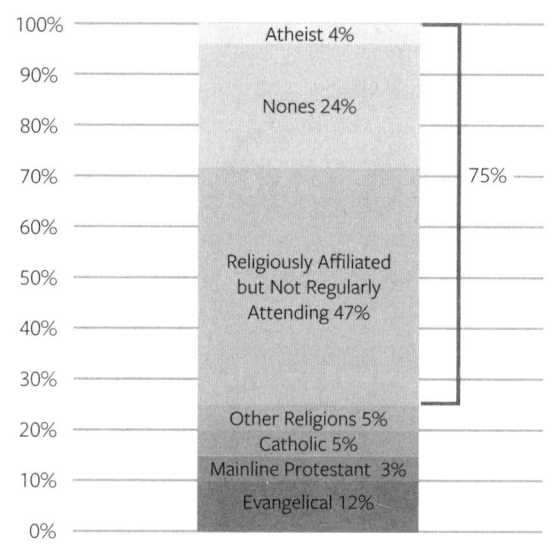

- Atheist 4%
- Nones 24%
- Religiously Affiliated but Not Regularly Attending 47%
- Other Religions 5%
- Catholic 5%
- Mainline Protestant 3%
- Evangelical 12%

(75% bracket covering the top three categories)

Note: The percentages in the lower four categories are based on people affiliated with each group and regularly attending services.

Sadly, as discouraging as these numbers are, they may be too optimistic. Attendance figures are notoriously difficult to obtain and assess.[66] Few denominations report or have the means to document the weekly attendance patterns of their local churches. In my own denomination, less than half of our churches annually report their weekly attendance numbers, and when they do, we don't really know if we are getting "the pastor's count" or "the deacons' count."

Even though my denomination is one of the few in America that continues to grow—and perhaps, to some degree because of that—institutional distrust, personal discouragement, and potential ego damage make many local church leaders reluctant to report regular attendance.[67] As a consequence, most national estimates of church attendance are gathered from surveys based on what people self-report about their attendance patterns.

There are a variety of reasons such self-reporting is undependable. One is that COVID has changed perceptions of what "regular attendance" means. Historically, pastors and parishioners have had differing perceptions of what it means. Those who rarely attend church may think of themselves as regular attenders if they are "pine tree and lilies" Christians—that is, only attending at Christmas and Easter. On the other hand, those who are highly committed to local church activities may not think of anyone as a regular attender who attends less than weekly.[68]

Almost everyone expects the pastor to think that regular attendance means going to church weekly. However, surveys of pastors indicate they now think of regular attenders as those who show up in person once or twice a month. Pastors (and church staff) also plan programs and curricula accordingly.[69]

Unquestionably, the disruptions of COVID and the availability of streaming services have made it much more common for the average parishioner to think that monthly in-person attendance counts as regular. Current surveys indicate that 41 percent of church people think regular means less than weekly.[70]

These variations in perceptions signal that trying to come up with a standard measurement of what regular attendance means is notoriously difficult and is influenced by individual expectations, traditional practices, and current trends. So, relying on what people *say* (i.e., self-report) about their attendance makes researchers dependent on the responses of people who may be tempted to report what they think their patterns ought to be, or what the pastor expects, or the past habits that formed their perception of their attendance, even if it varies from present patterns. All of these factors make it quite challenging to get at what is real.

The Real Majority

As mentioned in the preceding chapter, what is real in terms of what most people actually *do* on Sunday is likely far different from what they *say* about their worship patterns. One-fifth to one-fourth of Americans *say* that they are in worship services each week.[71] Historically, we have had few ways of confirming these personal reports. Yet, like so many other facets of our society, technology is changing what we can confirm or debunk. As indicated previously, researchers now have the ability to assess the movements of the general population by tracking smartphones. So, now we understand that if the patterns indicated by our cell phone movements on Sunday mornings are accurate, then 5 percent of all Americans of any religious tradition are actually engaged in weekly worship on that day.[72] This means the religious landscape in America according to our worship patterns looks to be more as the following chart illustrates:

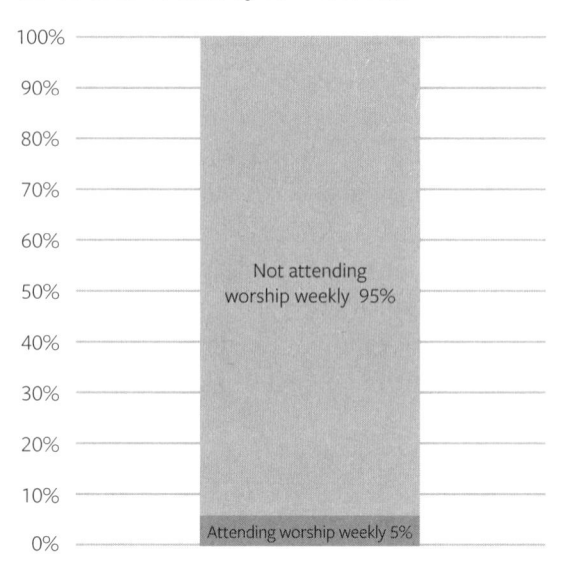

Population Percentages of Weekly Sunday Worship Attendance as Indicated by Cell Phone Data

Not attending worship weekly	95%
Attending worship weekly	5%

These statistics obviously mean that the changes in America's religious affiliations and habits have resulted in massive changes in faith expression. In one generation, American culture has shifted from 90 percent of the population identifying as Christian to less than half belonging to any church and 95 percent *not* engaged in weekly Sunday worship. With such dramatic shifts over so short a span, we should not be surprised that different generations may have very different perspectives of the world, their place in it, and how to express their faith according to current realities, challenges, and opportunities.

What's Real for Our Children

The realities of current affiliations and attendance patterns among those identifying as religious in our nation may be surprising, even shocking, for senior adults or those who became adults in the Moral Majority era (i.e., the 1970s and '80s when conservative religion and politics merged efforts to motivate America's Christian majority to vote for social change that would make America moral again). Quantifying these realities may provide a little more understanding of why the Moral Majority efforts ultimately seem to have had little effect upon the secularization of our society. There hasn't actually been a moral majority for many decades.

If what we intended to yoke together for political purposes was a majority of the American public who conscientiously and regularly embraced a historic, biblical faith in home, work, and worship, then we were harnessing shadows. My goal in saying such things is not simply to explain our present dismay or disappointment in an increasingly secular society, but to respond appropriately.

Responsible and caring reactions to the loss of a majority Christian influence in America must include understanding how great the pressures are upon Christian children, especially those who are trying to live faithfully in this present evil age. Christians who are age fifty and older were raised in an era when the vast majority of Americans thought of themselves as Christian. They attended worship services regularly and agreed with basic Christian values—even if those values were lived inconsistently. By contrast, our children and grandchildren are being raised in a society where Christian affiliation, practices, and belief are increasingly residual.

The effects are probably most plain when discussed in the context of personal experience. I began this chapter by reminding Christian adults of the era familiar to many of them, a time when everyone seemed to be a Christian. Such adults need to recognize that a Christian young person in a public high school today who is regular in church attendance, faithful in biblical standards of sexual purity, and orthodox in theology, may be the only such "Christian" they know—especially if 30 percent of their female friends say their gender is nonbinary, all of their male friends have normalized pornography usage, half of their church friends are sexually active, and most peers will hide their faith identity from the university they wish to attend lest their admission be jeopardized.[73]

In their life context, young people of this generation who remain faithful to their Savior need to be understood, supported, and celebrated by the generation that precedes them. Pastors and churches need to understand younger and older generations and minister to both. How we can do so, despite the generations' vastly different societal perceptions and church expectations, is the subject of the next chapters.

4

THE MATURE UNIFORM

My friend looked at me with a grimace after the sermon from the 40-year-old pastor who had just been called to lead a historic church. The new pastor had laid out his vision for the aging congregation to reach young families and minister in new ways to the community. Some in the congregation were obviously excited about new possibilities. My 62-year-old friend was not. He summarized his assessment of the new pastor with these simple words: "He won't put on the uniform."

I understood what the phrase meant. A prior generation had gone to war against cultural assaults on historic Christianity in our nation with a clear agenda that united Evangelical churches across denominations and across our country. Virtually every pastor of a Bible-believing church and every member of the church understood the agenda and "suited up" to fight the culture war in uniforms designed by heroes of the Lord's army.

Perceptions of the Mature

These heroes were the organizers of political campaigns, economic boycotts, life chains, and court actions that promised to help Bible-believing Christians drive out encroaching evils that were threatening the morals of our children, polluting the content of our entertainments, and unraveling the way of life epitomized in advertisements for Campbell's soup and

Kodak film. The "uniform" donned by faithful pastors of that generation who were doing their duty in the culture wars consisted of sermons on social issues that our heroes said needed to be addressed to turn back the forces of evil destroying our nation's morals and values.

The Great Loss

Just as the "Greatest Generation" had gone to war to rescue our world from evil outside our land, the duty and calling of the next generation was to protect secured territory from enemies within our borders that marched under the banners of liberalism, Hollywood, and secular humanism. Christian philosopher Francis Schaeffer identified and lamented the incursions of these spiritual enemies in a sobering message delivered to motivate churches for their cultural mission in the 1980s:

> The whole culture has been squandered and largely lost. Eighty years ago, there was a Christian consensus in this country; all the most devastating things . . . have come in the last 40 years. Anybody who here is 55 years of age [knows] all the most devastating things in every area of our culture, whether it be art or music, whether it be law or government, whether it's the schools, permissiveness and all the rest, all these things have come climactically in our adult lifehood. . . . But, the mentality of accommodation did not raise the voice, it did not raise the battle, it did not call God's people to realize that this is a part of the task to speak out into the culture and society against that which was being squandered and lost and largely thrown away. An accommodation mentality ecclesiastically . . . led to a lack of confrontation in our culture, society and in the country. As the great loss occurred . . . more and more things were lost, more and more things were allowed to be robbed, more and more things slid away.[1]

According to Schaeffer, our calling was to reclaim what had been lost. The enemy was a permissive society. Past failure was due to the church's accommodation to a secular culture. Ground to be reclaimed had once been secured by a Christian consensus that had kept our nation's morals and values from sliding away. Thus, the mission of the church was now to "raise the battle" and speak out "in our culture, society and in the country" with a voice of "confrontation" that addressed the issues of "the great loss."

Uniting churches from different traditions, denominations, and regions in a nationwide calling to reclaim the heart of America would not have been possible without the sense of loss that Schaeffer so well identified. He also accurately captured the perception of the churched people of his era that was described in the preceding chapter. At a time when 90 percent of Americans identified as Christians, it was no stretch to believe that finding ways to motivate the majority to organize, act, and vote according to the Christian consensus of their parents' generation would turn back the rising tide of unbelief.

The political movement that became known as the Moral Majority throughout the 1980s was birthed out of the perception that most people in America were Christian (or at least traditionally moral according to Christian values). This perception was shared by conservative church and political leaders who believed that a new Christian consensus could secure families, communities, and a traditional way of life from the threats of a secular humanism being advocated by liberal elites in government, education, media, and the arts. Thus, the goal of conservative church and political leaders was to convince the majority to act, voting for political candidates who would support the values of the church on social issues.

The Issues

Key issues united the Moral Majority in its opposition to secular philosophies and values. The issues are well-known to any who have led Evangelical churches over the last half century. Many of those churches—or at least a healthy proportion of their members—still expect their leaders to "put on the uniform" in loyalty to conservative causes by regularly addressing these issues in ways that are supposed to prove one's biblical faithfulness and cultural courage.

These issues were dealt with in virtually every national context, from local churches to school boards to corporation meetings to legislative halls to our nation's Supreme Court. The goal of liberal causes was to throw off perceived chains of oppression that limited choice and self-expression. The conservative agenda was to *take control* of hearts and the electorate by convincing the *moral majority* to take necessary steps to *halt* spiritual erosions and help organizations that would stem the great loss.

I expect that simply charting the common perceptions and expectations of Evangelicals during the Moral Majority era will bring a ready "aha" of recognition to those now in their fifties and older.

Evangelicals in Their Fifties and Older: Perceptions and Expectations

Long-standing perception: "I am a Christian in a *majority* Christian culture."

Mission: The church should work to help the majority *take control* of the culture.

Means: Help restore the nation's biblical values and *halt* the corrosive influences of:
  Abortion
  The Homosexual (now LGBTQ+) Agenda
  Pornography
  Illegal drugs
  Gambling
  Green movements
  Illegal immigration
  Racial discrimination

Abortion

I put abortion first on the list of "uniform" issues because nothing else has been of equal significance in uniting conservative Christians across denominations and regions into a single voice. Though the Moral Majority formally ended as an organization in 1989, its influence has clearly continued to unite and mobilize those in the Evangelical movement across the Reagan, Bushes, and Trump presidencies.

The Life Chains, Marches for Life, Sanctity of Human Life Sundays, annual gatherings at the capitols of our states and nation, pregnancy help clinics, adoption advocacy organizations, lobbying groups, political platform statements, the overturning of *Roe v. Wade*, and more ecclesiastical organizations and actions than I can list—all testify to the incredible unifying power of the fight against abortion. No other issue has been of equal import in bringing together diverse Protestant denominations into a cooperative movement with each other and with other faith traditions.

This is not to say that the issue has always united Evangelicals. Many individuals have been so committed to defending the defenseless that they have not been able to hear differing voices on strategies or time frames. As an example, C. Everett Koop, the Surgeon General during the Reagan administration and one of the pro-life movement's most articulate spokespeople, came under harsh criticism for disagreeing with the strategies of some pro-life groups. He later responded that he believed the Right to Life movement was undermining itself with "shrill" voices that damaged relationships and credibility.

Greater but similar concerns arose when civil disobedience and violence became instruments of a very few abortion opponents. I mention Koop's characterization only because it continues to have bearing on how some younger Evangelicals now respond to pro-life issues, as will be discussed shortly.

Homosexual Agenda

The leaders of the Moral Majority understood that the success of the gay rights movement would fundamentally change the moral standards of the United States. So, their opposition was strong both on the basis of biblical standards and the realization that fears of homosexual influence (in the terms of that era) would be a powerful galvanizing force for their own political gains. And they were right—at least for a time.

When the formal organization of the Moral Majority was at its height, the gay rights movement was still relatively small. Into the 1970s, homosexual practices were still illegal in most states. The Stonewall riots in 1969, which are generally considered to have ignited the modern gay rights movement, were the consequence of police trying to shut down a gay bar in New York City—a place none consider a center of conservative politics. From the 1970s forward, the gay rights movement advanced quickly,[2] even though some states retained anti-sodomy laws into the early 2000s.

The American Psychiatric Association removed homosexuality from its list of psychiatric disorders in 1973. The trajectory of the nation's attitudes and standards regarding all LGBTQ+ issues is evident in the changing military regulations that followed. Through the mid-1970s the military actively excluded or discharged anyone identifying as gay. In 1994, regulations officially changed to allow retention if individuals did not disclose their orientation. This "don't ask, don't tell" policy was repealed in 2011 under the Obama administration. By 2013, spousal and family benefits were extended to same-sex married partners in the military. The ban on transgender individuals was most recently rescinded in 2021, allowing those who don't identify with their biological gender to enlist and serve in the armed forces.

These trends in the military have only echoed changing attitudes and standards in the wider culture. In the 2015 *Obergefell v. Hodge* decision, the US Supreme Court ruled that the Fourteenth Amendment requires all states to grant same-sex marriages and recognize same-sex marriages granted in other states. The ruling seemed to indicate that Evangelical opposition to gay rights had failed politically. The great loss deepened.

Debates will continue in the Evangelical church as to why its opposition to the LGBTQ+ agenda failed (or whether it has failed in the hearts of the faithful) considering Americans overwhelmingly objected to homosexual expression as late as the mid-1990s. At that time, over two-thirds objected to what more than two-thirds now approve.[3] Why were our voices not heard in a culture where the majority still identified as Christian? Was the failure due to the triumph of secularism, the cleverness of the LGBTQ+ campaigns, the nominalism or apathy of the American church, the shrill voices of the religious right, a combination of all of these, or some other factor?

Regardless of the answer(s), it is apparent that our culture has rapidly changed in what it considers acceptable regarding sex and gender. It is also clear that Evangelical young people differ from the generations before them on homosexual issues. According to one study, only one-third (34 percent) of white Evangelicals age fifty and over favor same-sex marriage, but 51 percent of those ages 18–49 now favor it.[4] This means, of course, that the changing nature of the culture and church have to be weighed as Evangelical leaders consider how best to minister God's unchanging truth.

Pornography

I write these words not long after receiving word of the death of Donald Wildmon, a United Methodist preacher and founder of the National Federation for Decency and the American Family Association. Wildmon organized Christian boycotts of television networks, corporations, magazines, and retailers who marketed or sponsored sexually oriented materials—largely in the era before the internet.

Wildmon was a courageous culture warrior who proved to be visionary when he said, "What we are up against is not dirty words and dirty pictures. . . . It is a philosophy of life which seeks to remove the influence of Christians and Christianity from our society."[5] Tens of thousands of Evangelicals joined his boycotts and thousands of churches embraced his message. Even without the science to prove it, they understood instinctively from Scripture that the sexualization of our entertainments and habits would lead to lusts and addictions that would damage families and faith (2 Pet. 2:14–22).

Study after study now confirms the destructive effects of pornography on family and personal health.[6] Though the stats are difficult to confirm and highly debatable, the studies most likely to draw our attention show little difference between pornography use of born-again Christians and all others in our society.[7] One internet magazine summarized recent studies this way:

> The porn pandemic is engulfing the Christian world as well. The Barna Group discovered there is virtually no difference in the monthly porn use of non-Christian men (65 percent) versus Christian men (64 percent). Porn use is even worse among the younger Christian generation. In 2019, the Freedom Fight conducted a survey of more than 1,300 Practicing Christian college students from over thirty different campuses across the country. . . . Eighty-nine percent of the Christian men surveyed watch porn at least occasionally. Sixty-one percent view it at least weekly and 24 percent watch porn daily or multiple times a day.
>
> But this is not just a guy's problem. Porn use is also plaguing women in Christian colleges. Fifty-one percent of this group watch porn at least occasionally. Seventy percent of them either watched porn or had a sexual hookup in the last 12 months.[8]

More sophisticated research from The Gospel Coalition reminds us that these often-cited percentages are based on *self-identified* "Christians" and not Evangelicals who are consistent in worship and belief. This research concludes, "A statistic that implies a significant majority of Christian men are consumers of porn is alarming. But it becomes less surprising when you realize many of those 'Christian' men surveyed are nominally Christian or reject traditional sexual ethics."[9]

Apparently, only about a third of "devout Protestants" regularly use pornography (and here we have to assume that this category captures regular and committed Evangelicals).[10] That is still a sadly large number of those regularly with us in worship, but it's also evidence that the gospel does provide hope against sinful struggles. Researcher Lyman Stone concludes, "Today, Protestant men who attend church regularly are basically the only men in America still resisting the cultural norm of regularized pornography use."[11]

This is a more hopeful perspective, but it still requires us to consider the consequences of regular pornography use being seen as "the cultural norm." One obvious effect is that many men are suffering from the old hedonist dilemma of no longer being stimulated by constant exposure to what once gave them pleasure.[12] Pastors who counsel couples are well aware that heavy pornography usage creates marital dissatisfaction, dysfunction, and depression—effects that have been corroborated by secular researchers.[13]

We think of pornography as hypersexualizing our culture, but it is also desexualizing many of its addicts who need greater and greater sexual thrills until they can no longer be thrilled by sex at all—neither within nor outside of marriage. A common pattern of pornographic addiction in marriage is an increasing dissatisfaction with sexual intimacy with one's spouse, then perceiving one's spouse as a hindrance to satisfying sex, then perceiving digital sex as more satisfying and less complicated than human relationships, and then seeking endlessly for some form of digital sex to satisfy or at least stimulate.[14]

Young people who learn to relate to the opposite sex through pornography sabotage their future relationships by becoming accustomed to using others for personal pleasure rather than caring selflessly for another, thus depriving themselves of the kind of love that ultimately provides any relationship its deepest fulfillment and greatest satisfaction.[15] The sense of loveless passion or of being used that results from purely mechanical or selfish sex becomes so unfulfilling that the number of sexually active teens is plummeting—not on the basis of moral objection but on the basis of dissatisfaction with the experience or the pressures to perform according to advertised expectations.[16]

Young women who are introduced to sexual intimacy through pornography or experiences with boys mimicking it, seem to be retreating from traditional sexual identification in record numbers.[17] The number of women in their teens and twenties who identify as nonbinary is as high as

30 percent in some parts of the country (some of my pastor friends say it is much higher in their areas).[18] Causation is difficult to prove and undoubtedly multifaceted. Still, clinicians continue to report climbing caseloads of nonbinary adolescent females in this country and other Western cultures.[19]

Understanding rooted in biblical principles of how sin can invade and warp the health of mind and spirit provides possible explanations for many Christians. Women, who are exposed to the vileness and violence of today's pornography that is ramped up to capture increasingly desensitized males (and a growing number of females), may simply be saying to themselves, "If that is what sex is, then I want nothing to do with it."[20] Alternatively, young women, whom the Lord has created to need sensitivity and care, have become repulsed by men who want to use them pornographically and turn to other women who are also seeking tenderness.

Pornography cannot be the sole cause of such dramatic cultural shifts, but it is a major contributor to the unprecedented sexual confusion of rising generations. Pew surveys indicate that 5 percent of young people ages 18–29 no longer identify with the sex assigned them at birth—that is seventeen times higher than those age 50+.[21] The CDC's Youth Risk Behavior Surveillance System indicates that one in four high schoolers also do not identify as "straight."[22]

We should be saddened but not surprised—or uncaring. Today, young people—who are not emotionally ready for the committed relationships that actually make sex satisfy as God designed—are immersed in social media, peer perceptions, and pop culture expressions that tout sexual activity as the ultimate pleasure for youth. So, those who experiment sexually and feel dissatisfied, or who back away from pornographic images or relationships that seem demeaning, then wonder why they are not "normal."

For any young person asking that question today, there is an army of counselors, peers, and teachers mobilized to affirm and congratulate being same-sex attracted or other-sex made. Adults should know that at some point every adolescent wonders, "Am I normal?" But now, as teachers and peers push young people to think that their sexual questioning is actually a marker of sexual orientation or gender identity, young people are being pressed into same-sex identifications or permanently damaging transgender decisions that no child is ready to handle.[23]

If the figures are correct that nearly two-thirds of those who self-identify as Evangelicals are regular consumers of pornography—or even if the number was half that—then, knowing that researchers ignore R-rated images and only count what is X-rated as pornographic, there still is no question that the poisoning of God's intended purposes for passion is pervasive among us.

No Evangelical pastor, teacher, youth leader, or alert parent can deny that the images, words, and topics available to adults and children at hardcore internet sites or via everyday cable TV and streaming apps have led to a general coarsening of our culture, common dysfunction in our marriages, and wide-scale confusion for our children.[24] All of these factors contribute to the inescapable conclusion that, despite all the ridicule and invective that Donald Wildmon received as a smut crusader, he was right: "What we are up against is not dirty words and dirty pictures. . . . It is a philosophy of life which seeks to remove the influence of Christians and Christianity from our society."

Illegal Drugs

For the Moral Majority era and the two decades leading to it, parental fear of our children's use of illegal drugs stimulated many cautionary sermons. Pastors joined parents in decrying the counterculture mantra of "turn on, tune in, and drop out" that threatened to capture or kill their children. The perceived enemies of traditional life were the hippies, radicals, and druggies who were unconvinced that the compulsions of affluence, position, and power driving their parents' generation should dictate the life choices of subsequent generations.

Educational efforts attempted to teach all Americans of the gateway evils of marijuana that led to the greater threats of cocaine, LSD, and heroin. The last of these became particularly available and addictive for military personnel seeking escape from the pressures and horrors of their tours of duty during the Vietnam War. So, when returning veterans joined the counterculture habits of America's youth, President Nixon announced the "War on Drugs" that escalated under President Reagan's "Just Say No" campaigns.

The Reagan efforts, in particular, coincided with the rise of the Moral Majority's efforts to save America's children from various moral corruptions.

The efforts were not mere rhetoric. With the sermons and support of most Evangelicals and other churches, many billions of dollars of educational resources and law enforcement were directed at assessing and curtailing drug availability and use.

Those efforts resulted in the US incarceration rate more than quadrupling between 1980 and the early 2000s, with jail terms disproportionally assigned to those young, poor, and Black.[25] Urban Black communities especially suffered from the availability of cocaine, contributing in some states to half of all Black males being arrested by age 35 and a quarter being incarcerated for some period.[26] Still, the drugs did not stop.

When government intervention efforts and "get tough" mandatory sentencing policies proved largely unsuccessful, the nation ultimately lost its stomach for the mass incarcerations it could not afford, limit, or justify. Republicans and Democrats agreed to end the War on Drugs.[27]

Under the Biden administration, the House of Representatives passed the Marijuana Opportunity Reinvestment and Expungement (MORE) Act, removing marijuana from the Controlled Substances Act and directing the expungement of all related convictions. By mid-2023, over thirty states had decriminalized marijuana to some degree.

Now, a growing number of states have also decriminalized all illicit drugs, choosing to deal with drug abuse as a public health issue rather than a criminal offense. Sadly, neither mandatory sentencing nor the easing of law enforcement saved the nation from the opioid crisis (precipitated by the profiteering of drug companies and unscrupulous pain clinics) or the present battle with fentanyl (the synthetic opioid provided easily and cheaply from illegitimate sources). Not only is the synthetic fifty times stronger than heroin; it is terribly addictive and kills 150 Americans per day.[28] As a result, Evangelical pastors and church leaders have learned that our nation's drug problems do not only plague "street people" that so-called *respectable* churches can choose to ignore. Now, church leaders from all demographics must care for the lawyers, teachers, businesspeople, mechanics, bricklayers, and factory workers in our pews who first became opioid addicted under a doctor's prescribed care.

Only as the nation and its religious leaders have had to face the loss of our constituents have we been able to confess our failure to curb America's chemical addictions. With the head of our government's Drug Enforcement Agency, most church leaders recognize that, after more than a half century of trying to stop illegal drugs, we are only now facing what is being called the "most devastating drug crisis in our nation's history."[29]

Gambling

From the beginning of the twentieth century, Evangelical Protestants actively sought to curb unbiblical habits in society ranging from abuse of alcohol, to strip clubs and adult bookstores, to playing sports and shopping on Sundays. Blue laws and vice squads enforced the will of the Christian majority that sought to protect the young, the morally weak, the poor, and church attendance from businesses and entrepreneurs willing to take advantage of human vulnerabilities. The logic that led to these controls also led the Evangelical church to fight against gambling.

Early anti-gambling efforts sought to remove horse racing, dog racing, cock fighting, and gambling hall establishments that not only took advantage of the poor but were gathering grounds for the "unsavory" segments of our communities. However, shifting mores and advances in technology after World War II changed what American society was willing to limit and had the ability to regulate.

In my lifetime, blue laws that had prohibited retailers from being open on Sundays were first lifted for services and commodities deemed "necessary" (e.g., restaurants, gas stations), then for grocery stores, and then for all that was needed to make interstate travel safe and possible seven days a week. By the time all the exceptions had been allowed, Walmart was open seven days a week, being closed on Sunday was a marketing distinction of Chick-fil-A alone, and pastors were in trouble if the sermon went long enough to make parishioners late for the game or last in line at the local buffet.

In the process, gambling has also become respectable and acceptable. It wasn't always so. In the Moral Majority era, many churches joined efforts with conservative political forces to restrict the vice of gambling to protect the poor and those with addictive vulnerabilities. Statewide campaigns to limit lotteries, restrict casinos, and prohibit sports betting were often the subjects of sermons and petition drives in conservative churches. Churches and organizations as varied as the Evangelical Lutheran Church of America, the Billy Graham Evangelistic Association, the Biblical Counseling Coalition, the Protestant Reformed Church, the Southern Baptist Church, the Assemblies of God, and many others warned of the consequences of gambling and cited biblical principles about not taking advantage of the vulnerable.[30]

As technology made all forms of gambling available at all times, American attitudes changed from seeing gambling as a vice to seeing it as a form of entertainment and a means of gaining revenue for state governments without raising taxes.[31] In 2009, Gallup found that 58 percent of Americans said that gambling was morally acceptable; by 2023, approval increased to 70 percent.[32] Now, 44 states have casinos, 40 states have some form of legalized sports betting, and 45 states have lotteries.

The voice of the church has become less certain and less vocal about the evils of gambling in recent years. Fewer Evangelicals think that Scripture completely prohibits gambling.[33] Pastors are more inclined to speak about gambling as a decision to be based on prudence rather than as a clear biblical prohibition.[34]

Americans spend half a trillion dollars per year on *illegal* gambling (roughly five times what they contribute to church causes),[35] with another three-quarters of a trillion dollars spent on legal forms of gambling (roughly the same as Americans' total spending on K–12 public education).[36] Estimates are that 80 percent of adult Americans gamble, with many becoming addicted, including almost a million young people (ages 14–21) and 6 percent of all college students.[37] Yet, a recent study indicates that nearly two-thirds of Evangelicals do not think gambling—especially sports gambling—is wrong.[38]

Green Movements

Environmental issues would seem to be an unlikely focus of Evangelical church concerns. And, if we only consider *organized* opposition to green movements, the church's response does not compare with its activity relating to elements of the Evangelical uniform previously mentioned. Still, older congregants and pastors are likely to have strong, negative opinions about environmental movements, including perceived antibusiness pollution standards, Greenpeace, Ralph Nader, Rachel Carson, and most especially climate change advocates such as Al Gore.

There are historic reasons that an older generation of Evangelicals considers opposition to the so-called "green" movements to be an aspect of their faith uniform. The opposition has not been so much to forest protection as to political associations. The environmental advocates who rallied to defend snail darters, spotted owls, and a cleaner planet often did so using antibusiness or even anti-capitalist rhetoric.

In key states and regions, antibusiness stances threatened corporate profits and vital jobs. Those threats united business and labor populations in politically conservative strongholds to oppose tree huggers, greenies, and later climate activists. Already among threatened business and labor populations were the ordinary congregants of conservative Evangelical churches. Their green opposition was more about self-protection than scriptural opposition to creation care.

The additional opposition from so many church people was stimulated by environmentalism's anti-capitalist messaging that was too reminiscent of Evangelicalism's older enemies. Prior to the Moral Majority era of the 1980s, Cold War opposition to atheistic communism rocketed figures such as Billy Graham, Carl McIntire, and Billy James Hargis to Evangelical leadership. Waves of Communist fears stirred by McCarthyism, Russian nuclear threats, Eastern European and Chinese aggressions, and spy scandals gave Evangelicals strong cause for resistance organizations, protective schools, and political alignments that would remain effective footholds for later Moral Majority figures.

In time, Jerry Falwell, Pat Robertson, D. James Kennedy, and others would press for political alliances as well as church support on the basis of their opposition to godless Communism. The liberal voices in universities, which argued that not every nation needed democracy or US military protections, seemed to join with liberal theologies attacking Scripture and traditional faith in an unholy union determined to undermine our nation's freedoms and security.

The social gospel of Mainline denominations, which substituted good works as the church's primary mission instead of promoting faith in Jesus Christ, also sounded too much like the social agenda being pushed by liberal political movements that had locked arms with the environmentalists. For many Evangelicals, it simply seemed that the tree huggers and their allies were more concerned with preserving nature than the nation and protecting Mother Earth rather than glorifying our Father in heaven.

The strength and effects of these fears may seem unfounded to a contemporary generation that wonders whether its children or grandchildren will survive unaddressed climate woes. Still, for those of us raised when nuclear weapons were being shipped to Cuba and missile-defense silos were being buried under America's cornfields, the Communist threats were real and the liberal compromises plain. Just as the psyche of a present generation of schoolchildren has been shaped by active shooter drills, so the perceptions of an older generation were formed as we huddled in our school hallways and learned how to survive a nuclear holocaust.

Evangelical opposition to the green movements and their social allies has never really been whether or not to preserve forests. Snail darters were not the real concern; the liberals were. Even today, the kiss of death for any cause or persons who are questionable among Evangelicals is attaching a "liberal" label to them that sticks.

Illegal Immigration

Immigration concerns, much like environmental concerns, seem an unlikely piece of the Evangelical uniform. Informed Evangelicals know our Lord's mandate to his people: "You shall not oppress a sojourner. You know the heart of a sojourner, for you were sojourners in the land of Egypt" (Exod. 23:9; see also Zech. 7:10; Mal. 3:5). Yet, in a Christmas devotional a few years ago, when I identified Mary and Joseph as "transients" on their journey to Bethlehem, I caught more heat than I imagined possible for being so "political."

What causes America's Evangelicals—who are almost entirely descended from immigrants, who are regularly taught to respect all people as being made in the image of God, whose hearts so readily go out to those who are suffering, and who know the Golden Rule—to become so angry and animated in opposition to illegal immigration?[39] The key word in that question is "illegal."

While no one can deny that plain old prejudice and bigotry are the cause of some opposition to immigration among Evangelicals, the more common concerns relate to border and job security. With falling birth rates, our nation needs an influx of immigrants to maintain economic growth and prosperity. Yet, we cannot handle the numbers currently seeking entrance.

As I write this paragraph more than a quarter million immigrants have illegally crossed our nation's southern border in the past month—2.5 million in the last year.[40] Mayors in our nation's major cities, as well as leaders in communities along our border, say that they cannot provide for such large numbers of immigrants.

Evangelicals are not alone in believing that more must be done to protect our nation's boundaries for the sake of those on both sides of the border. More also needs to be done to protect the families, health, and dignity of those who are fleeing violence, oppression, and extreme deprivations in their homelands. Yet, we as a nation are divided on what needs to be done. So, conservative church people tend to align with the position of the political party they favor. In recent years, that has been the party most aligned with their moral concerns and zealous for greater immigrant and refugee restrictions.

Because we are "people of the Book," Evangelicals tend to favor the party that argues for upholding the rule of law. Because many of our people are working class, we tend to favor the party that argues for protecting jobs. Because we remain susceptible to prejudice, we may even listen to racist fears and xenophobic comments that are contrary to our faith.[41]

Since we have already suffered such large cultural losses previously described in this book, we also tend to fear that the influx of so many "different" people will further "threaten traditional American customs and values."[42] What an older generation may not understand is how such arguments can hold so little value for a generation that was raised distant from those customs and values and that evaluates compassion primarily based on news and social media images of suffering immigrant families.

Racial Discrimination

Of all the items on the list of social concerns that the Moral Majority generation hoped to correct or control, racial discrimination is the unlikeliest. Without question, the traditional makeup and mentality of the Evangelical church made it tardy or absent from efforts to bring racial justice to our nation. Some of our denominations, including my own, had individuals or documents stating that our founding purposes included maintaining segregation.[43]

Thankfully, a number of Evangelical denominations, including my own, have made statements of repentance for their complicity in the sins of slavery and the Jim Crow era, and for their indifference or opposition to the Civil Rights Movement.[44] These expressions of repentance have not simply been lip service.

Even though Mainline churches have more consistently preached against racial discrimination, the Evangelical church has made much greater advances in racial reconciliation. A Duke study funded by the Lilly Endowment reports,

> In 1998, only 1 in 100 mainline Protestant churches reached the no-one-group-has-more-than-80-percent threshold of diversity. In 2018–19, one in ten mainline Protestant churches met this threshold. . . . In 1998, only 7 percent of evangelical congregations were multiracial in this sense, but this percentage more than tripled to 22 percent in 2018–2019.[45]

These figures are not unqualified good news. The gap is much smaller when considering primarily white congregations of either Mainline or Evangelical churches. At least three-quarters of white Christians say that their churches are mostly white, including 80 percent of white Mainline Protestants and 75 percent of white Evangelical Protestants.[46] Mostly responsible for the diversity among Evangelicals are Pentecostal and Hispanic Protestants, and megachurches.[47]

Still, virtually all major Evangelical denominations now report some degree of racial diversity.[48] Most pastors see racial diversity as a biblical goal, despite their struggles to achieve it.[49] These are significant advances toward biblical fidelity in churches whose official teaching affirms the Bible's declarations of the divine image and personal dignity of all persons.

While it is impossible here to summarize all that has led to changes in Evangelical attitudes, if not actual membership makeup, much should be attributed to significant leadership examples, such as:

- Billy Graham's refusal to segregate his crusades.
- John Perkins's refusal to express hatred for his persecutors and opponents.

- Tony Evans's willingness to minister across racial lines (despite recently confessed unrighteousness in his life).
- The efforts of the National Association of Evangelicals to diversify its leadership in the 1990s and beyond.
- More recent efforts of The Gospel Coalition, and (most pointedly for the average person in the pews) the efforts of the Promise Keepers movement to make racial reconciliation a major goal of its gatherings and the commitments of their participants, especially in the 1990s but also into the present.[50]

I should note at this point that the Promise Keepers movement used the terminology of "racial reconciliation" to promote the biblical concepts of mutual love, respect, and justice. This terminology has stayed acceptable among most Evangelicals, even as the Critical Race Theory battles and critiques of the last half decade have made terms such as "racial justice," "ethnic diversity," and "intersectionality" suspect in many Evangelical camps—subjects to which we must return in chapter 5.

Concerns for the Mature

I began this chapter by noting that a healthy proportion of Evangelicals still expect their leaders to "put on the uniform" of social conservatism in loyalty to the goals of the Moral Majority. For many senior members of our churches (and not a few of their children and grandchildren), regularly addressing issues such as those identified above is still proof of their leaders' biblical faithfulness and cultural courage.

A consensus remains among almost all who call themselves Evangelical that a great loss has occurred, threatening faith and family. But hardly anyone agrees that there is now a *Christian* majority in the nation that can be mobilized to secure the traditional way of life whose passing Francis Schaeffer lamented. Different conclusions about how the Evangelical church should now engage cultural issues often divide churches, and often the divide is along generational lines.

An older generation listens in church for messages that affirm the rightness of culture war issues for which they fought and the continuing necessity of the practices and preaching of the Moral Majority era. However, a younger generation that often agrees with the biblical values of their seniors still questions their messaging, methods, and success in a culture without a Christian majority or consensus.

Such questions sound like either criticism or cowardice to an older generation that sacrificed to try to turn the nation back to its "Christian roots." Conversely, such accusations sound like stubbornness or insensitivity to a younger generation that wants to rescue family, friends, and neighbors from a pervasively paganized culture by communicating "Christ's heart."

The generations have much more in common than these tensions would suggest, but we need to understand how rising generations perceive their culture and their cultural engagement responsibilities before we can celebrate the contributions of all generations. The next chapter seeks to provide such understanding.

5

THE MINORITY MISSION

Ever since childhood, Christians in America who are now age fifty and older have perceived themselves to be in a majority Christian culture. Their children and grandchildren have not. Christians who are in their forties or younger have never known a day in their lives when they considered themselves to be in a Christian majority culture. Always they have perceived themselves to be a minority in a secular, pluralistic culture.

Perceptions of the Young

Such differing perceptions have profound effects on what each generation and its leaders consider their church's cultural engagement responsibilities. As we have already seen, the natural response to cultural corruption, when we believe that a moral majority objects, is to try to motivate the majority to take steps to roll back societal evils. In that context, encouraging and equipping the church to mobilize its members to take control of cultural institutions and power centers in their spheres of influence seems not only reasonable but biblically responsible.

However, if we believe that we are part of a Christian *minority* in a culture that is already controlled by relativistic philosophies and secular values, we will necessarily consider ourselves on a different mission. More in concert with first-century Christians in a pagan Roman culture, those seeking to bear witness to Christ in a majority non-Christian culture will think that their first priority is to make their faith *credible* to an unbelieving world.

The Great "Secularization"

How we make our faith credible requires some assessment of what opposes our faith. In this the generations are often aligned. Sounding much like the heroes of the Moral Majority a half century earlier, influential Evangelical pastor Tim Keller wrote a series of articles in 2022 based on the following assumptions:

> A process called "secularization" has been going on in western societies for several centuries, mainly among highly educated elites, though it gathered steam among the general population after World War II. . . . Secularization has two basic features:
>
> *The enforced privatization of religion.* Science and technology are considered the only ways to understand and solve human problems. Beliefs and values in religion are never to be invoked in serious public discourse. . . . This has made religion seem irrelevant to society.
>
> A *radical individualism.* The move from religion to use of one's reason . . . developed a view of the emancipated self that must be free to determine its own moral choices.[1]

The New Mission

By such statements, it could be argued that Keller and Schaeffer (see chapter 4) are still on the same page, seeing the same secular evils and critiquing them according to the same biblical values. In fact, Keller argues in the same series of articles, "The renewed church must be completely orthodox in its historic doctrine." But what is the path to such renewal? Keller charts this new and different course:

> It [the renewed church] will unite a commitment to social reform, listening to marginalized people and sacrificial ministry to the poor—with a deep commitment to evangelism, to new church planting, to apologetics, to sharp critiques of modern culture. It will combine a concern to contextualize the gospel to new cultures and to bring theology into dialogue with modern

thought—with an emphasis on theological retrieval and faithfulness to historic doctrines and traditions. . . .

It will need to listen carefully to what the Bible says about justice *and* to what non-white people in the U.S. say about their experience. . . .

By using the culture's own narratives of body positivity, consent, diversity, freedom, safety, and love—the church may find ways to present the biblical vision for sexuality in compelling terms that ground Christian sex ethics in a larger framework that attracts rather than repels. . . .

The renewed church may find a better way to speak about politics and the state. . . . It cannot live completely or mainly in any one of the current media "bubbles." It will need to weigh promising proposals privileging a distinct worldview—and adopt one that seeks to be more neutral, promoting the thriving and participation of multiple religions and worldviews in the public sphere.[2]

Again, there are striking parallels with Keller's statements and the Schaeffer agenda of the 1980s. Both claim that the church still needs to listen and act biblically as it fulfills an obligation to speak into "the public sphere." Where these men's calls to action vary is not in their theological foundations or mutual commitment to reasoned Christian apologetics but in their cultural applications. Keller has no doubt of the Bible's truth and the need for salvation through the provision of Jesus Christ. But his overarching goal is to attract nonbelievers, not repel them.

Keller gives no call for organizing a Christian majority. Instead, he suggests how to make the Christian message credible to an unbelieving society by arguing for "social reform," justice for non-white people, "finding ways to present the biblical vision for sexuality in compelling terms," "a better way to speak about politics," and even "promoting the thriving and participation of multiple religions and worldviews in the public square."

These were not the missional priorities of the Moral Majority. In fact, to many activists and advocates of the conservative agenda formed during the latter portions of the twentieth century, they will sound similar to the social gospel of the old Mainline church. Yet, each of these measures, and others that Keller offered, have the pointed goal of giving Christians the opportunity to present a reasonable and righteous faith to family, neighbors, and communities that are not Christian. His goal was not political pressure but cultural penetration; not taking control of society but making credible our faith, and thereby transforming our culture by converting or making allies of those who control its foundational values and belief structures.

Issues of the Young

The realities of our secular culture, more than the influence of Keller or any other Evangelical leader, have changed the perception, mission, and goals of the current generation of Evangelical preachers and the congregations they serve. Charting the expectations and issues that Evangelicals in their forties or younger commonly have for their churches may not bring as ready an "Aha" of recognition as the chart of the Moral Majority era in the previous chapter. Yet, for those who are in the rising generations in Evangelical churches, the list is likely to bring an exasperated sigh of, "That's right, but I don't think my parents' generation understands." Here's the list:

Evangelicals in Their Forties and Younger: Perceptions and Expectations

Lifelong Perception: "I am a Christian in a *minority* Christian culture."

Mission: The church should work to *make faith credible* to our friends and our culture.

Means: Present the reasonableness and righteousness of faith by *helping* with:
- Adoption and foster care
- Care for and witness to LGBTQ+ persons
- Victims of pornography and sex trafficking
- Substance addiction counseling and rescue
- Gaming and gambling addictions
- Creation care
- Refugee compassion
- Racial reconciliation and justice

I want to reemphasize that these are not universally held views among younger generations of Evangelicals. Even Keller acknowledges, "Within Evangelicalism there are a number of factions seemingly battling to the death over control of the movement."[3] As the next chapter will discuss, the influence of the Moral Majority era was not entirely social and political. The reason that so many Evangelicals got on board with the movement was that there are strong biblical arguments for much that was opposed.

Those arguments continue to make sense to many in the Evangelical movement—younger and older. And, as I will soon argue, there are biblical values that should and do continue to unite the generations, even when their approaches to cultural engagement vary. How those approaches vary is apparent when considering the issues that often top the agenda of leaders and congregants who want their churches to address cultural concerns.

Adoption and Foster Care

While many Evangelical churches continue to honor a Sanctity of Life Sunday in January to commemorate the horrors of *Roe v. Wade* and now celebrate its reversal, the number of Sundays dedicated to anti-abortion sermons is a small fraction of those similarly designated in the 1980s and '90s. The subject does not even make the list of "75 Most Popular Sermon Topics Being Preached Today" on the Sermon Search website.[4]

I have no way of knowing if my experience tracks with that of churches across the country, but as a leader of an Evangelical denomination, I know of very few churches still actively prioritizing anti-abortion efforts. Even though my position takes me to many conservative, Bible-believing churches, I rarely hear a sermon on the subject. That is not to say, however, that concern for sanctity of life and the preciousness of every human being made in the image of God has lessened.

What I hear instead of anti-abortion sermons is a drumbeat of sermons on the subjects of adoption and foster care. Not since the first century, perhaps, have Christian pastors and parents been so dedicated to proclaiming the love of their Lord by providing such care for the despised and abused of our society. Many have argued that Christianity spread rapidly in its earliest years because of the witness of Christian families rescuing unwanted children from the trash heaps of Roman society.[5] Now, the evidence is overwhelming that this generation of young Evangelical families is "putting its money where its theological mouth is" in caring for the nation's outcast children.[6]

Where a previous generation of Evangelical parents may have taken their children with them for a few afternoon hours to participate in a Life Chain or abortion clinic protest, the present generation is permanently opening their homes to children in need of adoption or foster care.[7] While there are statistical ups and downs in the numbers of Evangelical families making these commitments, pastoral encouragement remains strong.[8]

These commitments of families and finances indicate continuing dedication of younger Evangelicals and their leaders to the sanctity of life, even though the expression of the commitment is often quite hard and very different from the previous generation.[9] As an example, the church that I pastored for most of the last decade had many families involved in adoption and foster care.

I must acknowledge that this pattern of care began before I arrived and has continued since I left. My sermons were not what convinced families to make such sacrifices and show such compassion. What a previous generation did to defend the sanctity of life remained convincing. A younger generation heard, agreed, and committed to the same cause, but with a different perspective and with different methods. Each generation has contributed to the cause of life in ways appropriate for the culture they faced.

It is unlikely that pastors have studied statistics to determine how their messages should shift from an anti-abortion emphasis to a pro-adoption emphasis. Instead, their pastoral instincts are more likely to have caused them to perceive how their messages were being received in a changing culture. One reason, of course, that anti-abortion issues are not as numerous or as strident as they were a generation ago is that, as indicated in chapter 2, so many in the Evangelical church have participated in or been affected by abortions.

The other often-cited reason is that the more the anti-abortion message seems to wed the church to a political party, the more it can become offensive to a number of younger Evangelicals.[10] However, it is important to note that the objections are probably not as high as secular media report or as those already unaffiliated from the church perceive. It is actually the unchurched who are most likely to be put off by the church's political associations, affecting outreach more than current or continuing attendance.[11]

The Public Religion Research Institute reports that prior to COVID only 16 percent of young people who left their church said it was because they considered the church too political.[12] The Lifeway Institute (which tends to reflect more conservative views) and the Religion News Service (which tends toward more liberal perspectives) both indicate that if people depart, they are more likely to do so because they disagree with a church's particular political position rather than because the church is too political.[13] Young people tend to want their preacher to be more "woke" on social issues; however, disaffected older Evangelicals tend to leave local churches because the pastor is not "God-and-country" enough.[14]

Care for and Witness to LGBTQ+ Persons

One category of concern that younger Christians are more likely to disagree with their parents about is how to deal with LGBTQ+ issues.[15] Numerous studies affirm what has saddened many of our youth leaders and pastors in recent years. Evangelical youth disagree with their church's historic position on sexual attraction and gender-identity issues in significant numbers.

Pew researchers report, "The gap between younger and older evangelicals is perhaps most noticeable on LGBT issues. Evangelical Protestants who are Millennials (those born from 1981 to 1996) are considerably more likely than older evangelical Protestants to support same-sex marriage." Over half say that homosexuality should be accepted by society.[16]

One reason that young people tend to be more accepting is that they are much more likely to have friends and coworkers who identify as gay or transgender. Also, young people are the ones whose teachers, peers, and employers are much more likely to ostracize or penalize anyone with non-affirming views.

We also must acknowledge that the way the church has taught biblical sexual ethics has contributed to the generations' differing perspectives. Philosopher and theologian Tim Sansbury writes, "I wonder how much of the issue is that the older generations were so aligned on issues like 'homosexuality is wrong,' that it was hardly necessary to expound Scripture to show it. . . . Now, when so many churches are preaching very superficially, even theoretically, about sexual identity, younger Evangelicals may not have ever heard an expository argument versus a mere assumption about the biblical view."[17]

Finally, it is important to recognize that, according to the figures reported in earlier chapters, the rates of same-sex attraction, gender dysphoria, and nonbinary identification are at higher levels than for any previous American generation. Across the country, as much as 30 percent of young women in their teens and twenties now report nontraditional sexual attractions.[18]

Among all high schoolers, 26 percent similarly report, and 21 percent of all Americans in their twenties identify as LGBTQ+.[19]

A recent Gallup poll indicates that individuals in each younger generation are now roughly twice as likely to identify as LGBTQ+ as those in the preceding generation[20]—meaning that nearly half of those now under age twenty will ultimately identify as other than heterosexual, at least for a period of their lives. So, even if some churches consider these issues to be remote, they will soon be at the door. No pastor, family, church, or community leader will be able to address sex and gender issues uncaringly without doing damage to relationships that must be maintained for gospel witness.

Thus, in order to make the gospel credible in these times when any objection to non-biblical sexual relationships can be considered "hate speech" by those in and outside the church, more and more of the church's messaging is about taking the love of the gospel to those who assume we hate them. Decades ago, such love was expressed in finding ways to care for those with AIDS. In more recent years, care is being expressed by helping children and their parents deal with sexual confusion, trying to open "missional conversations" with gay communities,[21] and opposing transgender medical procedures for minors that irreversibly damage bodies and future reproduction.[22]

The days of people in the church cheering because they believed AIDS would wipe out homosexuals were a disgrace then and are incalculably offensive now. There was a time when people may have spoken derisively or disdainfully of "Sodomites" without knowing anyone who was same-sex attracted or confused, but that time has passed for all but the most culturally isolated or blind. The churches that will be most effective in gospel witness going forward are not those that cave to homosexual agendas or adopt LGBTQ+ ideology, but those that find ways to express Christ's heart to individuals who think the church is betraying them by holding to biblical standards.

Victims of Pornography and Sex Trafficking

Another day that has passed is one in which only the dirty and desperate used pornography. Again, as has been shown in previous chapters, no pastor of any sizable church can now assume that only a few congregants are regularly accessing sexually explicit materials. The availability and consumption of internet porn by vast numbers of church people has become a scourge to healthy attitudes about sex, proper regard for the opposite sex, and the profoundest joys of sexual expression in marriage.

The often-cited "Proven Men Porn Survey" found that 64 percent of men view pornography at least once a month, including 54 percent of men identifying as born-again Christians.[23] Such numbers indicate that it would be foolish today for Evangelical pastors to speak with scorn of those who experience sexual struggles. Too many of our people struggle. Instead, pastors have learned to address such pervasive temptation and sin by showing a heart of compassion and a path to health.

The heart of compassion is shown by proclaiming the grace that God offers to the broken and ashamed. This includes making clear the gospel's offer of pardon and power to those who are caught in the webs of sex trafficking, as well as to those who consume the evils of the sex trade—all are perceived as victims. Such proclamation strengthens hearts with regular affirmation of the gospel that frees us from slavery to sin (Rom. 6:6, 14), unites us to a Savior who forgives the worst and most repetitive of sins (Matt. 18:21–22; Luke 17:3–4; 1 John 1:9), and provides the power of his Spirit to overcome them (1 John 4:4).

The path of help is provided through peer and pastoral counseling that promises safety from exposure as well as biblical instruction, practical information about internet filters, accountability measures, and addiction counseling. Sometimes a church will not be trusted to provide such grace until it demonstrates its heart by a willingness to care for the most spiritually destitute by offering rescue to those in sexual slavery or alternative employment to those in the sex trade.

Providing these avenues of grace is not easy for church leaders, and the discussion of them can be distasteful for the upright and shame-inducing for those caught in the sin. Still, the pervasive sins of our age make it as necessary to have these discussions as it was for Amy Carmichael to tell the straitlaced churches of Victorian and Edwardian England of their responsibility to rescue children from temple prostitution in India.

Rescue is still our responsibility, but the methods cannot be the same when the sin is pervasive among us and not just thriving in a distant land or among disgraceful people. Talking about curbing the evils of pornography through rescue and counseling is a different approach than Donald

Wildmon's boycotts. Still, the ongoing conversations indicate that younger generations of church leaders yet identify pornography use and involvement as sin and are seeking to do what is most effective for fighting this pervasive moral evil in the current context.

Substance Addiction Counseling and Rescue

Conversations have also shifted about how the church deals with illegal drugs. Once it was easy for preachers distant from the hard realities of poverty, prejudice, and hopelessness to rail against drug dealers, street thugs, and a hippie culture that were "threatening our children." That was when the chief obligation of most Christian parents fighting drug use seemed to be pitying the few families whose children succumbed. Back then, the sermons against using marijuana, LSD, and cocaine were directed at stereotypical movie thugs, societal dropouts, back alley criminals, and delinquents troubling the nice kids at the local high school. Now, the opioid and fentanyl crises have brought the realities of addiction into all our neighborhoods, homes, and churches.[24]

Pastors have changed their messaging from condemnation of people they don't know to urgent appeals to the people they intimately know, begging strugglers to acknowledge their bondage and get help. As indicated in the previous chapter, we remain in "the most devastating drug crisis in our nation's history" that is claiming victims from all ages and walks of life.[25] The magnitude is hard to overstate. For example, drug addicts now outnumber high school students in San Francisco.[26]

I write these words almost numbed to the now-familiar pain that has resulted in so many lawyers, teachers, businesspeople, and church leaders in my own life and church becoming addicted or dying due to prescription opioids or fentanyl substitutes. I have known respected, professional adults to threaten and steal from their own aging parents to get money for the next hit. I have tried to comfort spouses and children who cannot recognize the husband and father of only a year ago—a man who now will transform from tearful child to angry monster in seconds to manipulate loved ones into providing funds for more drugs.

No informed pastor will deny this evil, but opposition to it cannot be expressed in the same voice as the Bible-banging harangue against the

The Minority Mission

liberal policies of weak politicians and irresponsible parents that was common through the early 2000s. Those sermons were against *them*; now the church must minister to *us*—her own loved ones.

Gaming and Gambling Addictions

If "gaming" is a new term for you, then you have identified your generation. The generation that never knew a day without Mario, *Minecraft*, or *Grand Theft Auto* is not only very familiar with video games but also knows their addictive power. In an age when screens can distract us from loneliness (even while reinforcing it) and from real-world pressures, interactive video games can create a sense of success, reward, and even community with fellow gamers.

The results for the introverted and awkward can be devastating. Many families have sent an academically promising child to college only to have him or her home again before the first semester is done. Away from parental guidance, gaming can initially seem to be a familiar respite from homesickness, adult responsibilities, and scholastic pressures. However, the dopamine hits that the brain receives from the gaming graphics and successes can lead to all-day and all-night addictive behavior that causes students to ignore relationships, studies, and consequences.

AddictionHelp.com estimates almost 10 percent of American children and teens are addicted to gaming; of the more than 10 million addicts, the majority are ages 18–34, with the average age being 24.[27] It seems that as adult responsibilities become more intimidating, adolescent distractions can become more appealing.

The commonness of social dysfunction in adolescents and young adults due to gaming has caused it to be of increasing concern to the church. Since most of those who are gamers have the education and resources to engage in the video universe, this addiction—unlike some others—is not as prevalent in segments of our society that face disadvantages and discrimination. Sixty-seven percent of all gamers in the US are Caucasian, 15 percent are Hispanic, 12 percent are African American, and 5 percent are Asian.[28] Of the 150–200 million gamers in the US, only 3–6.5 million are diagnosed with "gaming disorders," but 94 percent of those are male.[29]

Young people and their entertainments often make fun of the nerd universe that preoccupies so many of their friends, but they are keenly aware of the damage gaming inflicts among their peers—and to some measure their jibes at one another are intended as cautions. The most addictive types of games are those with role-play, battle and gunplay interaction, massive multiplayer involvement, and gambling.[30]

This last category is particularly poignant. Just as the subject of gambling seemed to go out of vogue in Evangelical preaching—because it had so little effect on society—anti-gambling messages have begun to reappear.[31] Such sermons are often tentative, as this generation of preachers tries to avoid the bluster of the past.[32] But now the goal is not to stop underworld-controlled casinos and state-governed lotteries; it is to protect college students from the epidemic of sports gambling (made legally available twenty-four hours a day through their phone apps).[33] Yet, here again, the focus of such sermons tends to be not so much about condemning profiteers and organizing voting campaigns but about cautioning students and offering counseling.[34]

Creation Care

While it may be obvious to an older generation that environmentalists and climate change activists can recklessly advocate measures that will destroy business and challenge the American way of life, such conclusions are not apparent at all to a generation regularly exposed to media images of melting glaciers, plasticized oceans, and massive deforestation.[35]

The "cultural mandate" that caught the ear of conservatives in the Moral Majority era was "fill the earth and subdue it, and have dominion over the fish of the sea and over the birds of the heavens and over every living thing that moves on the earth" (Gen. 1:28). The "creation mandate" that captures the concerns of the present generation includes, "The LORD God took the man and put him in the garden of Eden to work it and keep it" (Gen. 2:15). Dominion is the emphasis of the former; stewardship is the emphasis of the latter.

Climate change enters into the voting concerns of nearly 80 percent of Evangelicals ages 18–25, with 52 percent of that age group expressing that they are "very" or "extremely" concerned—almost the same degree of concern this generation expresses about terrorism.[36] Environmental protection concerns have moved beyond the ranks of a few progressive Evangelicals who read *Sojourners* magazine and have become mainstream for those generations that face the longest futures on the planet.

Refugee Compassion

Roughly the same percentage of young adult Evangelicals express concern over our nation's immigration policies (80 percent) as they do over climate change. However, the concerns are usually not the same as that of the generations preceding them.[37] For example, in recent political seasons, only 16 percent of young Evangelicals said that border control was extremely important to their vote,[38] whereas older Evangelicals, who are predominantly Republicans or Republican-leaning independents, identify border security as a major concern.[39]

Voters who focus on images of mass waves of illegal and undocumented immigrants crossing into our nation see threats to family safety, community budgets, and job security that require us to secure our borders. Voters who focus on images of individuals struggling through history's largest displacement of people across the world (over 100 million)[40] see suffering and remember the Golden Rule.[41] Of course, the latter are often younger voters who may not yet have had to think very deeply about economic and security issues in their lives. Nevertheless, they are thinking biblically, even if weighing matters differently from those who are older.

Christians, who often divide along generational (as well as political) lines in their focus, will defend their views by citing Scriptures about God establishing national borders and governments to provide for the welfare of citizens (Acts 17:24–27; Rom. 13:1–7; 1 Tim. 2:1–3) or, conversely, the biblical responsibilities to recognize the image of God in all humanity and to care for the stranger in need (Lev. 19:34; Matt. 25:34–40; Luke 10:29–37).

I am not here trying to make the biblical case for either position. The issues are complex and heartbreaking and cannot be resolved by anger or indifference. However, I am again making the case that different generations may perceive the church's priorities differently without necessarily being disloyal to Scripture.

We should applaud national leaders who are wrestling with how to provide national protection and international compassion in a broken world. We should also recognize how Christians from different generations may have different contexts affecting judgments about their church's priorities. Some will determine that their church should prioritize security. Others will decide that their church should prioritize mission. Prudence and Scripture indicate that neither can be ignored, and we should celebrate any generation that still seeks to be guided by God's Word and Christ's heart.

Racial Reconciliation and Justice

In our present context, no issue is more difficult to discuss nor more important to younger Evangelicals' concerns than this one. Despite advances in Evangelical attitudes toward and acceptance of racial minorities since the reconciliation efforts of the Promise Keepers and others, new tensions have divided the nation and the church.

Recent injustices toward George Floyd, Michael Brown, Breonna Taylor, and others have reignited old animosities through media storms that have touched every corner of our nation. The Black Lives Matter movement and 1619 Project have so pressed indicators of racial disparity into the cultural conversation that virtually every institution—political, educational, business, media, and church—has been forced to identify whether it aligns in support or opposition to racial justice.

The trendy educational response of Critical Race Theory (CRT) has moved from university lectures to public school curricula, requiring children to identify whether they are victims or oppressors on the basis of their skin color. Churches have struggled to respond well. The excesses and misunderstandings of CRT have led to bad behavior on both sides of the debate about its legitimacy.

Some in the church, not recognizing that CRT is just the latest critical theory (an academic designation for approaches to considering and critiquing history or society through the lens of a particular population's experience[42]), have lumped all past and present calls for racial justice into CRT plots. They do not realize that, prior to present debates about CRT, we had already experienced feminist, gay, Latino, Asian, colonial, and Communist critical theories, among others. Now we also have writers discussing "Biblical Critical Theory."[43]

What has caught the attention and ignited the animosity of key Evangelical leaders is the philosophical heritage of each of these critical theories, including CRT, in aspects of Communist/Marxist thought.[44] That association has set off old alarm bells. All the Cold War evil and fear that helped spark the growth of the Evangelical movement in the middle of the twentieth century has come roaring back into church consciousness.[45] As a consequence, it has recently become more difficult to talk about racial reconciliation and racial justice in the church without being accused of being a "woke" advocate of CRT—that is, a closet Communist or at least a compromising liberal.[46]

Those concerned for racial justice on school boards, on university faculties, in journalistic pursuits, and in government offices have sometimes been as guilty of creating needless division as those in conservative politics or churches have been of ignoring clear discrimination. In our polarized nation, it is easy to slap opponents and score political points with allies by identifying anyone who opposes CRT as a "racist" who doesn't want children to know Black history.

The tensions that surround discussions of race and CRT could lead one to conclude that the best way to deal with race in the church is to ensure that the church doesn't make too much of something so divisive. That would be a mistake.

The key difference between those over age fifty and those in their forties and below with regard to the Evangelical church's social engagement is *not* disagreement about the need for racial reconciliation and racial justice for all made in God's image. Thankfully, the majority of all generations are now united in regard for persons of all races; however, they are divided about its priority. Racial reconciliation was late on the agenda of the Moral Majority generation; it is first among the social engagement priorities of the younger generation.

Surveys indicate that 94 percent of young Evangelicals ages 18–25 believe racial issues are important for our nation to address; 54 percent say these issues are "very" or "extremely" important.[47] The CRT disputes have not dissuaded our young adults from believing what we taught them: "Red and yellow, black and white, all are precious in His sight. Jesus loves the little children of the world."

Younger pastors and their congregations believe what much of the world does about a nation whose Sunday worship time can still be characterized as "the most segregated hour in America": Racism can be seen as America's most obvious original and ongoing sin.[48] So, the church that teaches the necessity of repentance for sins must continue to address this one, but even more than previous generations have attempted.

Different Agendas

The following comparison of the likely agendas of Evangelicals from differing generations indicates why they often have trouble understanding or respecting one another. The first column identifies the agenda of those in their fifties and older, who grew up in the twentieth-century decades of Christian consensus. The second column represents the concerns of those in their forties and younger, who grew up in the late twentieth and early twenty-first-century decades of diminishing Christian influence. Those represented by the first column grew up thinking of themselves as Christians mostly surrounded by other Christians—or at least by those who shared Christian values. The second column represents younger generations of Christians who have never thought of themselves as part of a majority Christian culture but always as a minority in a pluralistic culture.

Comparison of Evangelical Generational Expectations and Issues

	Fifties and Older	Forties and Younger
Perception	"We are (or were) a *majority*."	"We are a *minority*."
Mission	Take *control* of culture	Make *credible* our faith
Means	Bring a *halt* to . . .	*Help* with . . .
	Abortion	Adoption and foster care
	Homosexual agenda	Care for and witness to LGBTQ+ persons
	Pornography	Liberating victims of sex trafficking and sex addiction
	Illegal drugs	Substance addiction counseling and rescue
	Gambling	Gaming and gambling addictions
	Green movements	Creation care
	Illegal immigration	Refugee compassion and care
	Racial discrimination	Racial reconciliation and justice

Often members of the older generation look across the aisle at younger pastors and leaders in their own churches or denominations who will not put on the Moral Majority uniform and conclude that the rising generation is composed of cowards, compromisers, and liberals. It is also common for younger leaders to examine the messages of their older counterparts and conclude that senior leaders are insensitive, out of touch, and hypocritical about gospel mission.

A younger generation thinks the older has sold out the church to the Republican Party. An older generation thinks the younger sold out their faith to liberal media and educators.

To get a sense of how deep and visceral the divisions may be, ask leaders in each group who their heroes are in the ongoing battle for the soul of America. An older generation will salute the efforts of Jerry Falwell, Pat Robertson, D. James Kennedy, Phyllis Schlafly, and Dr. James Dobson. Yet, those same names are seen by many younger pastors not as people who have aided the Evangelical movement but who have contributed to its current decline. The perspective of these younger leaders is the gospel cause was compromised by conflating the church's biblical mission with conservative politics and pursuing that altered mission through consumer marketing and the strategies of secular power.[49]

Older Evangelical leaders and congregants are hardly able to believe their ears when hearing these assessments, since they trusted, followed, and supported these culture warriors. Older Evangelicals will particularly question criticisms of Dr. Dobson.[50] Hundreds of thousands trusted his daily advice for raising their families and learned from his books, programs, and Truth Project how to confront the culture and vote for its correction. Yet, when younger leaders hear Dr. Dobson still declaring that a profane and immoral politician is "Christian" because of his political stance, they roll their eyes.

Some younger leaders will still repsect the past teachings and guidance of Chuck Colson and Francis Schaeffer. These were culture warriors who, when Scripture required it, took stances their peers deemed liberal, resulting in criticism from liberal ranks at some times and rage from conservatives at other times. By taking hits from both sides of the conservative/progressive wings of the Evangelical church, Colson and Schaeffer gained "street cred" from younger Evangelicals looking for guidance beyond the party line.

Who are the heroes of many younger Evangelical leaders today? They are the architects and advocates of the new agenda: Tim Keller, Ed Stetzer, Beth Moore, and many Gospel Coalition types focused on how Christians engage in contemporary mission, along with people like David French (now with *The New York Times*), Russell Moore (with *Christianity Today*), and Justin Giboney (of the AND Campaign) focused more on political or cultural engagement. All these leaders are concerned to make biblical faith credible to an increasingly secular culture.

Yet, even as I write the names of those most notable to younger leaders, I recognize that none of them have carried the same cultural weight as did Falwell, Robertson, and their constellation of peers who were able to unite the Evangelical church into a voting bloc that largely determined the election of four of the last seven presidents and the composition of the present Supreme Court.[51] In fact, some older leaders may grimace to hear persons like Keller and Stetzer cited on mission—or French, Moore, and Giboney on politics—out of worry that poor reflection on their necessarily nuanced perspectives might lead younger Evangelicals to compromise with our culture in their attempts to win it.

Common Ground

What is apparent when discussing the divides between generations is that the polarities dividing our nation are also finding expression in the Evangelical church. Is there any hope for pulling together as Christ's church to fulfill his mission? We will consider significant rays of hope in a later chapter, but key unifiers should already be apparent.

The Bible

All those who are informed and devoted Evangelicals of any generation are still looking to the Bible as their authoritative source of guidance. The first principle of the Bebbington quadrilateral (see chapter 3) still holds among those who are regularly and actively involved in their churches and consistently faithful to their families. We trust the Bible to be our only infallible rule of faith and practice, and we believe that mutual devotion to its truths will ultimately result in unity for Christ's church.

The Sanctity and Dignity of Life

Because we trust the Bible, Evangelicals are still committed across generations to the sanctity of life and the dignity of all made in the image of God. The generations may differ over whether those principles require them to prioritize condemning abortion or advocating adoption, but all agree that life is sacred and that the Lord loves all that he has made. The Lord's love and the fact that all humanity bears his image also unite us in affirming that dignity and justice must be afforded to all people. The generations may differ over how to respond to sexual confusion, refugee crises, and racial inequities, but all agree that hatred and bigotry are an obscenity on God's plan for humanity.

Mission

Finally, we agree that the glory of God and the goodness of his gospel are to be made known to all the world. We may differ on what we need to prioritize in our different contexts and eras to accomplish these goals, but Christians of every generation do not question that our Lord has mandated this mission for us. Whatever are the generational differences in the expressions of our agendas, concern for the eternal souls of our neighbors, families, and enemies remains our responsibility and calling. As we address the needs of individuals and the brokenness of our world, we are committed to our world knowing the glory of the Lord Jesus Christ and experiencing the grace of his kingdom.

6

THE ZEAL OF LOSS

Before we consider hope for the church signaled by the common ground that Evangelical Christians share across the generations, we need to consider a parcel of that common ground shared by unlikely partners. In the essay quoted previously, influential pastor Tim Keller made this observation shortly before his passage into glory:

> On the Right, a growing number of conservatives are attracted to the use of state power to stifle liberal and progressive points of view and promote Christianity (e.g., the fascination of Tucker Carlson with Victor Orban of Hungary). On the other hand most younger adults are progressive and their view of the state is that it should redistribute wealth, power, and status from the privileged groups to disadvantaged groups, especially racial and sexual minorities and women. . . . Many Christians today are splitting from one another over these warring views of the role of the state and the role of the church in politics.[1]

The divides are even broader. Michael O. Emerson, sociologist and scholar of American religion for more than three decades, indicates that he has never seen such an extraordinary level of conflict in the church. He says, "The conflict is over entire worldviews—politics, race, how we are to be in the world, and even what religion and faith are for."[2] Pointing at recent church controversies over politics, race, sexuality, and immigration, Aaron Renn writes, "Where once there was a culture war between Christianity and secular society, today there is a culture war within evangelicalism itself."[3] Though Keller's focus was more narrow, his words and experience are helpful in understanding these divides, their depth, and their sources.

Keller wrote of "warring views" from personal experience. His last years were clearly his most difficult in terms of criticism from within his own ranks. At the same time that he was being hailed by many Evangelicals for offering a reason for God that made sense to the modern mind, he was being accused by other Evangelicals of pursuing a liberal agenda. The attacks were particularly ironic and painful in that they were often based on the same evidence that Keller would have considered signs of the success of his goal of making credible the Christian faith.

In his final years, Keller was able to write articles and op eds for secular media as diverse and influential as *The Atlantic* and the *New York Times*. He spoke before the British Parliament, participated and prayed in nationally televised government ceremonies, grew churches at multiple locations in New York City that drew national celebrities and government officials, built bridges with leaders of other faith traditions, generated networks that planted hundreds of churches in international cities and nations where Christians are persecuted, sold millions of books through secular as well as religious publishers, and was nominated for numerous awards from both sides of the liberal/conservative religious spectrum.

Those accomplishments remain astounding and would seem to be clear evidence of the blessing of God that would be cheered by those who want the Christian faith to spread in a secular age. The eulogies that flowed upon Keller's death indicate that many did cheer. However, even as he was dying of pancreatic cancer, the criticisms and accusations intensified. Though some of the heat could be attributed to petty jealousies and the inescapable reality that "tall trees catch the wind," there were larger forces at work.

The New Right

Since Keller's denomination (and mine) identifies as conservative Presbyterian with largely Southern roots, it would be easy—but wrong—to stereotype his critics according to out-of-date clichés. The caricature of someone in our church who is objecting to efforts to make our faith credible to a secular society through intellectual arguments, cultural sensitivity, urban priorities, and multiethnic outreach would be an older Southern aristocrat who is dressed in a seersucker suit and looks a lot like Kentucky Fried Chicken's Colonel Sanders.

In reality, the criticism is more likely to come from young pastors in small churches who are dressed in plaid shirts and tight jeans, or from young professors in a cadre of Christian colleges whose constituents are the same Evangelicals who backed the MAGA movements of recent political campaigns. Many of these critics find strong motivation in the sense of loss that has been described in previous chapters.

To understand how powerful is this sense of loss and its effects on a younger generation of Evangelicals, consider again the charts we looked at in chapter 3.

Population Percentages as Indicated by Regular, *Self-Reported* Religious Affiliation

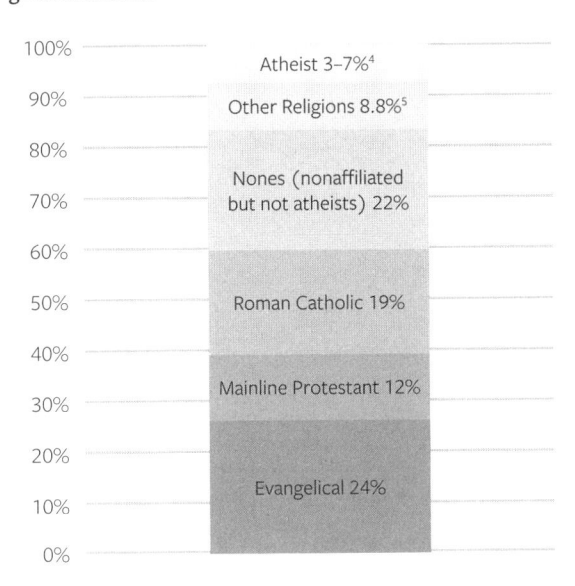

Atheist 3–7%[4]
Other Religions 8.8%[5]
Nones (nonaffiliated but not atheists) 22%
Roman Catholic 19%
Mainline Protestant 12%
Evangelical 24%

Add to the realities of these figures the understanding that they represent multiple denominations and ethnicities. If we only consider the influence of the often-cited "voting bloc" of white Evangelicals, then the percent at the bottom of the pile is even smaller. Only 14–15 percent of the population is composed of those identifying as white Evangelicals—a distant reality from the population proportion the Moral Majority hoped to turn into cultural clout.[6]

The numbers grow even more discouraging for Evangelicals who thought of themselves as having considerable influence in American society when we consider the actual church involvement of those who claim to be Evangelicals.

Population Percentages as Indicated by Affiliation and *Self-Reported* Regular Worship Attendance

Category	Percentage
Atheist	4%
Nones	24%
Religiously Affiliated but Not Regularly Attending	47%
Other Religions	5%
Roman Catholic	5%
Mainline Protestant	3%
Evangelical	12%

(75% bracket shown on right side)

Note: The percentages in the lower four categories are based on people affiliated with each group and regularly attending services.

We should remember when examining these charts that they are only about *self-reported* attendance. If we put aside considerations of who shows up in church and only count those who actually hold to traditional, orthodox Evangelical beliefs, then the number at the bottom of the second chart would fall below 8 percent (see chapter 3).

Robert Jones of the Public Religion Research Institute summarizes the impact of these shrinking constituencies: "If you look at [the white Evangelical] presence in the national religious landscape, it's actually quite diminished from what it was even 10 years ago. . . . I think it's still surprising to many Americans because of how visible this population has been, particularly during the [first] Trump administration."[7]

For Evangelicals who once considered their numbers great enough to leverage presidential elections, Supreme Court appointments, school board elections, public library collection selections, and many other features of our society, these present population realities alone would be enough to create a sense of desperation. But desperation is not the only possible response. Another response—the response behind so much of the criticism of Tim Keller and his allies—can be understood when we remember that the percentages above represent real people who are disgusted with the modern trends of our society.

Conservative Evangelicals are not simply upset that they have less voting clout. They are enraged that public school teachers are encouraging their children to normalize gay or transgender choices; that social media has made their teens and preteens vulnerable to immorality, predators, and suicide; that CRT advocates seem to be trying to make children feel guilty for the color of their skin; that entertainment corporations have so sexualized our society that chastity is scorned, all marriages are endangered, and our families are fracturing; that border laws are ignored; that patriotism is ridiculed; and that some of their own church leaders seem to want the approval of sectors of our world that are presumed responsible for all this pain.

Adding to the pain is the realization that younger Evangelicals will bear the brunt of our culture's opposition to biblical faith. The figures in the

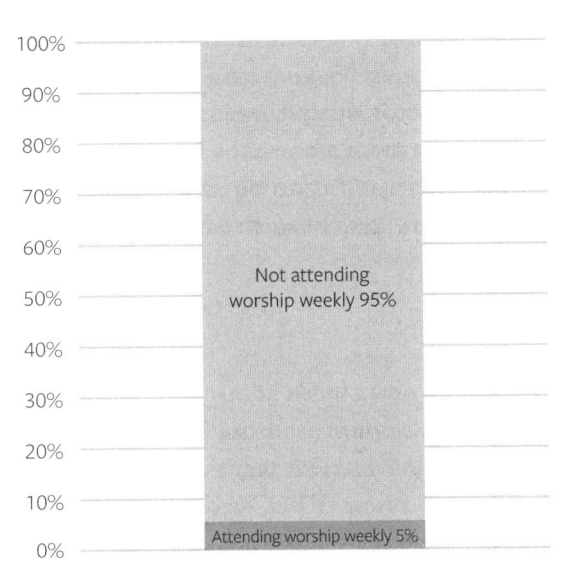

Population Percentages of Weekly Sunday Worship Attendance as Indicated by Cell Phone Data

Not attending worship weekly 95%

Attending worship weekly 5%

chart below remind us how alarmingly small is the segment of regularly involved Evangelicals in our society. But even this graphic is not adequate to represent the pressure on young people.

The 5 percent figure (which could optimistically be stretched as high as 9 percent weekly if midweek and weather factors are considered; see chapter 2 note 15) represents people from *all* generations and *all* faith traditions who attend church on a weekly basis. If we only consider the Evangelicals who are in their forties and younger as a part of this group, then the numbers are staggeringly small (well under 2 percent based on the proportions of Evangelicals to the general population). The Moral Majority of Evangelicalism's senior generation has become a tiny minority of young adults in this generation. Perhaps we can sense the pain and rage of both generations by using the above graphic to visualize a young, sincere Evangelical being crushed by the weight of societal unbelief (indicated by those not attending worship) as he or she tries to honor Christ in morality, marriage, child-rearing, and faith.

The New Responses

One response to the crushing weight of unbelief by faithful young adults (and probably the majority response) is the Keller option: Try to make faith credible to family, friends, and coworkers by giving a reasonable explanation for our faith while helping others see the emptiness and enslavement of the idols of our time—sex, power, money, and unfettered independence.[8] The other options have been labeled by what would initially seem to be unlikely references to early Roman Catholic saints who made very different choices about how they engaged their cultures in previous eras.

The Benedict Option

Though probably past its peak for discussion among Evangelicals, the Benedict option was proposed by Rod Dreher in his popular 2017 book as a Christian response to a post-Christian culture.[9] This approach to cultural engagement is loosely based on Saint Benedict's establishment of faith communities that were defined by commitments to regularized education, ritual, and discipline.

Resorting to such a separated community—shielded by shared practices, if not actually separate in location—remains a natural impulse for those who perceive the surrounding culture as a threat to their faith, ideals, and family. In its essence (and I confess that this simplicity is not altogether fair), the Benedict option is one of retreat into Christian subcultures for the sake of faith expression and family protection.

The Benedict option initially brings to mind pictures of isolated monks in desert monasteries, but the desire to circle into protective enclaves can at times be a temptation and at other times a necessity. There are always prudential decisions to be made as Christians deal with different levels and kinds of threats from a secularizing culture.

A generation ago, Francis Schaeffer warned against Christians isolating themselves into "corner cultures" that retreated from "salt and light" responsibilities for an unbelieving world. At the same time, his disciples became leaders in Christian school, homeschool, and classical school movements that sought to remove children from the seductions of relativistic education that Schaeffer so eloquently and vehemently decried.

The various L'Abri groups that grew in different countries, which were fashioned after Schaeffer's original Swiss community, themselves became expressions of a sort of Benedict ethic. Even though the intentions of those communities were initially to prepare young Christians for faithful living in secular society, these communities that first provided a "shelter" for societal preparation in some ways morphed into micro-societies for their own constituents.

The Boniface Option

The counterbalance to the Benedict option in conservative Christian discussions of the moment is the Boniface option. Again, loosely based on the biography of a Catholic saint—and probably to have a similar sounding name to counter the Benedict option rhetorically—the Boniface approach advocates confrontation rather than retreat.

Supporters of the Boniface option take notes for their cultural engagement from an event in the seventh-century saint's missionary endeavors. When he witnessed Germans mixing Christian worship with pagan worship, Boniface grabbed an axe and cut down a tree that was supposed to represent the power of Thor overshadowing the altar of Christ. The bravery of the missionary, and Thor's failure to send a lightning bolt of retribution, motivated the people of the region to renewed faithfulness.

For a number of younger Christians and their leaders, the Boniface option is not only instructive for cultural engagement in our pagan society but is also an answer to the pain that they feel. The goal of their cultural engagement is not so much designed to make our faith credible by "winsomely" revealing the emptiness of our culture's idols (the Keller option), but to boldly—even forcefully—demonstrate the powerlessness and foolishness of any moral or intellectual claims but Christ's.

Despite controversies and critiques of the "winsome wars" that so colored Keller's final years, the Evangelical leaders who followed the Moral Majority generation—and who now dominate most denominational and institutional leadership—have typically oriented their constituents to the mission of making our faith credible. However, the generation of young congregants and church leaders who now find themselves under the crush of our society's disregard and disdain are not always finding the winsome strategy convincing and may respond with their version of the Boniface option.

Sometimes unfairly, but not without some pastoral and political examples, this option is occasionally characterized as the "punch 'em in the mouth" approach to cultural engagement. Those who advocate this approach will often argue that the winsome advocates are not presenting the full picture of Scripture's instruction for cultural engagement.

They will agree that sometimes the Christ of Scripture was gentle and mild, but these church leaders are quick to point out that he also drove the money changers out of the temple. The Old Testament prophets spoke with biting sarcasm and said that the Messiah would come as a refining fire, and when he comes again, it will be with the sword of his Word on his thigh to do battle with his foes. This strident Jesus is invoked to validate telling Christians we must declare to opponents outside the church and compromisers within, "We won't take this anymore!"

Different Voices

Those who are looking for strong rhetoric have many outlets and some able voices.[10] Kevin DeYoung's discussion of Doug Wilson's resurging popularity (despite the latter's crudities and nontraditional Evangelical theology) is helpful for understanding the present Evangelical landscape.[11] DeYoung ascribes the delight Wilson's followers have in his frequent stridency as the allure of a "mood" that echoes populist angst and anger about our nation's moral erosion and family breakdown.

That mood is not unlike the attitudes that have surrounded some of Donald Trump's supporters in Evangelical ranks. If Evangelicals travel abroad, they will meet Christian brothers and sisters who cannot fathom why America's faithful are so supportive of a man whose profanities, family history, and character flaws would have been an immediate turnoff to any other generation of Evangelicals.

One older Evangelical woman expressed the reasons well to a news reporter on the eve of the Iowa Caucuses in 2023. She said, "I am not looking for a friend or a husband, I am looking for someone who will do what is right for our country." In the face of the overwhelming losses that Evangelicals have experienced in America in the last generation, we should be able to understand why many would want a fighter to represent them.[12]

When we grow accustomed to supporting political leaders who give voice to our angst, especially on the inflaming issues of sex and gender, then we should not be surprised when similar voices gain a hearing in the church. No one now questions that the polarities of our culture have affected the Evangelical world[13]—where, as indicated in chapter 2, people know their politics better than they know their theology.

Political rhetoric about "draining the swamp" of present government and "throwing out the bums" presently in office has worked its way into virtually all Evangelical denominations as populist concerns about cultural impotence and disadvantage affect both political and ecclesiastical leadership choices. The free-ranging anger resulting from the pain of loss that Evangelicals universally feel fuels a refining zeal that can readily be directed toward any leader or institution alleged not to be resisting secularism or liberalism strongly enough.[14]

Denominational leaders at a recent gathering of the National Association of Evangelicals unanimously acknowledged such polarities among their constituents. The battles in the larger denominations tend to be over LGBTQ+ issues; the smaller denominations are wrestling with cohabitation and divorce issues. Probably this is because the smaller denominations are still dominated by families who know each other well enough to make the larger society's gay, queer, and transgender issues seem remote—for now.

Generational Echoes

A further point to note, however, is that the anger and polarities are being expressed not simply by those of the Moral Majority generation but by the rising generations. Grandparents have no awareness of the Boniface option; their grandchildren do. Ryan Burge, whose statistics have been so helpful in previous chapters, explains why not all younger Evangelicals align with the "make credible" strategies of the majority of their present church leaders and peers:

> It would be wrong to assume that younger evangelicals are more moderate than their parents or grandparents. Because evangelicals are often defined in the larger culture by their opposition to abortion and same-sex marriage—two positions that are increasingly out of step with [non-evangelical] younger Americans—it stands to reason that only those who fully embrace all of the evangelical movement would still embrace that label. That means these younger evangelicals are likely more strident, outspoken, and unshakeable in their political beliefs than other young people.[15]

Where will they express that stridency? Some will spend hours every day on social media or in blogs not only criticizing the errors of their culture but also reserving special ire for the compromises and cowardice of those they consider to be traitors to the faith movement they have embraced. In this world of endless unrest and umbrage, gentleness is cowardice, kindness is compromise, and love of enemies is not Christlikeness—it is betrayal.[16]

How do such views become common, even praised, among a segment of younger Evangelicals? To answer fairly, we should remember how deserving of our respect and praise young people are who remain faithful when so much of their culture condemns their convictions as ridiculous or reprehensible. Those few young people who remain committed to orthodox Christianity in this culture are clearly swimming against the tide of their peers' choices and beliefs.

Generational Megaphones

When young people, who have sacrificed peer esteem and endured teacher and employer abuse for their faith commitments, do not see senior church leaders resisting cultural attacks on their faith with sufficient vigor, then anger results. Young pastors and Evangelical leaders are more likely to express this anger on the web for a number of reasons. First, they are much more familiar than senior leaders with social media megaphones and the internet culture that flames and trolls opponents. Second, younger Evangelical leaders often have very different aspirations and faith perspectives than the generation that preceded them.[17]

A previous generation of church leaders often approached their church careers similar to the way an executive would try to climb the ladder at General Motors. The goal was to start small and work your way up to bigger, better, and higher-paying positions. Few younger Evangelical leaders now approach the church that way. In an increasingly post-Christian culture, large churches are perceived as politically divided, institutionally protective, dangerous for families, and incapable of providing true Christian community.

For a rising generation that does not expect the affluence and societal acceptance their parents experienced and does not desire the churches of present leaders, their aspiration is a "parish" church of peer families that will support one another in faith, family, and community. Significance is not to be found in the *size* of one's church but in the *support* of one's church.

But if one's church is small and unlikely ever to be strong or flourishing in this increasingly unchurched culture that is disinterested in religion, what now motivates church leaders? The human heart still desires significance. Capable pastors still want to make a difference in the world, even if their churches have little future hope for influence in denomination or community. So, where can significance be found?

Researchers tell us that nearly 60 percent of young people today see social media influencing as a viable career, and they'd be willing to quit their current jobs for the chance to chase it.[18] Younger pastors and lay leaders are not immune from this impulse, even if they are opposed to the culture from which it arises. So, if large-church ascendancy is not the path to significance, what is? The path some choose is the one that leads to applause and approval from an audience of internet peers.

Sadly, when the internet becomes the medium for one's significance, then its standards easily become the ethics of one's conversations. For such conversations, no truism is more obvious than "the internet loves a scandal." Thus, for a segment of Evangelicalism's younger leaders, the chemistry of internet savvy mixed with the pain of loss, anger at winsomeness, and a need for significance is behind the criticism that Keller and his generation of church leaders have experienced in recent years.

Almost any pastor who is willing to become the Rush Limbaugh of a denomination—no matter how small their church or how inexperienced they are in ministry—can get a following for a time. Sadly, the need to keep the scandals fresh through sarcasm, ridicule, belittling, and accusation is the raw meat needed to keep feeding the beast of personal significance.

Biblical Honor

In the day of judgment, when all will be judged according to Scripture and not internet standards, regular readers of such online disrespect and social media demeaning may be surprised to discover that it is as much a sin to entertain dishonoring messages as to spread them (Ps. 1:1–2; Rom. 1:29–32; 1 Cor. 5:11). Encouraging others to publish such reports by boosting their readership helps goad writers into rhetoric that corrodes their own souls. Readers as well as writers are responsible for the damage of promoting what does not honor God (Prov. 14:14–15; 22:24–25). The Lord has given standards for how we make evil and wrongdoing known.[19] We do not honor him by ignoring how he commands us to pursue truth and justice.

As a pastor, I have said in a number of settings how much I grieve for young colleagues I love whose rants and ridicule have severely damaged their own ministries. If it will help only one capable and promising young pastor for me to write this again here, I humbly repeat this sad truth: Angry young leaders become bitter old leaders. They may be applauded by organizational allies in times of controversy but will be devoid of close friends and avoided by family in the course of life. Judgmentalism ultimately isolates and imprisons its source. If your significance comes from the belittling and mockery of others, the future is dark despite the spotlight on your present cleverness and commentary.

I have had the privilege and pain of being in some dimension of my denomination's national leadership most of my adult life. I am well accustomed to the criticisms and denunciations that "come with the territory." Most of the time such comments come from people who have never met me and never talked to me. Rarely do they cause my heart serious pain anymore. Still, my heart aches for the younger pastors and church leaders who spend so much time performing for the applause of their peers by trying to scandalize others.

By now, I have witnessed the usual path of such leaders dozens of times: They will end up leaving the church, leaving the faith, leaving their families, or even taking their life. You simply cannot indulge darkness in one part of life to define your significance and not have similar patterns of thought and expression touch other parts you hold dear.

Sin cannot be corralled. Uncharitable and ungodly speech will inevitably touch how you address your spouse, children, and congregants. This is not simply a caution for the pundits. As indicated above, readers who encourage writers to go down these paths to their own spiritual ruin may cheer and laugh at the latest clever skewer, but when the Judge of all the earth calls us to account, Christ's blood will need to cover reader guilt too (Prov. 17:4; 20:19; Eph. 5:11).

The New Nationalism

Younger leaders who do express versions of the Boniface option in opposition to the present culture's corruptions and the church's perceived compromises have another audience: sympathizers in the Moral Majority generation. As an older generation senses the loss of influence outside the church and loss of respect inside the church, it also senses new opportunity in the zeal of some of the younger influencers. This is especially true in a time when populist resentments behind anti-institutional political movements also put new wind in the sails of social conservatives who choose to express themselves in the context of the church.

Patriot Partners

In denominational life, this can mean that disappointed and disaffected Moral Majority–era leaders become mentors of zealous younger Evangelicals, passing the baton of ultraconservative values and politics to a new generation—a generation with attitudes and perspectives much more like some of their grandparents than either generation is likely to expect.[20] How those who are younger will process their social-conservative commitments over time has yet to be determined, but some of the effects are already apparent in their efforts to renegotiate what seemed to be settled issues of cultural engagement in national and church politics.

Nowhere is the coalescence of younger and older conservative values more evident than in current expressions of Christian Nationalism among all ages of Evangelicals. Though longitudinal surveys indicate that Christian Nationalism has diminishing influence in overall American culture—and is unknown among significant sectors of our electorate[21]—there are pockets of strong support among at least two unlikely religious partners: white Evangelical Protestants (66 percent) and Hispanic Protestants (55 percent).[22]

We need to add to these categories some Pentecostal movements that advocate what is sometimes identified as "Dominion Theology," the teaching that those filled with the Holy Spirit will ultimately control all human institutions if Christians are sufficiently committed to God's causes.[23] Some surveys indicate that up to 30 percent of Americans are open to these ideals of Christian dominance because they can appear to be a resurgence of conservative patriotism.[24]

At first glance, Christian Nationalism might seem merely to be a reprise of the Christian America themes of the Moral Majority era. Those efforts were popularized in books such as *The Light and the Glory* by Peter Marshall and David Manuel, and were given scholarly support in works such as Peter Lillback's *George Washington's Sacred Fire*. Such efforts sought to "Christianize" the democratic principles and religious beliefs of America's founders in order to further political efforts to hold America accountable to what many consider our nation's original principles.

Were all present expressions of Christian Nationalism merely a reiteration of those "Christian America" claims, we might applaud the principles and the patriotism advocated, even if we questioned some of the historical presumptions. However, the new Christian Nationalism frequently carries different freight even if it seems to fly the same flag.[25]

Political Expressions

Definitions that all will support can be hard to come by, but present expressions of Christian Nationalism typically include the ideas that God chose America to be a special nation for advancing his plans for all nations, that the federal government should promote Christian values, and that political processes should be employed to declare and govern the US as a Christian nation.[26]

Though there are many variations of Christian Nationalism, its core ideas seek to make Christian norms the standards of American society.[27] For Christians who want God's righteousness and justice to rule our lives and land, such goals sound commendable—and they are.[28] We should want our nation to be governed according to God's truth and righteousness, and we should seek and support leaders who desire the same.

Still, not all the issues are as simple as voting for candidates that consistently represent our faith commitments. We also have to consider what specific standards of conduct or worship should become law, to whom such laws would apply, and how they would be enforced. These are significant concerns for a nation that is not entirely composed of committed Christians, nor of Christians who always agree, nor of non-Christians who would accept the notion that they should have no say in what is righteous and just.[29]

Kingdom Views

It is one thing to vote for Christian leaders, defend freedom of religion, and even seek to legislate Christian values that an electorate approves. It is quite another to say only Christians can be leaders, only our religion should be defended, and a religious majority should mandate whatever it has the power to legislate. The first position encourages Christians to live their faith as a salt-and-light influence in a pluralistic culture. The second encourages Christians to impose their faith by rule and control over those less powerful. The first sees Christ's kingdom on earth as primarily spiritual until he returns; the second sees Christ's kingdom as spiritual and as dominant as the church and politics can make it before Jesus returns. Both positions must wrestle with what our Savior meant when he said, "My kingdom is not of this world" (John 18:36); but the issues are particularly thorny for those advocating forms of Christian Nationalism that are as much about power as they are about true patriotism.[30]

For many—not all—Christian Nationalism advocates, the Christian norms that should be re-embraced by our nation are based upon a gilded vision of either Colonial America or the Eisenhower years. The goal of some Nationalists is to return our nation to a more traditional way of life where men were men, women were moms, races lived separately, immigrants looked like "us," and traditional churches and morality were respected by all. These goals are to be achieved through convincing the majority of Americans to participate in democratic (or revolutionary) processes that ultimately put Christians, if not the church, in charge of a government that will make everyone honor our God's standards.[31]

If a number of these goals seem to echo familiar choruses sung by Moral Majority leaders a generation ago, then we are understanding why Christian Nationalism is getting a hearing in some older *and* younger Evangelical ranks. What's different? At least some forms of the new Nationalism ultimately put the church in charge of government. This is why the Theonomy, Reconstruction, Federal Vision, and Dominion Theology movements of the 1980s and 1990s are being resurrected by a new generation of pastors and Evangelical writers.[32]

Advocates are not simply arguing for patriotism or a return to the American way of life that was enjoyed in the 1950s. The ultimate goals are to enforce Christian standards of faith as the law of the land by the power of the state (and in some expressions, according to the direction of the church). American ideals of freedom of religion, freedom of speech, and minority rights are subordinated to a Nationalist version of what it means for Christ to have dominion over all of life.[33] This understanding ultimately makes the civil government synonymous with Christ's kingdom in the present age—a government defined by ecclesiastical control of political power. The church's influence over culture is not merely through spiritual commitments to gospel mission but through its legal control of government.

Chosen Models

Those who are theologically astute recognize this is not the American way of life but an unreflective imposition of Old Testament civil law, medieval structures of church government, or a misperception of Colonial America where Sabbath-breaking, fornication, child disobedience, and contrary faith were sometimes punished with stocks, lashes, imprisonment, banishment, or death. Commenting on the thought of pastor and theologian John Piper, Desiring God senior teacher Tony Reinke summarizes the core error of trying to turn our democracy into some form of theocracy:

> No single nation [now] carries out God's work on earth. "God no longer works through a people who are a political state or an ethnic entity to perform his kingdom-spreading, saving work." More particularly, he no longer deals with Israel "as the embodiment—ethnically and politically—of his kingdom on the earth (Matt. 21:43). He is giving the kingdom to a people who produce its fruits—namely, the church of Jesus Christ. And since God works through his Spirit by his word in a people called the church, they have no status as a political state, and they have no singular ethnic identity." In Christ, "God no longer works as a king exerting immediate authority over a people gathered as a political state or as a single ethnic identity."[34]

Few Christian Nationalists want to use modern Iran as their governing model, but the theocracy they advocate would inevitably lead to such a system. When the decisions of the church become the mandates of the civil government, then dictatorial rule rather than the power of the Spirit gets used to enforce faith and obedience. This is not the spirit of democracy but the essence of demagoguery.

The zeal of loss among younger Evangelicals who did not live through the Moral Majority era and are being crushed by the immoral majority of our nation can lead to a fight for rights that is less about democracy and more about achieving the might to make right. Pastor and author Kevin DeYoung's analysis of Stephen Wolfe's published defense of Christian Nationalism astutely identifies the underlying prejudices and militancy some younger Evangelicals' ideas encourage. DeYoung writes,

> The appeal of something like Christian Nationalism is that it presents a muscular alternative to surrender and defeat. . . . Wolfe isn't just arguing for

the establishment principle or for legislating both tables of the Mosaic law, he's justifying violent revolution . . . and calling for "the Great Renewal" [brought about] "through a Christian prince" . . . "a measured theocratic Caesarism" and a "world-shaker for our time."[35]

Such ideas threaten not only the American way of life but the testimony of the church in a world that will remain a mixture of good and evil until Christ returns. Katherine Stewart uses the writings of some self-proclaimed Christian Nationalists to identify the underlying principle of their cause this way:

> The legitimacy of the United States government derives from its commitment to a particular religious and cultural heritage, and not from its democratic form. It is . . . allegiance . . . to a belief in blood, earth, and religion, rather than to the mere idea of government "of the people, by the people, and for the people."[36]

Trusted church leader Dr. David Coffin, whose commentary has guided conservatives in both church and government for a generation, sounds this alarm about such forms of Christian Nationalism: "This view is alive and all too well, and by whatever name is Pagan, not Christian. It [such Nationalism] should be—by those who long for a decent community, marked by an ordered liberty for all—opposed by every means of legitimate argument (logical, biblical, historical, and practical). Pagan Nationalism is a threat to all that is good."[37]

The zeal of these comments by one who is usually mild-mannered helps to indicate the danger of ideas that would try to make America into Old Testament Israel without the reigning grace of our Savior. The absence of such grace is always the mark of zealots and too often is the stance of those whose goals have moved from spiritual redemption to cultural domination.[38] Their efforts become pagan not because they deny that there is a God but because they try to put him into the harness of their worldly ambitions.

Victims to Victors

If the rule of the nation becomes synonymous with the demands of the church, then those who see their political goals not supported by others in the church must brand their disagreeing brothers and sisters as their spiritual enemies. Political scientist Daniel Bennett pegs the errors of both conservative and liberal activists who confuse their cultural preferences with biblical principles:

> There is a tendency, a temptation, to believe that any Christian with whom we have political differences *must* be mired in faithlessness, error, or even sin. "Woe to you partisans, because you do not vote like me," is a sneakily enticing posture to adopt.[39]

Such postures become more seductive when fueled by a zeal that is a product of confidence one's cause is Christ's and one's opponents are complicit with those who have inflicted pain on one's own family, church, and nation. Christian leaders who believe they are cultural victims are particularly susceptible to the kind of zeal that excuses abandonment of Scripture's commands about charity, civility, and integrity in order to enforce their own preferred norms of morality.[40]

Many Evangelicals believe, with good cause, that they are the losers in the culture wars of the last half century. Many also believe that they have been persecuted beyond the requirement to honor, or even learn, Scripture's standards for establishing an alternate society that appeals to the world's wounded because it refuses to mimic their habits of speech, morality, and conduct, particularly with regard to love for our opponents or persecutors.[41]

The flaming voices of church leaders on social media are typically young males who feel that cultural respect and church recognition have passed them by. Taylor Combs explains,

> In recent years, the Left's message to women has been loud and clear: "We want you. You belong here. . . . You are not part of the problem." But the same movement has said to men—particularly white, heterosexual, Christian men: "You are the problem. Men are oppressors. They're abusers. They are not to be trusted."
>
> On the flip side, conservatives in America have played to men's sense of victimization by telling them: "We need you. You still have a role to play. . . . You are not part of the problem."[42]

When such victimization joins with a sense of empowerment on social media and in church politics, then whatever will fuel a restoration of respect and influence gains credence and acceptance. Ordinary standards of testing truth, giving the benefit of the doubt, or charitably interpreting what is ambiguous get subordinated to devouring and distributing whatever information supposedly provides privileged insight, hidden knowledge, or political leverage. Malice welcomes misinformation.[43]

Hope for Scorn

The worst expressions of this are the alt-right and QAnon movements (counterbalanced by Antifa adherents on the political left) that prey on the fear and pain of those who feel disenfranchised from cultural privilege. However, the more common expressions in the church are the vitriol and scandalmongering that can dominate denominational chatrooms, Facebook pages, and Twitter (X) accounts.

Social media scorn and sarcasm experts will often point to examples of invective from select biblical passages or persecuted saints to justify present expressions of disdain. They can, of course, find such examples and may feel that they have sufficient evidence to echo them in comments about brothers and sisters in Christ's church.

It would be wrong, of course, to argue that our Lord himself was never strident in expression or wrathful in his warnings. Yet, it is important to note that his greatest expressions of anger were toward religious zealots he *knew* were enemies of his Father or those in the church he *knew* were not living according to his standards.

Perhaps those who are most convinced of the need for strident and uncharitable expression inside and outside the church are also sure that their targets are Christ's enemies or clear hypocrites. I would encourage them to be *very* sure if they intend to stand before the Lord, or even their own congregations, and justify internet rhetoric that is designed to wound or belittle (Rom. 12:10). Above all, however, I pray that all will remember that when the Bible describes Jesus's ministry to sinners who needed him, it says he would not break a bruised reed nor join the accusers of the broken.

It will ultimately be the Spirit of Jesus more than human words that gives us and our world hope. To retain hope in the face of such fallenness inside and outside the church, in the next chapter we will consider the multigenerational blessings that the Lord has provided for us to celebrate.

7

HOPE FOR THE FUTURE

Leveraging Gospel Opportunities

Some measure of the speed of changes affecting the landscape of American Christianity can be seen in projections for the future of faith made in separate studies by the Pew Research Center. In 2015, Pew projected that two-thirds of the American population would still be Christian by 2050. Five years later, the Center indicated Christians were already less than two-thirds of the population (down from 90 percent in the early 1990s).[1]

Calculating forward with mathematical scenarios that take into account the growing ranks of the Nones, the shrinking birth rates of Christian families, and the recent rates of religious "switching," Pew more recently estimated that Christians are more likely to be less than half of the population by mid-century, and only about a third of the population by 2070.[2] If we were only to consider the math, then the question is not whether Christianity in the US will decline but how fast and to what degree.

Thankfully, our hope is not built on math alone but on the work of the Holy Spirit in the hearts of people he is calling to Christ from every tribe, language, people, and nation (Rev. 5:9). Whether 90 percent of the American population ever was or ever again will be Christian is not nearly so important as whether the church will endure as a faithful witness to the gospel of Jesus Christ for hearts that need him. Making a way for that gospel to be heard and believed remains the church's chief mission, one that the Holy Spirit will provide power to fulfill if we will recognize and pursue the opportunities that are before us.

Hope in the Larger Story

Demographics of the Spirit

Christian news commentator David French identifies hope as "locating oneself within a larger story, specifically a story that has a *past* that fills us with longing, a *future* that pays off on that longing, and then a *present* that engages our energies."[3] As discussed in previous chapters, the Evangelical church is very conscious of a past story (or past glory) that fills many of us with longing for those better days. Yet, having a present and a future hope is still needed to fulfill Christ's purposes.

The Moral Majority movement and its successors, which includes many present expressions of Christian Nationalism and Federal Theology, long for a Christian America that would make a past way of life our future. This "back to the future" vision is what communication analysts call a "fantasy theme appeal" that motivates by reminding constituents of better days in the past that they want to reclaim for the future. It would be difficult for any preacher or church leader not to look back with longing for the days when Ward and June Cleaver did not wonder about the sexual orientation of their children and everyone attended Christmas and Easter services to sing familiar hymns by heart.

Whether days when Christianity was the default position of Americans fighting communism, advancing capitalism, and living to impress boss and neighbor were *really* the most biblical in expression is another question. Still, no one should be faulted for longing for simpler and less worrisome times. Neither is it wrong to long for a better time in the future. The larger story that Scripture is unfolding throughout its many chapters and verses culminates in the rule of Christ where animosities are reconciled, wounds are healed, hatreds are halted, sin is pardoned, everything sad *does* come untrue, and the shalom of God is the experience of all.

The opportunity that the gospel provides to live eternally in that larger story is the hope that engages our energies to live faithfully in this present evil age, even when our politics may not have won in the most recent election cycle, our churches do not seem to prosper in our time, and we do not now see the heavenly consequences of today's efforts. The greatest and most trustworthy reality that is the basis of our enduring hope is our Lord's promise that our present labors are never in vain when we stand firm on his promises for his eternal purposes (1 Cor. 15:58).

Standing firm includes honoring the Lord's commands regarding conduct, speech, and compassion even if the world hates, derides, and persecutes us. If, by its similarity to the world in speech and conduct, the church bears no testimony of the alternative society that the Spirit of Jesus intends, then there will be no longing for our message and no desire for our community. While there is always a part of us that will be "seeking for some great thing to do or secret thing to know,"[4] the most powerful expression of Christ's reality remains the local church consistently living the gospel in Christian love and obedience.

Lesslie Newbigin rightly directed the church to its greatest societal influence when he wrote,

> I confess that I have come to believe that the primary reality of which we have to take account in seeking for a Christian impact on public life is the Christian congregation. How is it possible that the gospel should be credible, that people should come to believe that the power that has the last word in human affairs is represented by a man hanging on a cross? I am suggesting that the only answer . . . is a congregation of men and women who believe the gospel and live by it. I am, of course, not denying the importance of many activities by which we seek to challenge public life with the gospel—evangelistic campaigns, distribution of Bibles and Christian literature, conferences, and even books like this one. But I am saying that they are all secondary, and that they have power to accomplish their purpose only as they are rooted in and lead back to a believing community.[5]

In following paragraphs, I will seek to spell out some of the multigenerational opportunities that give me hope for the future flourishing of the gospel, but I must not proceed to the pragmatic and promising without rooting us in the principles of the gospel Newbigin cites. Ultimately, any hope of gospel progress depends upon the witness of Christians living faithfully in the body of Christ. Whether we win elections or turn the tide of a secular culture in our lifetime is up to God. But he has given us clear responsibilities for living in and building up churches that honor his Word, love his people, obey the Great Commission, and provide Christ's testimony to our surrounding communities and future generations.

These responsibilities cannot be fulfilled without hearts transformed by genuine love for Christ. It may be trendy to mock the "old time religion" that prioritizes a personal relationship with Jesus through being born again, trusting that his sacrifice paid the penalty for my sin, and living faithfully in the daily strength of the Holy Spirit. Still, no other gospel will rescue our hearts, claim our children, or transform our world according to God's design.

Some will scoff at such basics and doubt the practical power of placing such an emphasis on personal spirituality. They may claim that calling the church to its primary responsibilities of personal conversion, Christian living, and sacrificial mission will create a privatized faith with no meaningful concern for the world's evils or engagement with practical realities. To such claims I must politely but firmly respond, "That is impossible."

If we truly believe that we have been saved from an eternity in hell by the mercy of God made available through the grace of Christ's provision alone, then our hearts will beat with desire for our Savior's honor and care. Such love is what enables us to fulfill the Greatest Commandment of loving the Lord our God with all our heart, soul, and mind (Matt. 22:37). But never is this greatest of commandments an end in itself. If we love Jesus above all other loves, then our hearts will be compelled to love what and whom he loves.

What does our Lord love? Scripture declares that he loves all that he has made (Ps. 145:9, 17). So, creation care stirs in the hearts of those who love their Creator's handiwork. Whom does Jesus love? He loves the unlovely, the poor, the oppressed, orphans and widows in their distress, the homeless, the refugee, and the persecuted (Deut. 10:18–19; Ps. 82:3–4; Isa. 58:7; Luke 10:25–37; James 1:27). That is why the Greatest Commandment flows naturally and spiritually into the "second" commandment: "You shall love your neighbor as yourself" (Matt. 22:39). True conversion does not lead to a privatized, egocentric faith; rather, it fuels a heart of compassion that compels Christian efforts for the triumph of truth, justice, and mercy while also passionately pursuing transformation of one's thought, conduct, family, neighborhood, city, and world (Jer. 29:7; Mic. 6:8; Rom. 12:1–2; Gal. 6:10; 3 John 1:4).

Only the Christ-transformed and Spirit-filled heart can fulfill the obligations of giving honor to those who are undeserving of it, refusing to return evil for evil, letting the Lord alone exact vengeance, submitting to those who are in authority over us, and sacrificing self for the good of others (Rom. 12:9–21). These are society-transforming weapons in the Christian arsenal that do not deny the rightness of efforts to change public opinion, defend the defenseless, and turn out the vote for what is righteous. However, they are the only means that convert these human efforts from worldly pragmatics to expressions of Christ's heart and power.

In its earliest centuries, Christianity grew at a rate of approximately 40 percent per decade. At Pentecost, the Holy Spirit gave the New Testament church a launch of three thousand members (Acts 2:41), but that was hardly a significant portion of the Roman Empire. So, the Holy Spirit was not done. By AD 150, there were an estimated forty thousand Christians; however, a greater story was still unfolding, and by AD 350 there were as many as 34 million Christians in the known world. So, how did Christianity grow from 0.000015 percent of the population to more than half of the Roman population within three centuries?[6] Christian social scientist Rodney Stark explains:

> Christianity served as a revitalization movement that arose in response to the misery, chaos, fear and brutality of life in the urban Greco-Roman world. . . . [It] revitalized life in Greco-Roman cities by providing new norms and kinds of social relationships able to cope with many urgent urban problems. To cities filled with the homeless and impoverished, Christianity offered charity as well as hope. To cities filled with newcomers and strangers, Christianity offered an immediate basis for attachments. To cities filled with orphans and widows, Christianity provided a new and expanded sense of family. To cities torn by violent ethnic strife, Christianity offered a new basis for social solidarity. And to cities faced with epidemics, fires and earthquakes, Christianity offered effective nursing services.[7]

The clear lesson of early Christianity is that the church gained power without seeking it through military, political, or marketing means. Our faith predecessors became the world's most influential force for transforming culture simply by consistently living out the principles of Christ.

The message for us is that unless our efforts to expand the church's influence are pursued by gospel-directed hearts with Christ's priorities and character, our cultural battles will only be waged in worldly strength against the world's powers, and will be lacking the Spirit's fruit even if worldly success comes for a time (Gal. 5:22–23; 2 Tim. 3:2–5). As discussed in previous chapters and as the frequent news of wanderings by Christian leaders and their families indicates, much damage to the gospel has already been done by movements of politics and pride claiming the imprimatur of God without his character.

Fruit of the Spirit

With this gospel perspective we can now begin to consider the opportunities before us with the hope that is future confidence in the power of the Spirit. His power will always befuddle the math of human wisdom. So, let's begin by affirming what the Spirit can do. While it is true that the math indicates present trends will lead to an inevitable decline in Christian influence in our culture, math is not the only force at heaven's disposal. What the demographers cannot calibrate is how the gospel can overrule our math.

Children and Millennials Multiplying

For example, mere math does not factor the treasure that the family is to those whose hearts have been captured by the grace of our Lord and delight in opportunities to glorify him. As child-rearing becomes increasingly burdensome and distasteful to a selfish and secular culture,[8] the blessing that children are to those who delight in multiplying the glory of the image of God becomes more powerful and influential in the world (Gen. 1:22, 26; Ps. 127:3–5; 3 John 1:4).

Additionally, while most institutions of our society (science, business, government, education, law, media) are increasingly distrusted, the family remains trusted by most to be the best means of providing love and security in a frayed world.[9] This reality provides strong opportunities for advocating faith principles that strengthen family ties, especially among the young.[10]

One of the countertrends to the common assumption that those who are now younger will have lesser faith commitments than preceding generations is the worship trends of Evangelical adults of child-rearing ages. In post-COVID America, Millennial adults are the generation most likely to attend church. Though Millennials (those in their thirties to mid-forties) are less likely to be active in church than older generations, those who remain active in church fit the overall pattern of being more religiously conservative than their peers.[11] Of Millennials who self-identify as Evangelicals, 61 percent attend church at least weekly. That is higher than the 44 percent of Evangelical Gen Xers (those in their mid-forties and fifties) and the 54 percent of Evangelical Boomers (those in their sixties and seventies).[12]

The influence of these Evangelical Millennials has significantly affected the religious patterns of the overall generation they represent. As cited previously, from 2019 to 2022, the overall percentage of Millennials reporting weekly church attendance increased from 21 percent to 39 percent.[13] The growth in attendance among younger adults is not only an unanticipated shift,[14] it also signals important and hopeful changes for the future.

Surveys conducted in 2022 in the wake of COVID indicated that 52 percent of Millennials said that religion was "somewhat" or "very" important to them; among Generation Z it was 53 percent.[15] These surveys suggest that Generation Z is not less religious than Millennials. Researcher Ryan Burge summarizes, "There's just no real evidence that a 25 year old sees religion as much less important than someone who is 40 years old."[16]

The generation of Millennials that returned to church in greater numbers than any other generation after COVID is being followed by another generation that continues to value matters of the Spirit. When this latter generation has aged into its most significant child-rearing years, it may also be incentivized to join Millennials in the revitalization of the American church. In short, there is much cause to hope for spiritual vitality in the generations soon to be most populous in the American church.

The worship patterns of Evangelical Millennials are particularly significant when we recall the studies cited in chapters 1 and 5 about the influence of parents on children. Millennial parents whose faith commitments have been strengthened by swimming against the secularizing currents of their culture are now raising the Alpha generation (children born between 2010 and 2024).

Already we have seen that a large majority of children raised in homes where commitment to Christ is consistent and grace-filled continue to embrace their faith after their teen years.[17] Such lifetime ("sticky") faith is the belief system children are most likely to embrace in their middle teens and is most influenced by consistent Christian parenting that is reinforced by church leaders, especially young adults respected by teens.[18] Studies show that 72 percent of adult Evangelicals embraced their beliefs before the age of 18. The average age of belief commitment is 15, but half of today's young adults came to faith between the ages of 5 and 12.[19]

Yes, it cannot be denied that a significant proportion of Christian teens will become less spiritually committed as they move into young adulthood (see chapter 1). However, as already shown, these are far more likely to be from homes where faith is nominal or expressed in casual commitments. Those from homes where a conservative, biblical faith is consistently lived remain spiritually engaged in much larger proportions, and 17–27 percent of them will shift into a *higher* religious commitment over the transitional years into young adulthood.[20] In short, spiritually committed families are far more likely to produce spiritually minded teens who are much more likely to remain highly committed Christians in adulthood.

Salt and Light

Since Evangelical teens now outnumber any other Protestant group of religiously active teens by more than two to one,[21] those who continue to identify as Christians in the future are most likely to be those whose faith is Evangelical.[22] I am not here contending that the children of today's Evangelicals will be a majority of the overall culture, but rather that they will be the majority of non-Catholics who identify as Christians.[23] This is important because, as we have already witnessed through the efforts of the Moral Majority, our salt-and-light influence is not so much a matter of numbers but of a faithful Christian witness in a pluralistic society.

The reengagement of Millennial parents in biblical Christianity makes the likelihood of an Alpha generation energized for Christ by the influence of their parents more than just wishful thinking. Already we are witnessing possible effects of the significance of Evangelical commitments among young adults. During the COVID pandemic, "those under 40 were especially likely to go online for their church substitute."[24] A year after COVID, 45 percent of those who experienced online services continued to consider the internet approach better than the in-person approach to worship,[25] but this is not entirely negative.

The young adult generation that was most comfortable with technology was also most influenced by the online portals to faith that COVID provided. The opportunity to explore Evangelical faith without the commitment or intimidation of walking through a church door led to a significant reengagement of lapsed Evangelicals. In fact, "22 percent who were not attending church prior to the pandemic said they started watching church online."[26] This would equate to 3 percent of all Evangelicals. That's roughly two million adults—most of whom were of this younger generation.

Though proving all the connections is not possible, this Millennial resurgence is clearly one of the reasons pandemic dynamics that initially ravaged church attendance seem to have had little long-term, negative impact on faith.[27] In the face of grievous loss of life, the exhaustion of the medical community, the depression of mandated isolations (in the forms of remote office work, online schooling, organizational closures, and gathering restrictions), the political strife, and the polarization of church communities, "the percentage of Americans who say they don't believe in God only edged up 2 points" across the worst of the pandemic years (2018 to 2022).[28]

In that same period, there was also no growth in the percentage of Americans "identifying as religiously unaffiliated" in that specific time span, and no overall shrinkage of those identifying as Evangelicals.[29] More recent studies indicate that the growth of the Nones may be hitting a ceiling in our nation. The percentage of Millennials and Gen Z who are nonreligious actually dropped from 2020 to 2023, with the percentage of Gen X (mid-forties and fifties) who are nonreligious staying the same. So, even though the percentage of all Americans who identify as Nones grew from 34 to 36 percent in this same period, much of that growth must be attributed to the nominally religious of the Boomer and Builder generations.[30]

The Concentration Effect

These last observations are particularly significant for our future hope. At a time when there is no social benefit to claiming to be a Christian—and increasingly there is social cost—those who continue to embrace biblical faith are those most likely really to mean it, and many of them are in the rising generations. This is very unlike the past when being "Christian" meant simply fitting into the majority culture. So, if Christian identification in general is shrinking but Evangelical expression is holding its own—and being held by young people with ardent convictions—then Christianity would seem to be more and more represented in society by those reflecting its true character and teaching. There is much to suggest that this supposition is also more than wishful thinking.

While the overall expression of Christian faith has dramatically shrunk in recent decades, the Evangelical faith community, though suffering serious reductions, has not diminished to the same degree. Overall church association and membership have clearly eroded, but individuals who *say* that they are Evangelical still constitute roughly the same percentage of the American population. In 2010, 28 percent of those ages 18–35 identified as Evangelical. At the same time, 31 percent of those ages 36–64 so identified. A decade later, the younger segment had not significantly changed, and the number of older adults identifying as Evangelical actually increased to 34 percent of the overall population.[31]

These figures should not be used to deny the huge declines in attendance, membership, consistent Christian living, and commitment to the historic tenets of biblical faith. Still, there has not been nearly as significant a decline in those who *think of themselves* as holding to a biblical, Christian faith. The abandonment of Christian labels or beliefs is mainly among those whose denominations or institutions were no longer embracing the historic and orthodox tenets of Christian belief.

The result of a sustained community of belief among a culture of increasing unbelief is the reasonable possibility of a "concentration effect." Those who retain Christian labels are those more likely to be serious Christians, and their salt-and-light witness is less likely to be diluted by those who have carried Christ's name without embracing his truth in belief or behavior. If the concentrate remains true to Christ's character and priorities,

Hope for the Future

then what we have seen repeatedly in the history of the church may well be repeated: A dedicated remnant proves to be far more effective for Christ's purposes than a nominal majority.

Leading indicators of this future hope may lie in the wake of the pandemic that seemed statistically to have done such damage to American religious practices. Despite all the hand-wringing about how church attendance has been affected by COVID, the disease strangely seemed to halt—at least for a time—the hemorrhaging of faith among those who were still engaged. These realities should remind us that trials can fray faith *or* affirm its necessity. As the blood of the martyrs is the seed of the church, so also desperation can stir devotion.

Yes, recent political associations gave Evangelicalism an artificial and temporary bump in numbers, but the constant threat of life-altering disease also seemed to press many hearts toward hope in a Great Physician. Two years after the trials and tragedies of the pandemic, half of all Americans still said that they have no doubt that God exists, and 84 percent still identified themselves as "spiritual."[32]

Through the pandemic, older Evangelical believers mostly held their ground, and younger believers—especially Millennials—actually grew in spiritual dedication. Now, whether by instinct or observation, pastors are responding to the rising spiritual interests of young adults, recognizing that they are the future hope of our churches. Over two-thirds (72 percent) of Protestant pastors say they expect the attendance of 18-to-29-year-olds at their church to increase in the next five years.[33] This is not mere optimism. The stats back the expectations and should be the cause of significant reflection on how church practices and services can best minister to the next generation.[34] Many of these same pastors (two out of five) say their biggest concern for the future of their church is how it will reach young adults.

The concern is appropriate. In the last twenty years, the average attendance in American churches has dropped by more than half. The median attendance dropped from 137 in 2000 to 65 in 2021.[35] By 2023, the median had dropped to 60.[36] Not all churches are shrinking, of course. The larger a church is, the more likely it is to grow. But 21 percent of churches with fewer than 50 people have also grown.[37]

143

Opportunities for the Spirit

Identifying what causes church growth in a secularizing culture is vital for every church concerned with outreach and next-generation ministry. The greatest predictor of whether a church will grow is whether it is located in an area of rapid population growth.[38] Still, there are churches growing across the country in every size category, but these total only 30 percent of all churches in America. Midsize churches (101–250) appear to be those at greatest long-term risk of maintaining the congregations they have known, even though their financial condition can be healthy. Attracting new and younger members, not more dollars, is their chief challenge.[39]

Personal with Purpose

According to the Hartford Institute for Religion Research that surveyed fifteen thousand churches of many denominations and types in the US, those churches that are growing in different size categories have certain common denominators:

- A high percentage of member participation in weekly worship.
- A high percentage of giving to missions and charitable causes. (Giving experts tell us young adults want to know their money makes ministry impact and does not simply keep the church lights on and the minister paid.)
- An absence of conflict.
- Members observably living in Christlikeness toward one another and outsiders.[40]

In other words, the churches that are growing and appealing to new people and rising generations are those that prioritize personal involvement and Christ's purposes.

These realities kick in the head the common notion that the main thing churches need to do to attract young people is "rock out" the music and take off the Sunday ties. As underscored in previous chapters, young people who are pursuing biblical faith in our time—despite their lack of parental models and their struggles with a sexualized and coarsening culture—are courageously swimming against the current of their peer culture. These

Hope for the Future

rising generations are not playing around when it comes to their concern for spiritual growth, glorifying worship, missional impact, and the training of their children.[41]

Researcher Ryan Burge offers this analysis of the surging faith commitments of younger Evangelicals:

> One explanation is that evangelicalism is becoming more culturally distinct among younger Americans. The share of millennials and GenZ who have no religious affiliation is more than 40 percent now—nearly double the rate of Baby Boomers. Christians in their 20s who welcome the "evangelical" label place themselves in clear opposition to prevailing trends among their friends. It makes sense that only young people who feel spiritually connected to theological evangelicalism are willing to embrace it.[42]

Worship with Roots and Reach

Those still willing to embrace historic Christianity want to be well equipped to live it and to attend churches with evident appreciation for it. While it is true that younger adults have little patience for unbending traditions that neither touch the heart nor challenge the mind, the ancient-future influences of Robert Webber, the Gettys, CityAlight, Indelible Grace, and others have made it plain that young adults want worship that is rooted in the faith of our fathers as well as accessible to the hearts of their children.

The churches with growing multigenerational ministries typically fall into three basic categories with respect to their worship features: (1) large churches that can afford traditional instrumentation and worship professionals, appealing to traditional purists of each generation; (2) new churches and large churches offering contemporary worship, either because it can be done well quite affordably or because it appeals to a targeted slice of the adult population (especially the dechurched who are reacting against traditional pasts); and, most commonly, (3) blended worship that honors familiar features of the past and accessible qualities of the present.[43] Small and midsize churches only offering traditional worship rarely have the resources to compete with large churches' professionalism or amenities and are likely to appeal only to a local clientele of traditionalists growing older and shrinking in numbers.

Of course, there are personalities that will prefer traditional or contemporary worship, but blended is where most Millennials land, rooting their faith in enduring foundations while reaching for future impact upon friends and family. In an eroding culture, Millennials desire worship that is "lively" while providing a sense of history and stability.[44] They have little interest in refighting the worship wars over screens, hymnals, and drums, but expect their church's leaders to respect the contributions every generation can make to church worship and mission.

Churches with Exposition and Application

Young adults who are returning to the church are not simply yearning for what is appealing but desire what will strengthen and equip them for the challenges of life in their homes and in a non-Christian world. As a consequence—and often as a surprise to seniors—those under forty are more likely to want *significant* prayer times, *inductive* Bible studies, and *in-depth* sermons.[45]

At the very time senior congregants may be pressing the pastor to shorten Sunday messages (lest the Methodists beat the Presbyterians to the local buffet), Millennials and the generation following them are likely to be demanding more meat from the pulpit that includes serious exposition of Scripture and meaningful application to everyday life.[46] Congregations insisting on brevity because they "have heard it all before" are unlikely to reach those longing to be newly or more fully fed from God's Word.

Worship that is only a social gathering, a rehearsal of past traditions, or a legalistic check mark for community approval will not be a priority for young adults and young families preparing to face a world hostile to their faith. What they want is what every generation of faithful Christians has desired: worship and ministry of the Word that inspires personal love for Christ, gives personal guidance on how to live for Christ, and helps secure personal relationships that provide mutual support in Christian faithfulness.

What keeps Christ's priorities in place are ordained and lay leaders' consistent emphases on gospel-sensitive worship,[47] Christ-centered preaching,[48] grace-enabled discipleship,[49] *and* mission reaching beyond traditional boundaries and bigotries. Without a sense of mission beyond the present congregation and physical walls of the church, the church's priorities will inevitably become maintenance of a past way of life. By making such interests primary, senior leaders will unintentionally but inevitably depersonalize and distance the local church's ministry for those who are new and are looking for spiritual support, a caring community, and family guidance beyond the physical spaces and regular meetings of the church.

Addressing the Darkness

The present opportunity apparent in the resurging involvement of young adult Evangelicals underscores the importance of the church seizing the moment rather than throwing in the towel. As affluence, technology, and escapist media prove to be incapable of stemming our nation's scourges of depression, isolation, and hopelessness—but are instead stoking them—the human heart reaches out from such spiritual darkness for the light of the divine (Acts 17:27). So, we can choose to be depressed by the secular shadows or to be encouraged by the growing light in Evangelical ranks.

Of course, we do not know if the young adult interest will continue, but the common perception that the secularization of the next generation is inevitable only weakens the church and excuses nonstrategic thinking. Research shows that Millennial (young adults in their thirties and forties) and Gen Z (those in their teens and early twenties) generations are open to addressing spiritual concerns,[50] especially if spiritual mentors are personally interested in their well-being and show nonjudgmental understanding of their challenges.[51] The effects can be powerful. For example, if recent history proves predictive, one-third of those who leave the ranks of the Nones will switch to Christian convictions.[52]

Church leaders who recognize this "unprecedented cultural moment"[53] for inspiring the next generation of believers will not only lament the rapid decrease in the number of Americans who say they pray on a daily basis or who deny that religion is "very important," but will also see latent spiritual longing in these spiritual voids.[54] Young people want more than empty ambition or passing pleasure to give their lives meaning. As a consequence, leaders of Christian colleges report that "the current generation of students is more prayerful, mission-oriented, and concerned for whole-life commitment to Christ than any generation in living memory."[55]

Such reports are not isolated or merely anecdotal. When the unplanned and unorchestrated spiritual revival broke out at Asbury University in 2023, student visitors from 285 colleges and universities came to the campus within sixteen days.[56] More spiritual awakenings on campuses have since occurred.[57] Additionally, it is worth noting that those who are involved in campus ministries in their college years are three times more likely to stay in church after college.[58]

The contemporary secular approach to life is not proving more rewarding or satisfying than America's Christian heritage to the rising generations—or anyone else. Despite being largely free of nation-consuming wars and economic catastrophes, all age groups are experiencing epidemic levels of loneliness and depression.[59] The US government now recommends that all adults under the age of 65 be screened for anxiety disorders and that all adults be checked for depression.[60] Worry, of course, is not the plague of adults alone. The percentage of students who say they have "constant feelings of sadness or hopelessness" has been rising for a decade, with almost 20 percent of 12-to-17-year-olds receiving mental health treatment.[61]

A survey published by the CDC indicates that girls and LGBQ+ teens are at highest risk (the survey data did not reflect students who identify as transgender or nonbinary). Almost 60 percent of high school girls experience persistent feelings of sadness, and 30 percent report seriously considering suicide—a rate that nearly doubled in the decade from 2011 to 2021.[62] Almost 70 percent of teens who identify as LGBQ+ also reported "persistent feelings of sadness" and 45 percent say they have considered suicide.[63]

The Savior who urges us to cast all our cares upon him because he cares for us (1 Pet. 5:7) offers help to those struggling with anxiety and depression. He also offers support for parents and loved ones desperate to rescue children, family members, and friends from anxiety, anorexia, addictions, compulsive disorders, self-harm, sexual confusion, depressive illnesses, and the host of emotional and physical maladies that are the consequence of striving to be happy in the world through the worldly solutions of power, pleasure, or connecting with your inner child.

Christians should anticipate that such pervasive struggles and sadness in our society will cause people to be open to considering spiritual answers to their concerns—because that is precisely what is happening. Around two-thirds (66 percent) of Americans say they are open to spiritual conversations with a friend, including 41 percent who say they are very open.[64] The younger the adults are, the more willing they are to have such conversations. Even among the religiously unaffiliated, few say they're not open at all to having spiritual conversations with a *friend*. Only one in five (20 percent) aren't at all open to a conversation about faith with a friend. In addition, over half (51 percent) of Americans say they would even be willing to have such a conversation with a *stranger*—and COVID made 32 percent more willing to talk than they were before the pandemic.[65]

Spiritual hunger is not simply the fabrication of preachers. There really is a God-made hole in every heart that cannot be filled by the things of earth (Eccles. 3:11). Adults of all ages experiencing real-world struggles desire spiritual consolation that can only be provided by those whose churches are willing to wade into the muck. For example, as we saw back in chapter 4, Protestant men who regularly attend church seem to be the only men in America who continue to resist our culture's acceptance of pornography use as normal.[66] But equipping men to deal with their temptations requires church leaders who are willing to counsel, address, and restore those whose strength has been challenged or failed.

Gallup and others report that adults who are devout are more satisfied with their marriages, their sex lives, their families, and their lives in general than those who have pursued nonreligious paths and priorities.[67] However, navigating these concerns according to biblical principles requires churches that will address the most sensitive and controversial issues of our time. And, to no one's surprise, the younger the adult congregant, the greater is the demand that the church address the tough issues.[68]

Challenges of the Spirit

Churches that celebrate young people who are willing to seek honest answers to tough questions are those churches most likely to attract and hold the younger generations that are returning to worship settings or are continuing in them in the post-COVID world. Such churches will need to face some tough realities to reach and to keep these future generations.

Diverse Ethnicities

The first reality that we will need to face becomes evident as we become a bit more specific about the ethnicities of those Millennials whom the Barna Group reported are returning to the church in greater numbers than their Evangelical seniors. As indicated previously, after two years of COVID upheaval, the overall percentage of Millennials reporting weekly church attendance increased from 21 percent to 39 percent since 2019, as reported in 2022.[69] That's very encouraging.

Other research indicates that those who are theologically conservative are more likely to attend religious services regularly.[70] That is also encouraging. However, as of 2022, the percentage of non-white Millennials attending church weekly was 45 percent, compared to 35 percent of white Millennials.[71]

This data suggests that the increase in Millennial church attendance can largely be attributed to non-white Millennials. This is because attitudes about family, work, and sexuality among ethnic minorities may compete with social justice concerns in their political and religious alignment. Data clearly indicates that "high attending Black Protestants" do not fit the stereotype of holding to ideologically liberal views that would keep them from Evangelical church involvement.[72] Recent voting polls show that Hispanic and Latino voters are also shifting ideologically to the right (indications strongly confirmed in the 2024 presidential election),[73] and segments of the Asian community (especially those who are older) have historically been conservative about social and religious issues.[74] Barna researchers comment, "Studying this data may help leaders recognize either an opportunity or a blind spot in their ministries."[75]

The Millennial generation that is reconsidering church has already indicated its desire to have Christ's love of all peoples and nations reflected in the ministry and membership of its churches. Efforts to proclaim the gospel with little evidence of its power to overcome human pride and prejudice are not likely to claim the loyalties of our young adults or their children (see chapter 5).[76]

Immigration

Similar issues should be considered if Evangelicals are to make progress with new immigrant populations that will affect the future of all churches in the United States. According to Pew research from 2005, our nation's foreign-born population (36 million in 2005) was expected to rise to 81 million by 2050—that's growth of 129 percent. However, more recent studies looking at immigrants *and* their children estimate that number will be 156 million in 2050. That projection translates to 34 percent of the future population, compared to 26 percent of the present population.[77]

As previous chapters have indicated, Evangelical populations are conflicted about these immigration statistics. Our economic well-being requires that our population continues to grow, but with declining birth rates, such growth will require immigrant infusions.[78] At the same time, the number of refugees and migrants crossing our borders raises genuine alarm about our ability to absorb, employ, and educate unregulated multitudes of new people—and can lead to xenophobic and racist attitudes not worthy of the people whose Savior claims his people from all nations.

Not only is the health of our nation's economy likely to depend on immigrant populations, so also is the health of the Evangelical church. Nearly half of the world migrants are Christians.[79] Those who immigrate to the United States are typically more spiritually inclined than the resident American population—and are also more inclined to have larger families. As a consequence, the US Religion Census shows that religious groups with immigrant members grew the fastest over the past decade.[80]

Though church attendance has been in general decline across the nation, churches appealing to immigrants have seen steady growth. The modest sectors of growth in the Catholic church over the last ten years have been almost entirely attributable to Hispanic immigrants. However, there has been a steady decline in the share of US Latinos who identify as Catholic,[81] and church membership among Hispanic Americans is the lowest of any major subgroup,[82] making a people with a rich religious heritage seemingly ready for new gospel outreach by Evangelical churches with Christ's priorities. Admittedly, Hispanics who leave the Catholic church more typically align with no other faith group, but those looking for spiritual expression outside their historic patterns are finding a home in Evangelical churches.[83]

There is already significant evidence to support optimism about the potential for this people group to have a profound influence on the future of Evangelical faith in America. Ryan Burge points out that "the share of

Hispanic immigrants to the United States identifying as evangelical has increased significantly, from 22% in 2008 to 32% in the most recent data. There's also a noticeable rise in the evangelical share among second- and third-generation Hispanic Americans, with about three in ten stating they are evangelical."[84]

These percentage increases in Evangelical faith among Hispanic Americans become even more significant when considering that by 2060, 103 million Americans will be Hispanic—that is, 27 percent of the overall population.[85] If present numbers hold, this would also mean that the number of Hispanic Evangelicals will soon total a full third of the present number of Evangelicals across the United States.

For those who foresee the present secularizing of America bottoming out in the spiritual destitution that has historically led to revival,[86] the spirituality and birth rates of immigrant populations are commonly expected to be major contributing factors to our nation's spiritual turnaround. Such a turnaround will require that majority-culture, white Evangelicals see that adding ethnic minorities to their local church is more than a matter of shoring up their church's attendance numbers (or demonstrating its tolerance). Instead, we must all see the absolute necessity of becoming bodies of Christ that are maturing in the gospel by virtue of the spiritual contributions of diverse people groups.

In the Lord's wisdom, no ethnicity has a monopoly on Christian virtue or biblical understanding. We are all affected by our cultural benefits and our cultural blinders. We need one another to represent the fullness of Christ to one another and to the world (Eph. 1:22–23).

I got a taste of what I needed to learn while teaching a preaching course in Africa some years ago. The translation of the morning session did not go well. It was obvious that I was struggling with jet lag, my translator was struggling to communicate, and my students were struggling to understand.

After the lectures, my host took me to see some sights in the city and on our way back in the late afternoon we passed by the classroom. The students were still there. I asked my host why. He replied, "Some of us struggled with today's lesson. So, all the students stayed to help one another. No one will go home until everyone understands."

My individualistic, democratic, self-sufficient, American mind then struggled to absorb what I had just witnessed. Could it really be possible that a commitment to the body of Christ required that each person consider the good of the community as important as his or her own well-being? Could it be true that each member of the body deserved the support of all? Could it be that even the weakest members were to be considered indispensable to the ministry of the whole church? I have known 1 Corinthians 12:22 ("the parts of the body that seem to be weaker are indispensable") all my adult life. But I think not until that day did I begin to understand the fuller dimensions of its truth.

If the gospel is to shine among us—the gospel that teaches the divine image in all humanity, the infinite value of all for whom Christ died, and the necessity of each member of Christ's body for Christ's purposes—then we do not need merely to welcome those of different nations and ethnicities. The gospel does not *only* require that we not hate or discriminate. Nor does the gospel simply require that we learn to *tolerate* others. It is not even enough to *welcome* others with the offer to love and respect them if they become like us in conduct, habit, and language.

Ultimately the gospel requires that we open our hearts and church communities to others with the humble confession that we *need* them (Eph. 2:19–21). The background and understanding that God has granted to immigrating Christians through their cultures of origin will mature and refine the gospel understanding of the American church (even as our understanding is necessary for the maturing and refining of others' thought). This is because none of us can fully understand or express all the beauty and intricacies of the gospel without the involvement, instruction, and leadership of brothers and sisters from all the contexts of God's world mission (Eph. 3:8–10, 17–19).

Hoppers

In the great shuffle that occurred as people were shifting churches during and after the COVID pandemic, almost 20 percent of churchgoing people "hopped" to another church.[87] That fluidity of commitment among once dependable parishioners is threatening to all church leaders as we wonder what ill-considered word, practice, or decision will send people packing more readily than ever before. However, people's willingness to make a move for what they consider best for the spiritual development of themselves, their friends, and their families is also an opportunity to be seized.

If people are going to continue picking churches according to personal preferences and priorities rather than traditional affiliations, then why not design churches according to gospel priorities? We will surely lose some people who are worldly minded if we do, but we may gain those who are gospel minded. And if we do not, we will most certainly lose a biblically minded future generation.

Making our principles and practices plain to those who are looking for a church with gospel priorities will require more than a road sign with a denominational label or a catchy slogan. Some sources report that COVID patterns have led to 80 percent of newcomers exploring a church service online before attending.[88] Concerns about continued online streaming diminishing regular Sunday attendance should not be so overblown as to miss such opportunities. While it is true that about 10 percent of adults attend church only online since COVID,[89] the most consistent users of local church streaming services are regular attenders who need and appreciate an occasional alternative.[90]

Upheavals

I began this chapter with the analysis of Pew researchers who ran various population scenarios and concluded that all of them led to the likely decline of the church in America. Some of those scenarios considered what would happen if trends continued as they are, or if every child kept the faith of his or her parents, or if all immigration and emigration ceased, or if people stopped switching churches or faiths as mature adults.[91] These are savvy considerations calculated by smart people. They are also smart enough to know that only our God knows the future and that there are too many earthly and spiritual variables to consider for any honest human to make guaranteed predictions.

The integrity of the Pew researchers required them to set aside their calculations long enough to acknowledge that, although another Great Awakening seems unlikely, "Armed conflicts, social movements, rising authoritarianism, natural disasters, or worsening economic conditions are

Hope for the Future

just a few of the circumstances that trigger sudden social—and religious—upheavals."[92] Such "upheavals" are what Evangelicals call revivals. They cannot be predicted or manufactured, but they typically occur when all other hopes have failed and all other life pursuits have left people feeling empty.

Thus, the spiritual resurgence of the Millennials and Generation Z, the desire of young adults to seek Christian solidarity beyond racial barriers, the numerical growth and spiritual contributions of immigrants, the willingness of 84 percent of Americans still to see value in the spiritual, and the willingness of churched people to step beyond their traditional affiliations—all are good reasons to continue to believe that our Lord still has plans for present and future generations of his people.

Still, the best reason for hope is our Lord Jesus's promise, "I will build my church, and the gates of hell shall not prevail against it" (Matt. 16:18). We do not maintain hope for the church of Jesus Christ simply to secure the stature of *our* churches and Christian institutions. That would be mere selfishness. Rather, our hope resides in daily faithfulness lived with the biblical assurance that the church has been given divine power to radiate the glory and goodness of God in our lives and relationships (2 Pet. 1:3–8).

Only the Spirit knows the timing and pervasiveness of the next revival (and whether it will precede our Lord's return), but we know that revivals surge when the human spirit is lowest and all other hopes have proven false. We prepare for revival by believing in the power of the gospel and living it consistently and courageously in home and workplace until the Spirit falls upon his people in power. Our mission is to live with obedient hope, to teach our children well, and to love our neighbors for Christ's sake. We take heart from the opportunities that are before us and pray for encouragement and endurance until the Spirit displays his intentions for the next phase of God's plan.

8

HOPE FOR THE NATIONS

The Spirit in the World

When resistance to the gospel in our North American culture tempts us to discouragement, a global perspective of rising generations' disciple-making efforts and church-planting movements should reignite confidence in and commitment to the ongoing work of God's mission.[1] Christianity remains the largest religion in the world with 2.6 billion adherents and growing (compared to 1.8 billion Muslims and 1.1 billion Hindus).[2]

These totals or proportions will likely fluctuate in future years, but it is clear that the worldwide number of births to Christian mothers has outstripped all other religious groups in recent years.[3] While Pew researchers think Muslim births may outnumber Christian births in the future,[4] possibly making Islam the world's largest religion by 2100, their estimates are by no means certain.[5] Further, regardless of which religion is largest, no one questions that current trends indicate there will be far more Christians in the next generation, with at least another billion by 2050.[6]

What is presently undeniable is that the world's fastest-growing countries tend to be highly religious, and the religion with the greatest number of followers is Christianity.[7] The spiritual impact on our world will be felt far into the future generations should our Lord's return not come sooner. Currently, 90 percent of young people in the world are in the global

South—the very place that Christianity has grown the most over the past century.[8] Further, birth rates in these growing nations indicate that "the percentage of the global population that is religiously unaffiliated will shrink in the decades ahead—in contrast with the trends seen in the US and Western Europe."[9]

Birth rates and population movements are not the only dynamics to assess when considering what the Holy Spirit can do in coming generations. For example, the fastest-growing church in the world today is probably in Iran.[10] The church there is severely restricted and largely underground, but it is flourishing.[11] I witnessed a sign of that spiritual health recently when I participated in yet another ordination of a Muslim-born, Iranian pastor in my denomination. He joins a cadre of Iranians who evidence a profound Christian commitment, despite having been tortured to try to force him to disclose associates in his country.

These Iranians are only a few examples of the many Muslims who are coming to faith in Christ despite persecution and threat—and despite the often terrible witness of, and wars with, Western nations identified as "Christian." In fact, if there is any nation that rivals Iran for the fastest-growing church it is probably Afghanistan, where Taliban rule can make Christian identification a death sentence.[12] In these and similar nations, university students and young professionals are the ones most likely to question repressive regimes, morality police, and Muslim faith. As evidence, we should recognize that Iran and Afghanistan are not the only Muslim nations where Christianity is growing. Muslims are also coming to faith in Christ in regions as disparate as Algeria, Albania, Syria, and Kurdistan. In fact, more Muslims have come to Christ in the last two decades than in the previous fourteen centuries combined.[13]

This multigenerational tide of Christianity is not confined to the parts of the world that are traditionally Muslim. When Western missionaries were driven from China in Chairman Mao's Cultural Revolution two generations ago, common reason would conclude that Christianity was done in the world's most populous nation. But the Holy Spirit was not done. This Sunday more people will worship Jesus Christ in China than in the United States.[14] Yes, the Christians in China are a much smaller percentage of the total population than in America, but the Chinese population is so large that the proportion that is Christian totals a greater number of worshipers than in America.

This Sunday, more Christians will also worship Jesus in Africa than in the United States. At the beginning of the twentieth century there were only about seven million Christians throughout the continent of Africa. That was a small fraction of the total population spread across a land mass three times that of the United States. Today more than half of Africa (where 70 percent of the population is under age thirty) identifies as Christian. That is more than 700 million people—over *twice* the total population of America—who are mostly young and have yet to raise children.[15]

In 1900, twice as many Christians lived in Europe as in the rest of the world combined. By 2050, African Christians will total 1.3 billion people—almost three times the number of those in Europe who identify as Christian.[16]

There are 70 million Christians in India despite pressure and persecution from Hindu (80 percent) and Muslim (10 percent) populations.[17] If growth rates continue for the next generation, by 2050 there will be more Christians in Asia alone (560 million) that in all of Europe (497 million).[18]

In the last one hundred years, places where the majority of Christians live have moved from the established church lands of Western Europe and North America to the global South in Asia, Africa, and Latin America.[19] Today, almost 80 percent of the world's Evangelicals are Africans, Asians, and Latin Americans.[20] However, the results of this global spread of Christianity are not only apparent in the global South.

As migration and oppression move groups from majority-culture nations to seek Western affluence and safety, Christianity is being refreshed in nations where love for Christ has lagged. Now the biggest churches in London are African and Caribbean. The biggest churches in Texas are usually Hispanic. The biggest churches in my denomination, the Presbyterian Church in America, are Korean in heritage. All of these migrant movements skew the Christian population younger as the perils of transition from the majority world and the allure of better futures for families in Western societies sift the older generations and energize the faith of the younger.

These migrant movements also provide evidence that the Spirit is not done with future generations of Western nations where Christianity once thrived and resourced the world's greatest mission movements. Despite the common assessment that Europe is "post-Christian," there are pockets of thriving Christianity—often the echo effect of missions Europeans once spawned. A 2021 mission report from Lausanne sources explains,

> Latin-American migrants have planted thousands of churches in Spain, Portugal and beyond over the last thirty years. It is difficult to find a major European city that does not have a large Spanish speaking and/or Brazilian congregation. Similarly, Chinese churches can be found almost everywhere. African-initiated Pentecostal churches number in the thousands in Britain alone.[21]

Church-planting movements in intensely secular France are planting a new church every week. Similar efforts are being initiated in at least thirty other European nations. These efforts are being backed by organized prayer efforts in seventy-eight countries, with most participants from present or former European contexts.[22]

Because these efforts are often outside the programs and practices of traditional churches, they also trend in appeal to younger generations seeking meaning and hope in cultures where the promises of affluence, sexual freedom, and technology have led to empty selfishness and unrelenting isolation. Tens of thousands of teens have recently gathered for worship and exploration of the faith of their forefathers in nations such as Norway, Austria, Sweden, Croatia, Northern Ireland, and Germany, where orthodoxy has long been considered calcified and collapsed.[23]

My intention in citing these many signs of hope for the future of Christianity is, first, to encourage readers with rarely considered evidence of God's work in the rising generations of the world. Second, I want to underscore the principle that we do no greater damage to the mission of God in our day than when we read of the powerful witness and work of the Holy Spirit in the New Testament and label those accounts as merely ancient history or primitive hyperbole.

The Holy Spirit who was at work then is at work now. He does not work in the same way in every generation and nation, but he is never idle. Along with the testimony of Scripture, we have powerful, present evidence of Christianity's progress that should stir our belief in God's blessings upon current and future generations. Such belief should also cause established generations to celebrate the advance of the gospel in our time and recommit ourselves, our resources, and our efforts to Christ's work for future generations across the nations.

In considering how God is dealing with the present challenges to the gospel that we lament, it is neither right nor responsible to limit our assessment to present American contexts. While it is true that North America and Western Europe no longer contain the majority of the world's Christians, we (especially Christians in the United States) are still providing the majority of the resources and missionaries for global mission—and remain responsible for stewarding these blessings for Christ's purposes with future generations.[24]

The Spirit in History

Proper assessment of and encouragement for God's work today requires recollection and understanding of how the Spirit has worked through history. He clearly uses different means for different tasks and times. For example, the accounts of the Spirit's work in Scripture and in the early church should teach us dimensions of his activity that will keep us zealous for his cause and confident in his ultimate victory despite our world's resistance to Christ.

We must not give in to cynicism about present challenges being too big for God, having no past precedent, and precluding future generations of faith. Yes, we have witnessed great erosion of the testimony and prominence of the American church in the last few decades, but these are not the worst times ever. Our God has provided past victories in more terrible situations to give us fresh passion for his cause even in the face of great opposition.

Faithfulness will require that we not yield to supposed sophistication that contends the Bible is not realistic or sufficient for our time. Scripture records the spreading testimony of persecuted disciples and the profound influence of a beleaguered church in its earliest generations so that we will never forget what the Holy Spirit can do against all odds.

Had any of us stood at the foot of the cross, we would have said the suffering could not possibly be right. We would have assumed that the mission of our Savior had failed and that his work was done. It had only begun. Resurrection, ascension, and the blessings of Pentecost were only around the corner of God's plan. Yet, that plan also had twists and turns to prepare our hearts for the unanticipated work of the Spirit that exceeds our wisdom while fueling our faithfulness.

God's plan took shape as our risen Lord proclaimed to his disciples, "You will receive power when the Holy Spirit has come upon you, and you will be my witnesses in Jerusalem and in all Judea and Samaria, and to the end of the earth" (Acts 1:8). This expanding work of the Holy Spirit seemed obvious at first, as he blew upon the apostles with the sound of wind and signs of fire. Then, he ignited faith in thousands of people from different nations on the day of Pentecost, and many came to believe in Jesus in subsequent weeks (Acts 2).

So many believed in the apostles' testimony of the life, sacrifice, and resurrection of Jesus that even Jewish priests expressed faith in Christ (Acts 6:7). That's when the Jewish authorities had enough of this new movement. They began to persecute the fledgling church and hired a young zealot named Saul to crush it. He was very effective, going from house to house and dragging men and women off to prison. Then, by his own testimony, he called for those who persisted in their belief to be killed (8:1–3; 26:10).

Again, had we been present when those early believers were facing such cultural opposition, we probably would have thought that the cause of Christ was finished. But the Holy Spirit had just begun to fulfill God's purposes across nations and generations. The believers who escaped the clutches of Saul fled Jerusalem and became like seeds on the wind, taking the truth of Jesus beyond the Middle East to new generations in Africa, Asia, and Europe (Acts 13).

Within a few years, the very man who had driven Christ's followers from their homeland would be renamed Paul by the Spirit of Jesus. That same Paul would take the gospel of Jesus to the distant lands where those followers had fled, and then to farther lands where the fledgling churches commissioned him to go. As a result, Christianity would become the official religion of the Roman Empire within four centuries.

Belief sparked by the Holy Spirit led to opposition that deepened faith in Christ. The Holy Spirit then used that refined faith to spread the truths of the gospel to future generations. Over and over, we have seen the Spirit work this way in history.

When the saints of the European Reformation were taken to trial, imprisoned, and burned at the stake, it seemed that the light of the gospel had been extinguished. But through their martyrdoms such a flame was lit for Christ that heaven was illuminated for millions more who came to see that eternal salvation is by faith in his grace alone. From European shores, persecuted believers fled to the Americas, where Christianity would ultimately find its greatest financial and human resources for world mission.

The Spirit in Mission

As the opening pages of this chapter indicate, the examples of the Holy Spirit overcoming persecution, opposition, apathy, ignorance, and sin could be multiplied many times. Still, a backward glance is not all that is needed. The purpose for this book has been not only to make us clear-eyed about the challenges that generations of Christians have faced in the past and are facing in our present context, but also to surface the future opportunities the Holy Spirit is providing for reaching our world with the Good News of Jesus.

We should understand that the "religion" that pervades our nation and dominates the world is materialistic nominalism—the pursuit of material gain without any serious attention to God. Regardless of ethnic or national history, the tenets of the major religions of the world are firmly held and faithfully practiced by only a few religious elites. The vast majority of the world's populations are simply pursuing some form of affluence in the context of religious apathy, ignorance, superstition, or shallowness.

Although those who identify with no religion are actually shrinking in numbers across the globe,[25] most people among the nations are like most people in America: religiously affiliated by region, tradition, or political party but not faithful to, or articulate in, the distinctives of their scriptures, doctrines, and creeds.[26] Inevitably this means that most people will seek satisfaction not from their faith but from the attainment of "personal peace and affluence" that cannot satisfy the soul.[27] But if these many millions of people made in God's image ever tire of their worldly pursuits or despair of finding fulfillment in them, then their empty hearts will be prepared—even longing—for the contentment and peace that Christ can supply.

The great emptiness that is the product of all worldly pursuits is the great opportunity the Holy Spirit provides for churches that will not abandon trust in his provision and power for future generations. Even when it seems that other institutions or distractions might fill the void, epidemics of self-harm, chemical and digital dependencies, and despair among the young are shouting the necessities of the hope Christ Jesus alone provides.[28]

In our nation, we have seen that greater levels of affluence, leisure, and technology have led to unprecedented levels of isolation, depression, and dehumanizing self-indulgence among our young.[29] More than a half century ago, Robert Merton and Jacques Ellul prophesied,

> The technological society requires men to be content with what they are required to like, for those who are not content, it provides distractions—escape into absorption with technically dominated media of popular culture. . . . Progress then consists in progressive de-humanization—a busy, pointless, and, in the end, suicidal submission to technique [i.e., devices causing standardized results].[30]

Despite their warnings, we have remained "committed to the quest for continually improved means to carelessly examined ends."[31] As predicted, even with all the promises of prosperity and privilege afforded through today's technological advances, nothing has proven to be an adequate substitute for a personal relationship with Jesus for eternal peace of heart.

In other nations as well, we see that a depersonalized religion exercised *for* political control and atheism enforced *by* political control are almost equally effective in driving people to Christ. The nations where theocracies rule or dictators dominate are often those where Christianity grows the fastest.[32] In their own way, both theocracies and dictatorships demonstrate the futility of trusting a person, a government, an economy, or the military to provide security for the heart. Thus, we see the amazing growth of churches (often underground) in tightly controlled nations such as China, Turkey, Iran, Afghanistan, Indonesia, and others.[33]

Such church growth echoes New Testament accounts of the church's expansion by the power of the Spirit, as those thought to have little cultural importance nevertheless risked personal safety or position to speak God's truth to those who needed it (e.g., Acts 3, 7, 13, 22, 24, 26). As we unpack the significance of these lessons today, we must remain mindful of how those considered least influential in our contexts may have the greatest impact on the future of the church.

Currently, young people under age thirty account for 50 percent of the global population.[34] Half of that group (25 percent of the total population) are under fifteen, with only 10 percent of the world's population over sixty-five.[35] Because of declining birth rates, the global population will rapidly age, but there is a present opportunity that the church must not miss.[36] Since we know that young people are simultaneously most open to the gospel and most likely to retain the faith that they embrace in their teens, focused efforts to make Christ known to this younger generation are likely to have the greatest impact on the future of our faith.

A generation ago, mission strategists led the Evangelical church in identifying the 10/40 Window of unreached people groups that needed focused attention for the church to take the gospel to all nations. We should celebrate the generation whose insights and commitments launched and led that great movement. Still, the challenge of today is a 30/50 window—the opportunity to reach those under the age of thirty who make up 50 percent of the world's population.

These billions are presently at the life stages in which they are most open to the gospel and most likely to make a lifetime commitment to it. Additionally, they have unprecedented access to the Scriptures. In part, this is because of the valiant translation efforts of Western Christian organizations (three-quarters of the world's people now have access to the full Bible in their own language).[37] In addition, the mission baton is now being carried in increasing numbers from those nations that were once the focus of Western missions (especially Brazil, Korea, and Nigeria).[38] The gospel is also spreading because of the digital Bible applications now available in many languages that are being used by many millions of young people on their cell phones.[39] Innovative mission efforts focusing on sharing the gospel through oral means that are more reflective of the pre-print or oral-preferencing cultures in which Christianity multiplied in its early centuries are further accelerating efforts to make Christ's claims known "throughout the whole world" (Matt. 24:14).[40]

The Spirit of Hope

For these reasons and many more, we should celebrate not only the generations that are rising but also the older generations that have maintained Christ's witness and care enough to provide the resources and love that can make him known to billions more. As has always been the case, the Lord calls each generation in its time for his purposes. Each is vital for his cause, and each should be celebrated for its faithfulness to the particular calling Christ gives for the glory and greatness of his name in the midst of changing challenges and opportunities.

The present challenges to our Christian witness have been detailed in the earlier chapters of this book. Christianity is clearly on the decline numerically in Western culture and in our nation. The health of the church and the consistency of Christian witness in the United States have seriously eroded in recent decades and resulted in declining attendance, membership, and personal commitment that was almost unimaginable at the turn of this century. Our children and grandchildren face a world in which they have few Christian peers and are likely considered odd, ignorant, or evil for holding to views of morality, marriage, and sexuality that the vast majority of Americans in their parents' and grandparents' generations once considered normal. If rising generations also believe that salvation from sin, death, and hell is by faith in Jesus Christ alone, they will be further ostracized in the pluralistic culture that surrounds them and disadvantaged by the institutions that educate, employ, and entertain all others in our society.

Hope for the future of faith does not lie in statistical analysis but in spiritual assessment of how our Lord has worked throughout Scripture and church history. When human achievements fail to satisfy, human philosophies fail to comfort, and human distractions fail to relieve, then the human heart seeks solace and security beyond the world's solutions. What should give us hope in this present evil age is the openness rising generations in this country and throughout the world have to the claims of the gospel. There are opportunities apparent in the number of Millennials returning to worship with their children in these post-COVID years, in the apparent plateauing of the Nones, in the willingness of younger generations to discuss spiritual matters, in the spirituality of increasing immigrant populations, in the growth of churches that are sensitive to the needs of next generations, and even in the despondency of our culture that has not been countered by irreligion, nontraditional sexual trends, technology, affluence, or politics.

Finally, there is the opportunity to take hope from the pervasive influence of the Spirit in the larger world. Whether Christianity will remain the world's largest religion is uncertain, and whether recent rates of conversions to Christ among non-Christian peoples will increase is unknown, but the simple effect of birth rates among Christians worldwide indicates that—should our Lord tarry—there will be another billion saints on this earth within a generation. The church of Jesus Christ will continue to have a profound impact on the nations, communities, families, and individuals of this world.

As faith is built on observation of God's faithfulness to generations past, and trust is confidence of his ongoing grace in our present context, so also biblical hope is faith in God's power to accomplish his future plans. Our hope is not merely optimistic wishing; it is strong confidence that the Lord will continue to bring to completion his plan to disciple the nations until all the world unites in glorifying our Savior (Hab. 2:14; Phil. 1:6). Churches that trust God's promises will rejoice to entrust new generations with this mission of God and will celebrate every opportunity to understand, equip, and resource their future faithfulness.

QUESTIONS FOR REVIEW AND DISCUSSION

Introduction: Celebrating the Faith of Generations

1. Why do you think the Bible says there is no greater joy than knowing that our children walk in God's truth (3 John 1:4)?
2. What reasons do you see in Scripture for us to ensure that our churches become multigenerational?
3. What instructions or suggestions do you see in Scripture that will help your church last more than one generation?
4. What multigenerational resources do you see in your church?
5. What sorts of people help churches to become multigenerational?
6. What attitudes or concerns keep churches from becoming multigenerational?
7. What happens to churches that do not become multigenerational?
8. Who are the Gene Mintzes in your church or in your life?

Chapter 1: Our Generational Challenges

1. What does the loss of truth in our culture mean to you?
2. What is some evidence that you see in your community or family of the loss of capital-T truth?

3. What might be some examples in the church of the loss of truth?
4. How does the loss of truth affect your relationships at work?
5. How does the loss of truth affect young people around you?
6. Is the loss of truth harder on those older or those younger in the church? Explain your answer.
7. How does the loss of truth affect the way people think about church or the commitment they have to their church?
8. If people don't believe in a capital-T truth, what do they tend to believe?
9. If people don't believe in a capital-T truth, what does that do to their relationship with God?
10. If people don't believe in a capital-T truth, what do they think about a church that does? What do they think about people who do? Are these dynamics harder on young people or mature adults?
11. What are some things we can do in the church or in our homes to support rising generations of Christians?

Chapter 2: Our Church Challenges

1. In your experience, are there fewer people attending church these days? Why do you think this is so?
2. Is there a lesser attendance of both young and old, or is this dynamic more apparent in one of these groups? Why do you think this is so?
3. What are some evidences of fewer mature people attending church regularly?
4. What are some reasons contributing to fewer mature people attending church as regularly now as they did a few decades ago?
5. How did (and does) the COVID pandemic affect the number of mature believers attending your church (or churches you know)?
6. What is the magnitude of the loss of mature people attending your church (or churches you know)?
7. What are the effects upon the church of the loss of significant numbers of mature Christians?

Questions for Review and Discussion

8. What are the effects on future generations of the loss of significant numbers of mature believers in your church or in your community?
9. Which do people in your church know better: their theology or their politics? What effects does your answer have on present and future generations?
10. What can your church do to encourage mature believers to continue in church attendance?

Chapter 3: Our Cultural Challenges

1. Did you ever feel as though Christians were in the majority in our culture? When was this, and what gave you that impression?
2. Has anything changed in your impression of the percentage of Christians in our culture? If so, what has changed?
3. If there has been a loss in the magnitude of professing Christians in our church, what generations will struggle the most with the change? Why?
4. Are you surprised at the magnitude of the loss of Mainline churches? Why do you think they have experienced such losses?
5. Are you surprised at the magnitude of the loss of Evangelical churches? Why do you think they have experienced such losses?
6. What does a committed Evangelical believe? What does a nominal Evangelical believe?
7. How is it possible that Jews, Hindus, and even Atheists are calling themselves Evangelicals in our present culture?
8. Does the rise of the Nones surprise you? What are the effects of the rapid rise of the Nones on your church, your family, and the generations coming after yours?
9. How does what people *say* about their church attendance compare to their actual church attendance? What do you think will be the effects of so few of those who call themselves Evangelicals attending church regularly?

10. Can it be true that only 3 percent of Americans attend church weekly now? If so, what are possible effects on our churches, our children, and our prayers?

Chapter 4: The Mature Uniform

1. What do you think are features of the "mature uniform" worn by mature adults in your church?
2. What were the issues being addressed by the Moral Majority during the era of Jerry Falwell, Pat Robertson, James Dobson, and D. James Kennedy, among others?
3. Was there anything wrong with the issues that were being addressed by the Moral Majority?
4. Was there anything wrong with the way that the Moral Majority addressed issues?
5. How has the era of the Moral Majority affected the alignment of the Evangelical church with political parties? How has this alignment affected the nation? How has this alignment affected the church?
6. How did you or your church respond to the concerns of the Moral Majority at its peak?
7. How is your church responding to the concerns of the Moral Majority now?
8. How are different generations in your church responding differently to the concerns of the Moral Majority? Are these differences good or bad? Are the people with the differences good or bad?
9. How are different generations in your church responding to the "great loss" experienced by the Moral Majority generation?

Chapter 5: The Minority Mission

1. Why does a generation that is under age 50 view the world so much differently than Christians who matured in their faith during the Moral Majority era?

Questions for Review and Discussion

2. How has the loss of a Christian majority in America affected secular perceptions and lifestyles in the church and outside the church?
3. What are some likely effects upon the mission priorities of a generation that views itself as a Christian minority in a pluralistic majority culture?
4. What are the likely social and moral concerns of Christians now in their forties or younger?
5. How do the social and moral concerns of Christians in their forties and younger compare to the social concerns of Christians who matured in the Moral Majority era?
6. What led to these differences? How do these differences affect the way the two generations sometimes evaluate one another's faith commitments? What can bring a healthy perspective to these evaluations?
7. How important is a commitment to Scripture to both generations?
8. In what ways are the differing agendas of committed older and younger Evangelicals reflective of their mutual commitment to Scripture, life, and mission?

Chapter 6: The Zeal of Loss

1. Prior to reading this book, would you have been aware of the different agendas of committed Christians in their forties and younger compared to those 50 and older? How would you have explained those differences previously?
2. Prior to reading this book, would you have been aware of the magnitude of the opposition to a biblical worldview and lifestyle choices that is upon our young people? How would you have evaluated the pressure of this opposition previously?
3. Prior to reading this book, would you have felt the pain of loss that many Christians who matured in the Moral Majority era experienced? How would you have explained that pain to a generation over age fifty? How would you explain it to a generation in their forties and younger?

Questions for Review and Discussion

4. Prior to reading this book, would you have understood the pain of loss that many Christian young people now experience in our increasingly secularized culture? How would you have explained that pain to a generation over age fifty? How do you see that pain in a younger generation?
5. Why might the zeal of loss felt by a younger generation turn some to more strident expression in their Christian commitments?
6. How does this strident expression from young leaders sometimes appear in the church, in social media, or in denominational life?
7. How does this strident expression sometimes turn into some form of Christian Nationalism or institutional suspicion?
8. In what ways does the pressure on young people create societal perspectives that may make them more like their grandparents than their parents?

Chapter 7: Hope for the Future

1. What aspects of the work of the Holy Spirit are not evident in surveys?
2. What does the Holy Spirit use in the life and ministry of the church to build the kingdom of God?
3. What are some aspects of the Holy Spirit's work in Scripture and history that help you maintain hope for the future of Christ's church, despite the numerical and faith challenges of the Evangelical church?
4. What is some evidence of the fruit of the Spirit in the American church today?
5. What is some evidence of the fruit of the Spirit in rising generations today?
6. What are some ways that the American church may need to adjust to bear the fruit that the Holy Spirit is raising in our nation today or in the future?
7. What is the "concentration effect" that signals how important it is for the Evangelical church to support the faith of its young people?

Questions for Review and Discussion

8. What is the demographic that has been most faithful in returning to church since the COVID pandemic?
9. What are some characteristics of churches that have returned to health since the pandemic?
10. What are some characteristics of churches that are now drawing future generations to worship and ministry?

Chapter 8: Hope for the Nations

1. What are some aspects of the Holy Spirit's work in the world that help you maintain hope for the future of Christ's church, despite the numerical and faith challenges of the Evangelical church in our nation?
2. Why is it a mistake to look at the amazing blessing of the Holy Spirit on the New Testament church and conclude that such is only "ancient hyperbole" or not relevant to our time?
3. How should the present work of the Holy Spirit in the world affect our understanding of what he can do in our nation and our time?
4. What are some of the places/nations where the Holy Spirit is more powerfully at work in our time?
5. What should the places/nations where the Holy Spirit is most powerfully at work in our day teach us about faithfulness in times of loss, oppression, apathy, or persecution?
6. When do revivals typically occur?
7. How should the fact that half the world's population is at ages most impressionable for hearing gospel truth that lasts affect our mission priorities?
8. How should the role that each generation can play in supporting Christ's mission affect our support and celebration of all generations?

NOTES

Chapter 1 Our Generational Challenges

1. Riley Beggin and Zachary Schermele, "Pressure Mounts on Ivy League Universities to Address Antisemitism After Presidents Testify; Calls for Resignation," *USA Today*, December 8, 2023, https://www.usatoday.com/story/news/education/2023/12/08/harvard-mit-upenn-leaders-asked-to-quit/71856298007/.

2. Ben Pierce, "Connecting with the New Global Youth Culture," *Lausanne Global Analysis* 8, no. 2 (March 2019), https://lausanne.org/content/lga/2019-03/connecting-with-the-new-global-youth-culture.

3. *State of the Great Commission: Report Prepared for Lausanne Global Congress Seoul 2024* (Lausanne Movement, April 2024), 53–55 (available as a free pdf download at https://lausanne.org/report); Jim Davis and Michael Graham with Ryan P. Burge, *The Great Dechurching: Who's Leaving, Why Are They Going, and What Will It Take to Bring Them Back?* (Grand Rapids: Zondervan, 2023), 73.

4. Hannah McClellan, "Pastors Wonder About Church Members Who Never Came Back Post-Pandemic," *Christianity Today*, September 26, 2023, https://www.christianitytoday.com/news/2023/september/COVID-study-church-attendance-change-pews-people.html; Megan Brenan and Jeffrey M. Jones, "Ethics Ratings of Nearly All Professions Down in U.S.," Gallup, January 22, 2024, https://news.gallup.com/poll/608903/ethics-ratings-nearly-professions-down.aspx; also, Davis and Graham, *The Great Dechurching*, 72–73.

5. Timothy Dalrymple, "The Splintering of the Evangelical Soul," *Christianity Today*, January 6, 2022, https://www.christianitytoday.com/ct/2021/april-web-only/splintering-of-evangelical-soul.html.

6. David French, "Why Do They Hate Us? Race, Christian Nationalism, and White Evangelical Alienation from America," *The Dispatch*, December 20, 2020, https://thedispatch.com/newsletter/frenchpress/why-do-they-hate-us/.

7. Communications Staff, "SBTS Convocation: Mohler Urges Confessional Resolution in the Face of Change," August 24, 2016, https://www.sbts.edu/news/sbts-convocation-mohler-urges-confessional-resolution-face-change/.

8. Davis and Graham, *The Great Dechurching*, 5, italics in original.

9. Aaron Earls, "Most Teenagers Drop Out of Church When They Become Young Adults," Lifeway Research, January 15, 2019, https://research.lifeway.com/2019/01/15/most-teenagers-drop-out-of-church-as-young-adults/.

Notes

10. Earls, "Most Teenagers Drop Out"; Aaron Earls, "20 Vital Stats for Ministry in 2020," Lifeway Research, January 7, 2020, https://research.lifeway.com/2020/01/07/20-vital-stats-for-ministry-in-2020/.

11. Barna, "Six Reasons Young Christians Leave Church," September 27, 2011, https://www.barna.com/research/six-reasons-young-christians-leave-church/.

12. "Most Twentysomethings Put Christianity on the Shelf Following Spiritually Active Teen Years," Barna, September 11, 2006, https://www.barna.com/research/most-twentysomethings-put-christianity-on-the-shelf-following-spiritually-active-teen-years/.

13. Ryan Burge, "Most 'Nones' Still Keep the Faith," *Christianity Today*, February 24, 2021, https://www.christianitytoday.com/news/2021/february/nones-religious-unaffiliated-faith-research-church-belief.html.

14. Reported in David Roach, "Church Attendance Dropped Among Young People, Singles, Liberals," *Christianity Today*, January 9, 2023, https://www.christianitytoday.com/news/2023/january/pandemic-church-attendance-drop-aei-survey-young-people-eva.html.

15. Ryan Burge, "The Religiosity of High School Seniors, 1976–2022," Graphs About Religion, March 28, 2024, https://www.graphsaboutreligion.com/p/the-religiosity-of-high-school-seniors?utm_source=post-email-title&publication_id=1561197&post_id=142510816&utm_campaign=email-post-title&isFreemail=true&r=grh36&triedRedirect=true&utm_medium=.

16. Suzette Lohmeyer and Anna Deen, "A Mass Exodus from Christianity Is Underway in America. Here's Why," *VirtueOnline*, December 17, 2022, https://virtueonline.org/mass-exodus-christianity-underway-america-heres-why; "Religious Landscape Study: 18–29 Year Olds," Pew Research Center (2014), https://www.pewresearch.org/religion/religious-landscape-study/age-distribution/18-29/; "New Data Suggests Over 40 Percent of Self-Identified Evangelicals Attend Church Once a Year or Less," *Relevant*, April 8, 2021, https://relevantmagazine.com/faith/church/new-data-suggests-over-40-percent-of-self-identified-evangelicals-attend-church-once-a-year-or-less/.

17. Jeffrey M. Jones, "U.S. Church Membership Falls Below Majority for the First Time," Gallup, March 29, 2021, https://news.gallup.com/poll/341963/church-membership-falls-below-majority-first-time.aspx.

18. Jim Denison, "Why Is Loneliness as Dangerous as Smoking?," The Daily Article, May 3, 2023, https://www.denisonforum.org/daily-article/loneliness-dangerous-smoking/.

19. Ryan Burge, "How America's Youth Lost Its Religion in 1990s," Religion News Service, April 13, 2022, https://religionnews.com/2022/04/13/how-americas-youth-lost-its-religion-in-1990s/.

20. Jessica Grose, "Americans Under 30 Don't Trust Religion—or Anything Else," *New York Times*, November 25, 2023, https://www.nytimes.com/2023/11/25/opinion/religion-nones-gen-z.html.

21. Burge, "How America's Youth Lost Its Religion."

22. Camilo Ortiz and Lenore Skenazy, "This Simple Fix Could Help Anxious Kids," *New York Times*, September 4, 2023, https://www.nytimes.com/2023/09/04/opinion/anxiety-depression-teens.html.

23. Lohmeyer and Deen, "Mass Exodus from Christianity"; Lifeway Research, "Church Dropouts: Reasons Young Adults Stay or Go between Ages 18–22," January 2019, https://research.lifeway.com/wp-content/uploads/2019/01/Young-Adult-Church-Dropout-Report-2017.pdf.

24. In later chapters we will analyze this data more closely. This general assessment is cited by David Roach, "Church Attendance Dropped Among Young People, Singles, Liberals," *Christianity Today*, January 9, 2023, https://www.christianitytoday.com/news/2023/january/pandemic-church-attendance-drop-aei-survey-young-people-eva.html.

25. Jennifer Benz, Lindsey Witt-Swanson, and Daniel Cox, "Faith After the Pandemic: How COVID-19 Changed American Religion," Survey Center on American Life, January 2023, https://www.americansurveycenter.org/research/faith-after-the-pandemic-how-COVID-19-changed-american-religion/.

Notes

26. Stephen Bullivant, *Nonverts: The Making of Ex-Christian America* (New York: Oxford University Press, 2022), 10.

27. Bullivant, *Nonverts*, 113–27; Lohmeyer and Deen, "Mass Exodus from Christianity."

28. Yonat Shimron, "Study: Unaffiliated Americans Are the Only Growing Religious Group: The Catholic Church Saw the Largest Decline in Religious Affiliation of Any Religious Group in 2023," Religion News Service, March 27, 2024, https://religionnews.com/2024/03/27/study-unaffiliated-americans-are-the-only-growing-religious-group/.

29. Andrew Wilson, *Remaking the World: How 1776 Created the Post-Christian West* (Wheaton: Crossway, 2023); Carl Trueman, *Strange New World: How Thinkers and Activists Redefined Identity and Sparked the Sexual Revolution* (Wheaton: Crossway, 2022); Carl Trueman, *The Rise and Triumph of the Modern Self: Cultural Amnesia, Expressive Individualism, and the Road to Sexual Revolution* (Wheaton: Crossway, 2020); Danny Olinger, "Presbyterians and Nonverts: 100 Years after *Christianity and Liberalism*," *New Horizons* 24, no. 9 (October 2023): 4.

30. Davis and Graham, *The Great Dechurching*, 163.

31. Jonathan Haidt, *The Anxious Generation: How the Great Rewiring of Childhood Is Causing an Epidemic of Mental Illness* (New York: Penguin, 2024), 114–42; Denison, "Why Is Loneliness as Dangerous"; Jim Denison, "Harvard's Arthur C. Brooks on the Secret to Happiness," The Daily Article, September 6, 2023, https://www.denisonforum.org/daily-article/arthur-c-brooks-secret-to-happiness/.

32. Ortiz and Skenazy, "This Simple Fix"; Denison, "Why Is Loneliness as Dangerous."

33. Adelle Banks, "Young People Define 'Sacred Moments' Broadly: From God to Nature to Relationships," Religion News Service, November 7, 2023, https://religionnews.com/2023/11/07/young-people-define-sacred-moments-broadly-from-god-to-nature-to-relationships/.

34. Davis and Graham, *The Great Dechurching*, 160.

35. Vern Bengston, "Families and Faith," *Guideposts*, accessed March 7, 2024, https://guideposts.org/positive-living/friends-and-family/family/families-and-faith/.

36. Matthew Brown, "Faith in the Family: How Belief Passes from One Generation to the Next," *Deseret News*, December 26, 2013, https://www.deseret.com/2013/12/26/20532051/faith-in-the-family-how-belief-passes-from-one-generation-to-the-next/; Ying Chen and Tyler J. VanderWeele, "Associations of Religious Upbringing With Subsequent Health and Well-Being From Adolescence to Young Adulthood: An Outcome-Wide Analysis," *American Journal of Epidemiology* 187, no. 11 (November 2018): 2355–64, https://doi.org/10.1093/aje/kwy142; John Roberto, "The Importance of Family Faith for Lifelong Faith Formation," *Lifelong Faith* (Spring 2012), https://www.lifelongfaith.com/uploads/5/1/6/4/5164069/family_faith_formation.pdf; Catherine Wilson, "Building Lasting Faith in Kids: Proven Ideas from Sticky Faith Research," Focus on the Family Canada, accessed July 31, 2024, https://www.focusonthefamily.ca/content/building-lasting-faith-in-kids-proven-ideas-from-sticky-faith-research; Bob Smietana, "Young Bible Readers More Likely to Be Faithful Adults," Lifeway Research, October 17, 2017, https://research.lifeway.com/2017/10/17/young-bible-readers-more-likely-to-be-faithful-adults-study-finds/; Vern L. Bengston with Norella M. Putney and Susan Harris, *Families and Faith: How Religion Is Passed Down Across Generations* (New York: Oxford University Press, 2013), 7, 77–78, 186; E. L. Idler, *Religion as a Social Determinant of Public Health* (New York: Oxford University Press, 2014), 218–20; and Glenn T. Stanton, "Are Young People Leaving the Church in Droves?," Focus on the Family, September 23, 2017, https://www.focusonthefamily.com/faith/are-young-people-leaving-the-church-in-droves/. Also see Glen Stanton, "Leading Factors Leading to Lasting Faith!," Focus on the Family, July 24, 2010, https://www.focusonthefamily.com/faith/leading-factors-leading-to-lasting-faith/, which is a good summary of the older, but important, research of Christian Smith in *Souls in Transition: The Religious & Spiritual Lives of Emerging Adults* (New York: Oxford University Press, 2009), 220–24, and "Faith in Flux: Change in Religious Affiliation in the U.S.," The Pew Forum on Religion and Public Life, April 2009.

37. "What Makes Faith Stick During College?," Fuller Youth Institute, September 5, 2011, https://fulleryouthinstitute.org/blog/what-makes-faith-stick-during-college.

Notes

38. See May 10–June 15, 2023, survey of approximately eight thousand Christian college alumni covering a previous twenty-two-year period, conducted by the Institutional Research Office of Covenant College, as cited in the Administration Report from the President's Office in an email to the author dated April 9, 2024.

39. Pew Research Center, "U.S. Teens Take After Their Parents Religiously, Attend Services Together and Enjoy Family Rituals," September 10, 2020, https://www.pewresearch.org/religion/2020/09/10/u-s-teens-take-after-their-parents-religiously-attend-services-together-and-enjoy-family-rituals/; Jesse Smith, "Transmission of Faith in Families: The Influence of Religious Ideology," *Sociology of Religion* 82, no. 3 (Autumn 2021): 332–56; Smietana, "Young Bible Readers"; Bengtson, *Families and Faith*, 76–79, 132–33, 181; Karen Whiting, "Grow Together in Faith with Family Prayer," Focus on the Family, accessed July 29, 2024, https://www.focusonthefamily.com/parenting/grow-together-in-faith-with-family-prayer/; Christian Smith and Phillip Kim, "Family Religious Involvement and the Quality of Parental Relationships for Families with Early Adolescents," A Research Report of National Study of Youth and Religion, no. 5 (2003), https://youthandreligion.nd.edu/assets/102508/family_religious_involvement_and_the_quality_of_parental_relationships_for_families_with_early_adolescents_.pdf; Richard Ross, "Three Predictors of Whether Kids Will Stick with Church or Leave," ChristNow.com, June 2, 2016, https://christnow.com/three-predictors-whether-kids-will-stick-church-leave/; Brad Wilcox and Nicholas H. Wolfinger, "Better Together: Religious Attendance, Gender, and Relationship Quality," Institute for Family Studies, February 11, 2016, https://ifstudies.org/blog/better-together-religious-attendance-gender-and-relationship-quality.

40. Carol Pipes, "How Can Churches Keep Teenagers Connected?," Lifeway Research, January 15, 2019, https://research.lifeway.com/2019/01/15/how-can-churches-keep-teenagers-connected/; Smietana, "Young Bible Readers"; Bengtson, *Families and Faith*, 74–79, 127; Wilson, "Building Lasting Faith in Kids"; Marjorie Lindner Gunnoe and Kristin A. Moore, "Predictors of Religiosity among Youth Aged 17–22: A Longitudinal Study of the National Survey of Children," *Journal for the Scientific Study of Religion* 41, no. 4 (December 2002): 613.

41. Fuller Youth Institute, "The Sticky Faith Research," accessed July 29, 2024, https://fulleryouthinstitute.org/stickyfaith/research.

42. Paul Vermeer, "Religion and Family Life: An Overview of Current Research and Suggestions for Future Research," *Religions* 5, no. 2 (April 14, 2014): 402–21, https://doi.org/10.3390/rel5020402; Bengtson, "Families and Faith."

43. Christian Smith and Amy Adamczyk, "Parents Set the Pace for Their Adult Children's Religious Life," *Christianity Today*, January 6, 2022, https://www.christianitytoday.com/ct/2022/january-february/smith-adamczyk-evangelism-parents-children-religious-belief.html.

44. Stanton, "Leading Factors Leading to Lasting Faith."

45. Lifeway Research, "Parents & Churches Can Help Teens Stay in Church," August 7, 2007, https://research.lifeway.com/2007/08/07/parents-churches-can-help-teens-stay-in-church/; Jen Bradbury, "Sticky Faith: What Keeps Kids Connected to Church?," *The Christian Century*, May 29, 2013, https://www.christiancentury.org/article/2013-05/sticky-faith.

46. Lifeway Research, "Parents & Churches Can Help Teens Stay in Church."

47. Holly Catterton Allen, Christine Lawton, and Cory L. Seibel, *Intergenerational Christian Formation: Bringing the Whole Church Together in Ministry, Community, and Worship*, 2nd ed. (Downers Grove, IL: InterVarsity, 2023), 16–17, 93–144; Matt Reynolds, "When Helping Children Hurts," *Christianity Today Books Newsletter*, March 7, 2024; Bengtson, *Families and Faith*, 101.

48. John Roberto, *Lifelong Faith: Formation for All Ages and Generations* (New York: Church Publishing, 2022), 6.

49. Josh Packard and Kevin Singer, "Uncertain and Unbundled: Are You Ready for Gen Z?," *In Trust* (Autumn 2021), https://www.intrust.org/in-trust-magazine/issues/autumn-2021/uncertain-and-unbundled/.

50. Gerard R. Roche, "Much Ado About Mentors," *Harvard Business Review*, January 1979, https://hbr.org/1979/01/much-ado-about-mentors; Nick Sonnenberg, "5 Generations Are Now Working Together: Here's How Smart Leaders Are Making the Most of It," Executive Network,

Notes

February 24, 2023, https://www.shrm.org/executive-network/insights/5-generations-now-working-together-heres-how-smart-leaders-making.

51. Davis and Graham, *The Great Dechurching*, 163.

Chapter 2 Our Church Challenges

1. Pew Research Center, "Modeling the Future of Religion in America: How U.S. Religious Composition Has Changed in Recent Decades," September 13, 2022, https://www.pewresearch.org/religion/2022/09/13/how-u-s-religious-composition-has-changed-in-recent-decades/.

2. Jim Denison, "Why Do We Hiccup? Some Surprising Unsolved Mysteries and the Bias Against Religion," Denison Forum, November 15, 2019, https://www.christianheadlines.com/columnists/denison-forum/why-do-we-hiccup-some-surprising-unsolved-mysteries-and-the-bias-against-religion.html.

3. Aaron Zitner, "America Pulls Back from Values That Once Defined It, WSJ-NORC Poll Finds," *Wall Street Journal*, March 27, 2023, https://www.wsj.com/articles/americans-pull-back-from-values-that-once-defined-u-s-wsj-norc-poll-finds-df8534cd.

4. ChurchTrac, "The State of Church Attendance: Trends and Statistics [2023]," accessed January 13, 2024, https://www.churchtrac.com/articles/the-state-of-church-attendance-trends-and-statistics-2023.

5. Bob Smietana, "Gallup: Fewer Than Half of Americans Belong to a Church," *Christianity Today*, March 29, 2021, https://www.christianitytoday.com/news/2021/march/gallup-church-membership-decline-minority-nones-us.html.

6. Smietana, "Gallup: Fewer Than Half."

7. Jeffrey M. Jones, "U.S. Church Membership Falls Below Majority for First Time," Gallup, March 29, 2021, https://news.gallup.com/poll/341963/church-membership-falls-below-majority-first-time.aspx.

8. Smietana, "Gallup: Fewer Than Half."

9. Jones, "U.S. Church Membership."

10. Jones, "U.S. Church Membership."

11. Pew Research Center, "Modeling the Future."

12. Pew Research Center, "In U.S., Decline of Christianity Continues at a Rapid Pace," October 17, 2019, https://www.pewresearch.org/religion/2019/10/17/in-u-s-decline-of-christianity-continues-at-rapid-pace/.

13. C. Kirk Hadaway, Penny Long Marler, and Mark Chaves, "What the Polls Don't Show: A Closer Look at U.S. Church Attendance," *American Sociological Review* 58, no. 6 (December 1993): 741–52.

14. Gina Christian, "Gallup: Just 3 in 10 US Adults Regularly Attend Religious Services," OSV News, March 28, 2024, https://www.osvnews.com/2024/03/28/gallup-just-3-in-10-us-adults-regularly-attend-religious-services/.

15. By factoring in weather and midweek services, the researcher estimated that weekly attendance could be as high as 9 percent—still far lower than what people self-report. See John Longhurst, "Cellphone Activity Clarifies Actual Church Attendance Levels," *The Free Press*, June 29, 2024, https://www.winnipegfreepress.com/arts-and-life/life/faith/2024/06/29/cellphone-activity-clarifies-actual-church-attendance-levels. Earlier cell phone studies estimated weekly attendance at less than 5 percent. See Devin Pope (@Devin_G_Pope), "Part 3: Religion in America: Evidence from Cellphone Data," X, July 14, 2023, 11:07 a.m., https://twitter.com/Devin_G_Pope/status/1679870211841826817.

16. Jason DeRose, "The Importance of Religion in the Lives of Americans Is Shrinking," NPR, May 16, 2023, https://www.npr.org/transcripts/1176206568.

17. Ryan Burge, "Religion Data Wonk: Just How Bad Is Denominational Decline?," Religion Unplugged, June 15, 2023, https://religionunplugged.com/news/2023/6/12/just-how-bad-is-denominational-decline; Ryan Burge, "Nondenominational Churches Are Adding Millions of

Notes

Members. Where Are They Coming From?," *Christianity Today*, August 5, 2022, https://www.christianitytoday.com/news/2022/august/nondenominational-growth-mainline-protestant-decline-survey.html.

18. Lydia Saad, "Catholics' Church Attendance Resumes Downward Slide," Gallup, April 9, 2018, https://news.gallup.com/poll/232226/church-attendance-among-catholics-resumes-downward-slide.aspx.

19. Pew Research Center, "How the Pandemic Has Affected Attendance at U.S. Religious Services," March 28, 2023, https://www.pewresearch.org/religion/2023/03/28/how-the-pandemic-has-affected-attendance-at-u-s-religious-services/.

20. Ed Stetzer, presentation at National Association of Evangelicals Spring 2021 meeting, and personal correspondence, March 2, 2022.

21. Aaron Earls, "Churches Are Open but Still Recovering from Pandemic Attendance Losses," Lifeway Research, November 8, 2022, https://research.lifeway.com/2022/11/08/churches-are-open-but-still-recovering-from-pandemic-attendance-losses/.

22. "How COVID Affected the Church (and Didn't)," *CT Pastors*, October 11, 2023.

23. Jennifer Benz, Lindsey Witt-Swanson, and Daniel Cox, "Faith After the Pandemic: How COVID-19 Changed American Religion," Survey Center on American Life, January 2023, https://www.americansurveycenter.org/research/faith-after-the-pandemic-how-COVID-19-changed-american-religion/.

24. Barna, "A New Chapter in Millennial Church Attendance," August 4, 2022, https://www.barna.com/research/church-attendance-2022/.

25. Hannah McClellan, "Pastors Wonder About Church Members Who Never Came Back Post-Pandemic," *Christianity Today*, September 26, 2023, https://www.christianitytoday.com/news/2023/september/COVID-study-church-attendance-change-pews-people.html.

26. Aaron Earls, "Church Switchers Highlight Reasons for Congregational Change," *Ministry Watch*, November 9, 2023, https://ministrywatch.com/church-switchers-highlight-reasons-for-congregational-change/.

27. Barna, "New Chapter in Millennial Church Attendance."

28. Ed Stetzer, personal communication.

29. McClellan, "Pastors Wonder About Church Members"; Aaron Earls, "Who Are 'Evangelicals' and Why Knowing That Matters for Your Church," Lifeway Research, July 26, 2021, https://research.lifeway.com/2021/07/26/who-are-evangelicals-and-why-knowing-that-matters-for-your-church/.

30. Stetzer, personal communication.

31. Danielle Kurtzleben, "Are You an Evangelical? Are You Sure?," NPR, December 19, 2015, https://www.npr.org/2015/12/19/458058251/are-you-an-evangelical-are-you-sure.

32. David French, "Did Donald Trump Make the Church Great Again?," The Dispatch, September 19, 2021, https://thedispatch.com/newsletter/frenchpress/did-donald-trump-make-the-church/.

33. Larry Eskridge, "How Many Evangelicals Are There?," Institute for the Study of American Evangelicals, last updated 2012, accessed January 11, 2024, https://web.archive.org/web/20160130062242/http://www.wheaton.edu/ISAE/Defining-Evangelicalism/How-Many-Are-There.

34. Eskridge, "How Many Evangelicals Are There?"; Earls, "Who Are 'Evangelicals'?"; Kurtzleben, "Are You an Evangelical?"; Barna, "Survey Explores Who Qualifies as an Evangelical," January 18, 2007, https://www.barna.com/research/survey-explores-who-qualifies-as-an-evangelical/; Ligonier Ministries, "2022 Results Now Available: The State of Theology," September 19, 2022, https://www.ligonier.org/posts/2022-state-of-theology.

35. Earls, "Church Switchers."

36. Barna, "Two in Five Christians Are Not Engaged in Discipleship," January 26, 2022, https://www.barna.com/research/christians-discipleship-community/; Lifeway Research, "Protestant Churchgoer Views on Livestreaming," September 2022, https://research.lifeway.com/wp-content/uploads/2023/06/Sept-2022-American-Churchgoers-Livesteaming-Report.pdf.

37. Jim Davis and Michael Graham with Ryan Burge, *The Great Dechurching: Who's Leaving, Why Are They Going, and What Will It Take to Bring Them Back?* (Grand Rapids: Zondervan, 2023), 171.

38. Earls, "Who Are 'Evangelicals'?"

39. Pew Research Center, "Global Survey of Evangelical Protestant Leaders: Evangelical Beliefs and Practices," June 22, 2011, https://www.pewresearch.org/religion/2011/06/22/global-survey-beliefs/; Ligonier Ministries, "Evangelicals Deeply Confused About Core Christian Beliefs," October 16, 2018, https://www.prnewswire.com/news-releases/evangelicals-deeply-confused-about-core-christian-beliefs-300731811.html.

40. Burge, "Nondenominational Churches Are Adding."

41. Davis and Graham, *The Great Dechurching*, xxii.

42. Burge, "Religion Data Wonk."

43. Ryan Burge, "Where Protestants and Catholics Go When They Leave Their Churches," *Christianity Today*, February 20, 2018, https://www.christianitytoday.com/news/2018/february/how-protestants-catholics-leave-church-change-religion-cces.html.

44. Earls, "Church Switchers."

45. Earls, "Church Switchers."

46. Earls, "Church Switchers."

47. Thomas Reese, "The Hidden Exodus: Catholics Becoming Protestants," *National Catholic Reporter*, April 18, 2011, https://www.ncronline.org/news/parish/hidden-exodus-catholics-becoming-protestants.

48. Ryan Burge, "How Does Religion Influence Decisions About Marriage and Family," Graphs About Religion, September 5, 2024, https://www.graphsaboutreligion.com/p/how-does-religion-influence-decisions; Bryan Chapell, *Christ-Centered Preaching: Redeeming the Expository Sermon*, 3rd ed. (Grand Rapids: Baker Academic, 2018), 187.

49. Tim Sansbury, personal conversation, March 9, 2024.

50. Cited in Jason S. Carroll and Brian J. Willoughby, "The Myth of Sexual Experience," Institute for Family Studies, April 18, 2023, https://ifstudies.org/blog/the-myth-of-sexual-experience-.

51. David Ayers, "Sex and the Single Evangelical," Institute for Family Studies, August 14, 2019, https://ifstudies.org/blog/sex-and-the-single-evangelical; Burge, "How Does Religion Influence Decisions About Marriage and Family."

52. Jessie Smith and Nicholas Wolfinger, "Testing Common Theories on the Relationship Between Premarital Sex and Marital Stability," Institute for Family Studies, March 6, 2023, https://ifstudies.org/blog/testing-common-theories-on-the-relationship-between-premarital-sex-and-marital-stability.

53. Rachel K. Jones, "People of All Religions Use Birth Control and Have Abortions," Guttmacher Institute, October 19, 2020, https://www.guttmacher.org/article/2020/10/people-all-religions-use-birth-control-and-have-abortions.

54. Francesca A. Marino, "Age Variation in Cohabitation, 2022," Bowling Green State University National Center for Family & Marriage Research, Family Profile No. 28 (2022), https://doi.org/10.25035/ncfmr/fp-22-28.

55. Marino, "Age Variation."

56. Lois Collins, "The Perils of Cohabitation and Why Timing Is Linked to Later Divorce," *Deseret News*, May 1, 2023, https://www.deseret.com/2023/5/1/23697802/living-together-cohabitation-before-marriage-linked-divorce/.

57. Collins, "Perils of Cohabitation."

58. Collins, "Perils of Cohabitation."

59. Smith and Wolfinger, "Testing Common Theories."

60. Smith and Wolfinger, "Testing Common Theories."

61. Carroll and Willoughby, "Myth of Sexual Experience."

62. Jessica Harris, "5 Reasons Purity Rings and Pledges Don't Work," Covenant Eyes, August 9, 2021, https://www.covenanteyes.com/blog/5-reasons-purity-rings-and-pledges-dont-work/; Brittney McNamara, "Girls Who Pledge Abstinence Are Actually More Likely to Get Pregnant Than Those Who Don't," *Teen Vogue*, May 22, 2016, https://www.teenvogue.com/story/abstinence-pledge-purity-ring-more-likely-to-get-pregnant.

Notes

63. Catherine E. Shoichet and Parker Leipzig, "More Baby Boomers Are Living Alone. One Reason Why: 'Gray Divorce,'" CNN.com, August 5, 2023, https://www.cnn.com/2023/08/05/health/boomers-divorce-living-alone-wellness-cec/index.html; Krista K. Westrick-Payne and I-Fen Lin, "Age Variation in the Divorce Rate, 1990–2021," National Center for Family and Marriage Research, November 16, 2023, https://www.bgsu.edu/ncfmr/resources/data/family-profiles/westrick-payne-lin-age-variation-divorce-rate-1990-2021-fp-23-16.html.

64. Susan L. Brown and I-Fen Lin, "The Graying of Divorce: A Half Century of Change," *Journals of Gerontology Series B: Psychological Sciences and Social Sciences* 77, no. 9 (September 2022): 1710–20, https://academic.oup.com/psychsocgerontology/article/77/9/1710/6564346.

65. Glenn Stanton, "FactChecker: Divorce Rate Among Christians," The Gospel Coalition, September 25, 2012, https://www.thegospelcoalition.org/article/factchecker-divorce-rate-among-christians/.

66. Stanton, "FactChecker"; Megan Cooper, "Breaking Down Divorce Rates by Religion (and What They Tell Us)," Love to Know, June 2, 2023, https://www.lovetoknow.com/life/relationships/divorce-statistics-by-religion; Pew Research Center, "Religious Landscape Study: Marital Status," accessed July 30, 2024, https://www.pewresearch.org/religion/religious-landscape-study/marital-status/; Charles E. Stokes, "Findings on Red and Blue Divorce Are Not Exactly Black and White," Institute for Family Studies, January 22, 2014, https://ifstudies.org/blog/findings-on-red-and-blue-divorce-are-not-exactly-black-and-white/; Jerry Z. Park, Joshua Tom, and Brita Andercheck, "CCF Civil Rights Symposium: Fifty Years of Religious Change: 1964–2014," Council on Contemporary Families, accessed April 11, 2024, https://sites.utexas.edu/contemporaryfamilies/2014/02/04/50-years-of-religious-change/.

67. Glenn Stanton, "Divorce Rate in the Church—As High as the World?," Focus on the Family, August 15, 2011, https://www.focusonthefamily.com/marriage/divorce-rate-in-the-church-as-high-as-the-world/; S. Michael Houdmann and staff, "Is the Divorce Rate Among Christians Truly the Same as Among Non-Christians?," Got Questions, April 14, 2023, https://www.gotquestions.org/Christian-divorce-rate.html.

68. Stanton, "Factchecker: Divorce Rate Among Christians"; Houdmann, "Is the Divorce Rate Among Christians Truly the Same as Among Non-Christians?"

69. Stanton, "Factchecker: Divorce Rate Among Christians"; Houdmann, "Is the Divorce Rate Among Christians Truly the Same as Among Non-Christians?"

70. Cooper, "Breaking Down Divorce Rates by Religion."

71. Mark Travers, "The 'Empty Nest Divorce' Trend, Explained by a Psychologist," *Forbes*, September 1, 2023, https://www.forbes.com/sites/traversmark/2023/09/01/the-empty-nest-divorce-trend-explained-by-a-psychologist/; Jack Carney-DeBord, "Why More Couples Are Getting a Gray Divorce," Jack's Law Office, accessed July 30, 2024, https://ohioexecutivedivorce.com/blog/gray-divorce; Shoichet and Leipzig, "More Baby Boomers Are Living Alone."

72. Bella DePaulo, "What Do Most People Over 50 Do After Divorce? Stay Single," *Psychology Today*, February 26, 2023, https://www.psychologytoday.com/us/blog/living-single/202302/what-do-most-people-over-50-do-after-divorce-stay-single.

73. Earls, "Church Switchers."

74. Davis and Graham, *The Great Dechurching*, 9.

75. DePaulo, "What Do Most People Over 50 Do After Divorce?"

76. Shoichet and Leipzig, "More Baby Boomers Are Living Alone"; Rhitu Chatterjee, "Americans Who Live Alone Report Depression at Higher Rates, but Social Support Helps," NPR, February 15, 2024, https://www.npr.org/sections/health-shots/2024/02/15/1231585339/depression-cdc-study-loneliness.

77. "Unmarried and Single Americans Week: September 17–23, 2023," United States Census Bureau, accessed July 30, 2024, https://www.census.gov/newsroom/stories/unmarried-single-americans-week.html.

Notes

78. Elizabeth Woodson, "Single Christians Have Common Needs—the Same Needs All Christians Have," *Christianity Today*, March 4, 2024, https://www.christianitytoday.com/ct/2024/march-web-only/solo-planet-anna-broadway-global-singleness-marriage-church.html.

Chapter 3 Our Cultural Challenges

1. Pew Research Center, "Modeling the Future of Religion in America," September 13, 2022, https://www.pewresearch.org/religion/2022/09/13/how-u-s-religious-composition-has-changed-in-recent-decades/; David O'Reilly, "What Is the Future of Religion in America?," *Trust Magazine*, February 7, 2023, https://www.pewtrusts.org/en/trust/archive/winter-2023/what-is-the-future-of-religion-in-america.

2. Jeffrey M. Jones, "U.S. Church Membership Falls Below Majority for First Time," Gallup, March 29, 2021, https://news.gallup.com/poll/341963/church-membership-falls-below-majority-first-time.aspx.

3. Ed Stetzer, presentation at National Association of Evangelicals Spring 2021 meeting, and personal correspondence, March 2, 2022.

4. Ryan Burge, "Nondenominational Churches Are Adding Millions of Members. Where Are They Coming From?," *Christianity Today*, August 5, 2022, https://www.christianitytoday.com/news/2022/august/nondenominational-growth-mainline-protestant-decline-survey.html.

5. Ryan Burge, "The Catholic Church Is in Trouble in Places Where It Used to Dominate," Graphs About Religion, October 12, 2023, https://www.graphsaboutreligion.com/p/the-catholic-church-is-in-trouble.

6. The Cooperative Election Study is a nationally representative annual sample survey of more than 50,000 American adults stratified by state and administered by the data and analytics group YouGov.

7. Burge, "Catholic Church Is in Trouble."

8. Jonah McKeown, "Where Catholics Live in the United States, Explained in Four Charts," Catholic World Report, January 2, 2023, https://www.catholicworldreport.com/2023/01/02/where-catholics-live-in-the-united-states-explained-in-four-charts/.

9. Burge, "Catholic Church Is in Trouble."

10. McKeown, "Where Catholics Live."

11. Ryan Burge, "Why It's Unlikely U.S. Mainline Protestants Outnumber Evangelicals," Religion Unplugged, July 12, 2021, https://religionunplugged.com/news/2021/7/12/why-its-unlikely-us-mainline-protestants-outnumber-evangelicals; Danny Olinger, "Presbyterians and Nonverts: 100 Years After *Christianity and Liberalism*," *New Horizons* 24, no. 9 (October 2023): 4; Ed Stetzer, "If It Doesn't Stem Its Decline, Mainline Protestantism Has Just 23 Easters Left," *Washington Post*, April 28, 2017, https://www.washingtonpost.com/news/acts-of-faith/wp/2017/04/28/if-it-doesnt-stem-its-decline-mainline-protestantism-has-just-23-easters-left/.

12. Ryan Burge, "Religion Data Wonk: Just How Bad Is Denominational Decline?," Religion Unplugged, June 15, 2023, https://religionunplugged.com/news/2023/6/12/just-how-bad-is-denominational-decline.

13. Ryan Burge (@ryanburge), "The annual rate of decline from 1984 through 2022 is almost exactly 4% per year," X, May 9, 2023, 9:03 a.m., https://twitter.com/ryanburge/status/1655921435624325122.

14. Greg Smith, "End of Presbyterianism: Farewell PC(USA)?," So What Faith, May 12, 2023, https://sowhatfaith.com/2023/05/12/end-of-presbyterianism-farewell-pcusa/.

15. Burge, "Why It's Unlikely."

16. Burge, "Why It's Unlikely"; Yonat Shimron, "The UMC Lost a Quarter of Its Churches—Most in the South," Religion News Service, January 26, 2024, https://www.religionnews.com/2024/01/26/the-umc-lost-a-quarter-of-its-churches-most-in-the-south-reflecting-political-patterns/.

17. Quoted in Terry Mattingly, "Episcopal Leaders Ponder Church's Groundhog Day Nightmares," *Knoxville News Sentinel*, December 17, 2020, https://www.knoxnews.com/story

Notes

/entertainment/columnists/terry-mattingly/2020/12/17/episcopal-leaders-ponder-churchs-declining-attendance-terry-mattingly/6534905002/.

18. Olinger, "Presbyterians and Nonverts."

19. David E. Campbell, Geoffrey C. Layman, and John C. Green, *Secular Surge: A New Fault Line in American Politics* (New York: Cambridge University Press, 2020), 3–4.

20. The text of the Auburn Affirmation can be viewed on the Presbyterian Church in America Historical Center website, https://www.pcahistory.org/documents/auburntext.html.

21. Gregory Smith, "About Three-in-Ten U.S. Adults Are Now Religiously Unaffiliated," Pew Research Center, December 14, 2021, https://www.pewresearch.org/religion/2021/12/14/about-three-in-ten-u-s-adults-are-now-religiously-unaffiliated/.

22. Smith, "About Three-in-Ten U.S. Adults."

23. Burge, "Why It's Unlikely."

24. Smith, "About Three-in-Ten U.S. Adults"; Jim Denison, "Why Do We Hiccup? Some Surprising Unsolved Mysteries and the Bias against Religion," The Daily Article, November 15, 2019, https://www.christianheadlines.com/columnists/denison-forum/why-do-we-hiccup-some-surprising-unsolved-mysteries-and-the-bias-against-religion.html.

25. David French, "Did Donald Trump Make the Church Great Again?," The Dispatch, September 19, 2021, https://thedispatch.com/newsletter/frenchpress/did-donald-trump-make-the-church/.

26. Daniel A. Cox, "The Coming Evangelical Christian Decline," Survey Center on American Life, September 8, 2022, https://www.americansurveycenter.org/newsletter/the-coming-evangelical-christian-decline/; Danielle Kurtzleben, "Are You an Evangelical? Are You Sure?," NPR, December 19, 2015, https://www.npr.org/2015/12/19/458058251/are-you-an-evangelical-are-you-sure; Aaron Earls, "Who Are the Evangelicals and Why Knowing That Matters for Your Church," Lifeway Research, July 26, 2021, https://research.lifeway.com/2021/07/26/who-are-evangelicals-and-why-knowing-that-matters-for-your-church/.

27. Jack Jenkins, "Survey: White Mainline Protestants Outnumber White Evangelicals, While 'Nones' Shrink," Religion News Service, July 8, 2021, https://religionnews.com/2021/07/08/survey-white-mainline-protestants-outnumber-white-evangelicals/.

28. Earls, "Who Are the Evangelicals?"

29. Ryan Burge, "The Rise of the Non-Christian Evangelical," Graphs About Religion, February 26, 2024, https://www.graphsaboutreligion.com/p/the-rise-of-the-non-christian-evangelical; Jim Denison, "Atheist Richard Dawkins Calls Himself a 'Cultural Christian,'" The Daily Article, April 4, 2024, https://www.denisonforum.org/daily-article/atheist-richard-dawkins-calls-himself-a-cultural-christian/.

30. Earls, "Who Are the Evangelicals?"

31. Daniel A. Cox, Jennifer Benz, and Lindsey Witt-Swanson, "Faith After the Pandemic: How COVID-19 Changed American Religion," Survey Center on American Life, January 5, 2023, https://www.aei.org/research-products/report/faith-after-the-pandemic-how-COVID-19-changed-american-religion/.

32. "New Data Suggests over 40 Percent of Self-Identified Evangelicals Attend Church Once a Year or Less," *Relevant*, April 8, 2021, https://relevantmagazine.com/faith/church/new-data-suggests-over-40-percent-of-self-identified-evangelicals-attend-church-once-a-year-or-less/.

33. "New Data Suggests over 40 Percent"; Earls, "Who Are the Evangelicals?"

34. Bob Smietana, "Many Who Call Themselves Evangelical Don't Actually Hold Evangelical Beliefs," Lifeway Research, December 6, 2017, https://research.lifeway.com/2017/12/06/many-evangelicals-dont-hold-evangelical-beliefs/.

35. David W. Bebbington, *Evangelicalism in Modern Britain: A History from the 1730s to the 1980s* (London: Unwin Hyman, 1989), 2–17.

36. Barna, "Survey Explores Who Qualifies as an Evangelical," January 18, 2007, https://www.barna.com/research/survey-explores-who-qualifies-as-an-evangelical/.

Notes

37. Timothy Keller, "The Decline and Renewal of the American Church: Part 2—The Decline of Evangelicalism," Gospel-Changed Minds (Winter 2022), https://quarterly.gospelinlife.com/the-decline-of-evangelicalism/.

38. Smietana, "Many Who Call Themselves Evangelical Don't Actually Hold Evangelical Beliefs."

39. Barna, "Survey Explores Who Qualifies as an Evangelical"; French, "Did Donald Trump Make the Church Great Again?"

40. Ligonier Ministries, "2022 Results Now Available: The State of Theology," September 19, 2022, https://www.ligonier.org/posts/2022-state-of-theology.

41. Yonat Shimron, "Poll: Americans Growing More Secular by the Year," Religion News Service, December 14, 2021, https://religionnews.com/2021/12/14/poll-america-growing-more-secular-by-the-year/; Smith, "About Three-in-Ten U.S. Adults."

42. Thomas Costello, "7 Church Attendance Statistics That Should Drive You to Prayer," REACHRIGHT, September 16, 2016, https://reachrightstudios.com/church-attendance-statistics-drive-prayer/.

43. Gallup, "How Religious Are Americans?," December 23, 2021, https://news.gallup.com/poll/358364/religious-americans.aspx.

44. Gallup, "How Religious Are Americans?"

45. Bob Smietana, "Gallup Poll: More than Half of Americans Rarely Go to Church," Religion News Service, March 25, 2024, https://religionnews.com/2024/03/25/gallup-poll-more-than-half-of-americans-rarely-go-to-church/.

46. James Denison, "Abortion Pills Called 'Lifesaving Care,'" The Daily Article, March 6, 2023, https://www.denisonforum.org/daily-article/abortion-pills-called-lifesaving-care/.

47. Gallup, "How Religious Are Americans?"; Smith, "About Three-in-Ten U.S. Adults."

48. Pew Research Center, "Modeling the Future."

49. Ryan Burge, "How Many Atheists Are There in Your State?," Graphs About Religion, March 25, 2024, https://www.graphsaboutreligion.com/p/how-many-atheists-are-there-in-your?utm_source=post-email-title&publication_id=1561197&post_id=142410958&utm_campaign=email-post-title&isFreemail=true&r=grh36&triedRedirect=true&utm_medium; Stefani McDade, "New Atheism Is Dead. What's the New New Atheism?," *Christianity Today*, August 14, 2023, https://www.christianitytoday.com/ct/2023/september/new-atheism-is-dead.html; Aaron Earls, "Reversing the Shrinking Share of Americans Who Regularly Attend Church," Lifeway Research, June 15, 2023, https://research.lifeway.com/2023/06/15/reversing-the-shrinking-share-of-americans-who-regularly-attend-church.

50. I have included Mormons and Jehovah's Witnesses with other non-Christian religions in this statistic. Without Mormons and Jehovah's Witnesses, non-Christian religions are about 6 percent of the American population according to Pew Research (Smith, "About Three-in-Ten U.S. Adults"). This means that those identifying with non-Christian faiths and those identifying as LGBTQ+ are roughly in equal proportions in contemporary America. See Jim Denison, "Candace Cameron Bure Ridiculed for Biblical Morality," The Daily Article, November 17, 2022, https://www.denisonforum.org/daily-article/candace-cameron-bure-ridiculed-for-biblical-morality/.

51. Yonat Shimron, "Study: Most Americans Are Spiritual but a Growing Number Say They Are Not Religious," Religion New Service, December 7, 2023, https://religionnews.com/2023/12/07/study-most-americans-are-spiritual-but-a-growing-number-say-they-are-not-religious/.

52. Burge, "How Many Atheists Are There in Your State?"

53. Byron R. Johnson and Jeff Levin, "Religion Is Dying? Don't Believe It," *Wall Street Journal*, July 28, 2022, https://www.wsj.com/articles/religion-is-dying-dont-believe-it-nones-others-surveys-faith-institutions-atheists-agnostics-practice-minority-11659017037.

54. McDade, "New Atheism Is Dead"; Vivek H. Murthy, "Our Epidemic of Loneliness and Isolation: The U.S. Surgeon General's Advisory on the Healing Effects of Social Connection and Community," Office of the U.S. Surgeon General (2023), https://www.hhs.gov/sites/default/files/surgeon-general-social-connection-advisory.pdf.

Notes

55. Campbell, Layman, and Green, *Secular Surge*, 3.
56. Gregory A. Smith et al., "Religious 'Nones' in America: Who They Are and What They Believe," Pew Research Center, January 24, 2024, https://www.pewresearch.org/religion/2024/01/24/religious-nones-in-america-who-they-are-and-what-they-believe/.
57. See the earlier figures in Smith, "About Three-in-Ten U.S. Adults."
58. Bob Smietana, "Gallup: Fewer Than Half of Americans Belong to a Church or Other House of Worship," *Christianity Today*, March 29, 2021, https://www.christianitytoday.com/news/2021/march/gallup-church-membership-decline-minority-nones-us.html.
59. Timothy Beal, "Can Religion Still Speak to Younger Americans?," *Wall Street Journal*, November 14, 2019, https://www.wsj.com/articles/can-religion-still-speak-to-younger-americans-11573747161; "Religious Landscape Study: 18–29 Year Olds," Pew Research Center, accessed July 30, 2024, https://www.pewresearch.org/religion/religious-landscape-study/age-distribution/18-29/.
60. Ryan Burge, "Dropping Out of Everything: An Increasing Number of Americans Are Just Done," Graphs About Religion, April 22, 2024, https://www.graphsaboutreligion.com/p/dropping-out-of-everything?utm_source=post-email-title&publication_id=1561197&post_id=143360780&utm_campaign=email-post-title&isFreemail=true&r=grh36&triedRedirect=true&utm_=.
61. Kathryn Post, "Who Are the 'Nones'? New Pew Study Debunks Myths about America's Nonreligious," Religion News Service, January 24, 2024, https://religionnews.com/2024/01/24/who-are-the-nones-new-pew-study-debunks-myths-about-americas-nonreligious/; Aaron Earls, "20 Vital Stats for Ministry in 2020," Lifeway Research, January 7, 2020, https://research.lifeway.com/2020/01/07/20-vital-stats-for-ministry-in-2020/.
62. Earls, "Reversing the Shrinking Share."
63. Stephen Bullivant, *Nonverts: The Making of Ex-Christian America* (New York: Oxford University Press, 2022), 9, 95.
64. "How U.S. Religious Composition Has Changed in Recent Decades," Pew Research Center, September 13, 2022, https://www.pewresearch.org/religion/2022/09/13/how-u-s-religious-composition-has-changed-in-recent-decades/; and Jim Davis and Michael Graham with Ryan Burge, *The Great Dechurching: Who's Leaving, Why Are They Going, and What Will It Take to Bring Them Back?* (Grand Rapids: Zondervan, 2023), 5.
65. Quoted in Davis and Graham, *The Great Dechurching*, 35.
66. Burge, "Why It's Unlikely."
67. Burge, "Religion Data Wonk."
68. ChurchTrac, "The State of Church Attendance: Trends and Statistics [2023]," accessed January 13, 2024, https://www.churchtrac.com/articles/the-state-of-church-attendance-trends-and-statistics-2023.
69. Aaron Earls, "Churches Are Open but Still Recovering from Pandemic Attendance Losses," Lifeway Research, November 8, 2022, https://research.lifeway.com/2022/11/08/churches-are-open-but-still-recovering-from-pandemic-attendance-losses/; Earls, "Reversing the Shrinking Share."
70. ChurchTrac, "State of Church Attendance."
71. ChurchTrac, "State of Church Attendance"; Earls, "Churches Are Open"; "Religion," Gallup, accessed July 30, 2024, https://news.gallup.com/poll/1690/Religion.aspx.
72. John Longhurst, "Cellphone Activity Clarifies Actual Church Attendance Levels," *The Free Press*, June 29, 2024, https://www.winnipegfreepress.com/arts-and-life/life/faith/2024/06/29/cellphone-activity-clarifies-actual-church-attendance-levels. Earlier cell phone studies estimated weekly attendance at less than 5 percent. See Devin Pope (@Devin_G_Pope), "Part 3: Religion in America: Evidence from Cellphone Data," X, July 14, 2023, 11:07 a.m., https://twitter.com/Devin_G_Pope/status/1679870211841826817; Steve Goldstein, "People Who Say They Go to Religious Services Weekly Are Probably Lying, Study Finds," Morningstar, April 16, 2024, https://www.morningstar.com/news/marketwatch/2024041661/people-who-say-they-go-to-religious-services-weekly-are-probably-lying-study-finds; Kevin Drum (personal blog), "How Many People

Really Attend Church?," July 6, 2023, https://jabberwocking.com/how-many-people-really-attend-church/; Jana Riess, "How Many Mormons Are Actually in Church Every Week in the US?," Religion News Service, February 16, 2024, https://religionnews.com/2024/02/16/how-many-mormons-are-actually-in-church-every-week-in-the-us/; Earls, "20 Vital Stats for Ministry in 2020."

73. "Are U.S. Colleges Hostile to Christian Students?," Beliefnet, accessed January 15, 2024, https://www.beliefnet.com/news/home-page-news-and-views/are-us-colleges-hostile-to-christian-students.aspx; Jessilyn Lancaster, "Agenda Exposed: Christian Students Rejected, Failed and Expelled for Faith in Jesus," Charisma News, July 15, 2015, https://www.charismanews.com/us/agenda-exposed-christian-students-rejected-failed-and-expelled-for-faith-in-jesus.

Chapter 4 The Mature Uniform

1. Dr. Francis Schaeffer, "A Day of Sober Rejoicing," address delivered at the 10th General Assembly of the Presbyterian Church in America, June 16, 1982, PCA Historical Center, https://www.pcahistory.org/mo/schaeffer/JandR.html.

2. Jim Denison, "How America Changed Its Mind on Gay Marriage," Denison Forum, June 3, 2024, https://www.denisonforum.org/daily-article/how-america-changed-its-mind-on-gay-marriage/.

3. "LGBTQ+ Rights," Gallup, accessed January 18, 2024, https://news.gallup.com/poll/1651/gay-lesbian-rights.aspx.

4. Yonat Shimron, "Young Evangelicals Are Leaving Church. LGBTQ Bias May Be Driving Them Away," Religion News Service, August 6, 2021, https://religionnews.com/2021/08/06/young-evangelicals-are-leaving-church-resistance-to-lgbtq-equality-is-driving-them-away/.

5. Danielle Silliman, "Died: Donald Wildmon, Champion of Christian Boycotts," *Christianity Today*, January 4, 2024, https://www.christianitytoday.com/news/2024/january/obit-donald-wildmon-american-family-boycott-tv-sex-7-eleven.html.

6. Mark Legg, "What Does the Bible Say About Pornography? Can You Break Free from Sexual Temptation?," Denison Forum, May 15, 2023, https://www.denisonforum.org/resources/what-does-the-bible-say-about-pornography-can-you-break-free-from-sexual-temptation/.

7. Samuel L. Perry and Andrew L. Whitehead, "Do People in Conservative States Really Watch More Porn? A Hierarchical Analysis," *Socius* 6 (2020), https://doi.org/10.1177/2378023120908472.

8. Ted Shimer, "How Porn Is Rewiring the Brains of a Generation," *Relevant*, November 2, 2022, https://relevantmagazine.com/life5/porn-is-rewiring-a-whole-generation-christians-included/.

9. Joe Carter, "FactChecker: Do Christian Men Watch More Pornography?," The Gospel Coalition, June 8, 2020, https://www.thegospelcoalition.org/article/factchecker-do-christian-men-watch-more-pornography/.

10. Lyman Stone, "The Truth About Conservative Protestant Men and Porn," Institute for Family Studies, June 19, 2019, https://ifstudies.org/blog/the-truth-about-conservative-protestant-men-and-porn.

11. Stone, "Truth About Conservative Protestant Men."

12. "How Porn Is Rewiring the Brains of a Generation," *Relevant*, accessed January 18, 2024, https://relevantmagazine.com/life5/porn-is-rewiring-a-whole-generation-christians-included/.

13. Stone, "Truth About Conservative Protestant Men."

14. CBC Radio, "'Digisexuality' Emerges as a New Sexual Identity," CBC, January 25, 2019, https://www.cbc.ca/radio/spark/the-spark-guide-to-human-ai-interaction-1.5192455/digisexuality-emerges-as-a-new-sexual-identity-1.4988400.

15. CBC Radio, "Digisexuality"; Matt Frad, "10 Shocking Stats About Teens and Pornography," Covenant Eyes, January 2, 2024, https://www.covenanteyes.com/2015/04/10/10-shocking-stats-about-teens-and-pornography/.

16. Michael J. New, "Teen Sexual Activity Continues to Decline, a New CDC Report Shows," *National Review*, December 19, 2023, https://www.nationalreview.com/corner/teen-sexual-activity-continues-to-decline-a-new-cdc-report-shows/.

Notes

17. Abigail Shrier, *Irreversible Damage: The Transgender Craze Seducing Our Daughters* (Washington, DC: Regnery, 2020), 22–23; Pamela Paul, "As Kids, They Thought They Were Trans. They No Longer Do," *New York Times*, February 2, 2024, https://www.nytimes.com/2024/02/02/opinion/transgender-children-gender-dysphoria.html?unlocked_article_code=1.Wk0.9s7-.3h9LVajJ1W3x&smid=em-share; Michelle Conlin, Robin Respaut, and Chad Terhune, "A Gender Imbalance Emerges Among Trans Teens Seeking Treatment," Reuters, November 18, 2022, https://www.reuters.com/investigates/special-report/usa-transyouth-topsurgery/.

18. Shrier, *Irreversible Damage*, 32.

19. Amelia Gentleman, "'An Explosion': What Is Behind the Rise in Girls Questioning Their Gender Identity?," *The Guardian*, November 24, 2022, https://www.theguardian.com/society/2022/nov/24/an-explosion-what-is-behind-the-rise-in-girls-questioning-their-gender-identity.

20. Luke Gilkerson, "Internet Safety: Teens Are Using Porn at Alarming Rates," Covenant Eyes, October 30, 2020, https://www.covenanteyes.com/2013/12/03/internet-safety-teens-looking-at-porn/.

21. Anna Brown, "About 5% of Young Adults in the U.S. Say Their Gender Is Different from Their Sex Assigned at Birth," Pew Research Center, June 7, 2022, https://www.pewresearch.org/short-reads/2022/06/07/about-5-of-young-adults-in-the-u-s-say-their-gender-is-different-from-their-sex-assigned-at-birth/.

22. YRBSS—United States, 2021 Supplementary Tables, "Table 4: Number and Percentage of Students, by Sexual Identity," Centers for Disease Control, last reviewed April 27, 2023, https://www.cdc.gov/yrbs/results/2021-supplementary-tables.html.

23. Guy Layfield, "Is There Really a Transgender 'Craze' Seducing Our Daughters? A Review of Abigail Shrier's *Irreversible Damage*," Renew.org, accessed January 18, 2024, https://renew.org/is-there-really-a-transgender-craze-seducing-our-daughters-a-review-of-abigail-shriers-irreversible-damage/.

24. Russell Moore, "Why Character Doesn't Matter Anymore," *Christianity Today*, March 22, 2024, https://www.christianitytoday.com/ct/2024/march-web-only/ned-flanders-douglas-wilson-russell-moore-character.html.

25. "Incarceration Statistics," Vera, accessed January 20, 2024, https://www.vera.org/incarceration-statistics.

26. Shawn Bushway et al., "Barred from Employment," *Science Advances* 8, no. 7 (February 18, 2022), https://www.science.org/doi/10.1126/sciadv.abj6992; see also Salem State University and Worcester State University, "2020 Massachusetts Uniform Citation Data Analysis Report," February 7, 2022, https://www.mass.gov/doc/2020-massachusetts-uniform-citation-data-analysis-report/download.

27. Nicholas Kristof, "Republicans and Democrats Agree: End the War on Drugs," *New York Times*, November 7, 2020, https://www.nytimes.com/2020/11/07/opinion/sunday/election-marijuana-legalization.html.

28. From the U.S. Centers for Disease Control and Prevention as reported by the National Center for Health Statistics' National Vital Statistics System, https://www.cdc.gov/stopoverdose/fentanyl/index.html. Estimates for 2020 are based on provisional data. Estimates for 2015–2019 are based on final data available at https://www.cdc.gov/nchs/nvss/vsrr/drug-overdose-data.htm.

29. Anne Milgram, "Fiscal Year 2024 Request for the Drug Enforcement Administration," Department of Justice, April 27, 2023, https://www.dea.gov/sites/default/files/2023-04/HHRG-118-AP19-Wstate-MilgramA-20230427.pdf.

30. Emily Belz, "Super Bowl Betting Is a $7.6 Billion Problem Fewer Evangelicals Care About," *Christianity Today*, February 11, 2022, https://www.christianitytoday.com/news/2022/february/super-bowl-betting-gambling-evangelicals.html.

31. Bob Smietana, "Why Faith Leaders Lost the Battle Against Online Sports Betting," Religion News Service, February 5, 2024, https://religionnews.com/2024/02/05/why-faith-leaders-lost-the-battle-against-online-sports-betting/.

32. Smietana, "Why Faith Leaders Lost the Battle."

Notes

33. Lisa Cannon Green, "Is Sports Gambling Moral? You Bet, Americans Say," Lifeway Newsroom, January 22, 2016, https://news.lifeway.com/2016/01/22/is-sports-gambling-moral-you-bet-americans-say/.

34. Belz, "Super Bowl Betting"; Kyle Worley, "Sports Betting Has Become Too Prevalent for Christians to Ignore," *Christianity Today*, September 19, 2024, https://www.christianitytoday.com/2024/09/sports-betting-online-gambling-christians-sin-bible-money/.

35. "New AGA Report Shows Americans Gamble More Than Half a Trillion Dollars Illegally Each Year," American Gaming Institute, press release, November 30, 2022, https://www.americangaming.org/new/new-aga-report-shows-americans-gamble-more-than-half-a-trillion-dollars-illegally-each-year/.

36. "National Income and Product Accounts," Bureau of Economic Analysis, December 21, 2023, https://apps.bea.gov/iTable/?reqid=19&step=3&isuri=1&1921=underlying&1903=2017; "https://www.americangaming.org/researchAGA Commercial Gaming Revenue Tracker," American Gaming Institute, January 18, 2024, https://www.americangaming.org/resources/aga-commercial-gaming-revenue-tracker/; Will Yakowicz, "U.S. Sets Gambling Record in 2022 With More Than $54.9 Billion in Revenue," *Forbes*, January 13, 2023, https://www.forbes.com/sites/willyakowicz/2023/01/13/us-set-gambling-record-in-2022-with-more-than-549-billion-in-revenue/?sh=48c27b0867cc.

37. "5 Alarming Gambling Addiction Statistics," Addictions.com, August 3, 2023, https://www.addictions.com/gambling/5-alarming-gambling-addiction-statistics/.

38. Michael Foust, "Mohler Warns: Evangelicals Becoming Lukewarm on Gambling," *Christian Headlines*, February 15, 2022, https://www.christianheadlines.com/contributors/michael-foust/mohler-warns-evangelicals-becoming-lukewarm-on-gambling.html; Worley, "Sports Betting Has Become Too Prevalent for Christians to Ignore."

39. Robert P. Jones, Daniel Cox, Betsy Cooper, and Rachel Lienesch. "How Americans View Immigrants and What They Want from Immigration Reform: Findings from the 2015 American Values Atlas," Public Religion Research Institute, March 29, 2016, http://www.prri.org/research/poll-immigration-reform-views-on-immigrants/.

40. Camilo Montoya-Galvez, "U.S. Border Officials on Track to Process over 300,000 Migrants in December," CBS News, December 31, 2023, https://www.cbsnews.com/news/us-mexico-border-migrants-processed-december-record/; Colleen Long, "The Mayors of Five Big Cities Seek a Meeting with Biden About How to Better Manage Arriving Migrants," Associated Press, November 1, 2023, https://apnews.com/article/migrants-big-cities-biden-democratic-mayors-border-f498da66af8fb0ff8df653969f3f7a7a.

41. Rebecca Shabad, "Trump on 'Poisoning the Blood' Remarks: 'I Never Knew That Hitler Said It,'" NBC News, December 22, 2023, https://www.nbcnews.com/politics/donald-trump/trump-poisoning-blood-remarks-never-knew-hitler-said-rcna130958.

42. Jones, Cox, Cooper, and Lienesch, "How Americans View Immigrants."

43. William H. Frazer, "The Social Separation of the Races," *Southern Presbyterian Journal*, July 15, 1950, 6–7; "First Presbyterian Church of Jackson, Miss. Declares Itself on Segregation," *Southern Presbyterian Journal*, July 7, 1954, 8; Morton Smith, "The Racial Problem Facing America," *Presbyterian Guardian* 33, no. 8 (October 1964): 125–28; John E. Richards, "As God Is One" (sermon), July 25, 1965, sent by First Presbyterian Church of Macon, GA, to all PCUS churches and published in *The Historical Birth of the Presbyterian Church in America* (Liberty Hill, SC: Liberty Press, 1987), 51–59; Morton H. Smith, *How Is the Gold Become Dim: The Decline of the Presbyterian Church, U.S., as Reflected in Its Assembly Actions* (Steering Committee for a Continuing Presbyterian Church, 1971), 20–21, 170–74.

44. Committee on Mission to North America, Pastoral Letter on Racism, approved at the March 2004 MNA Committee Meeting as the Committee's Recommendation to the Thirty-Second General Assembly, in *Minutes of the Thirty-Second General Assembly of the Presbyterian Church in America* (2004), Appendix H, Attachment E, 427–57, https://www.pcahistory.org/topical/race/2004_pastoral_letter_on_racism.pdf; Sean M. Lucas and J. Ligon Duncan III, Personal Resolution on Civil Rights Remembrance, in *Minutes of the Forty-Third General Assembly of*

Notes

the Presbyterian Church in America (2015), 16–17, 71–77, 81–82; then *Minutes of the Forty-Fourth General Assembly of the Presbyterian Church in America* (2016), Appendix M, 329–30; Appendix V, Attachment 1, 673–88, https://www.pcahistory.org/topical/race/2015_Personal%20Resolution%20on%20Civil%20Rights%20Remembrance.pdf; Overture 43 from Potomac Presbytery, "Pursuing Racial Reconciliation and the Advance of the Gospel," in *Minutes of the Forty-Fourth General Assembly*, 74–78, 646–48; Overture 44, "Creation of the PCA Unity Fund," in *Minutes of the Forty-Fourth General Assembly*, 46–47, 261–62; Overture 55 from Mississippi Valley, "Confession of the Sin of Racism, and Commitment to Christian Unity," in *Minutes of the Forty-Fourth General Assembly*, Appendix V, 669–72, https://www.pcahistory.org/topical/race/2016-55.pdf; Report of the Ad Interim Committee on Racial and Ethnic Reconciliation, in *Minutes of the Forty-Sixth General Assembly of the Presbyterian Church in America* (2018), Appendix V, 596–668, https://www.pcahistory.org/topical/race/2018_report_ethnic_and_racial_reconciliation.pdf.

45. Kevin D. Doughtery, Mark Chaves, and Michael O. Emerson, "Racial Diversity in U.S. Congregations, 1998–2019," National Congregations Study-IV, October 12, 2020, https://sites.duke.edu/ncsweb/files/2020/10/Racial-Diversity-in-U.S.-Congregations-1998-2019.pdf.

46. Russell Contreras, "American Churches Remain Largely Segregated—with One Exception," Axios, May 18, 2023, https://www.axios.com/2023/05/18/religion-protestant-evangelical-hispanic-latino.

47. Contreras, "American Churches Remain Largely Segregated."

48. "Religious Landscape Study: Racial and Ethnic Composition Among Evangelical Protestants by Religious Denomination," Pew Research Center, accessed January 22, 2024, https://www.pewresearch.org/religion/religious-landscape-study/compare/racial-and-ethnic-composition/by/religious-denomination/among/religious-tradition/evangelical-protestant/.

49. Marissa Postel, "Most Pastors See Racial Diversity in the Church as a Goal but Not Reality," Lifeway Research, February 15, 2022, https://research.lifeway.com/2022/02/15/most-pastors-see-racial-diversity-in-the-church-as-a-goal-but-not-reality/.

50. Patrick Glynn, "Racial Reconciliation: Can Religion Work Where Politics Has Failed?," *American Behavioral Scientist* 41, no. 6 (1998): 834–41; Richard Hunt, "Free Resources from Promise Keepers to Challenge Racism—and the Power of Racial Reconciliation," K-LOVE, September 9, 2020, https://www.klove.com/news/faith/free-resources-from-promise-keepers-to-challenge-racism-and-the-power-of-racial-reconciliation-16110.

Chapter 5 The Minority Mission

1. Timothy Keller, "The Decline and Renewal of the American Church: Part 2—The Decline of Evangelicalism," Gospel-Changed Minds (Winter 2022), https://quarterly.gospelinlife.com/the-decline-of-evangelicalism/.

2. Timothy Keller, "The Decline and Renewal of the American Church: Part 4—The Strategy for Renewal," Gospel-Changed Minds (Summer 2022), https://quarterly.gospelinlife.com/american-church-the-strategy-for-renewal/.

3. Keller, "Decline and Renewal of the American Church: Part 2."

4. Stephen Coté, "75 Most Popular Sermon Topics Being Preached Today," Sermon Search, January 4, 2022, https://www.sermonsearch.com/articles-tips/sermon-ideas/75-most-popular-sermon-topics-being-preached-today/.

5. Larry W. Hurtado, *Why on Earth Did Anyone Become a Christian in the First Three Centuries?* (Milwaukee: Marquette University Press, 2016), 75, 108–9; Katy Faust, "Children and the Christian Revolution," *World*, October 20, 2023, https://wng.org/opinions/children-and-the-christian-revolution-1697747323.

6. Bob Smietana, "Adoption, Foster Care Commonplace in Churches," Lifeway Research, January 24, 2018, https://research.lifeway.com/2018/01/24/adoption-foster-care-commonplace-in-churches/.

Notes

7. Jedd Medefind, "New Barna Research Highlights Christian Adoption & Foster Care Among 3 Most Notable Vocational Trends," Christian Alliance for Orphans, February 12, 2014, https://cafo.org/new-barna-research-highlights-christian-adoption-foster-care-among-3-most-notable-vocational-trends/.

8. Aaron Earls, "Fewer Christians Know Families Who Foster or Adopt, *Christianity Today*, May 22, 2023, https://www.christianitytoday.com/news/2023/may/adoption-foster-care-church-goers-children-lifeway-study-re.html.

9. Kristin T. Lee, "Adoption Was Beautiful, Precious, and God-Ordained. Then I Adopted," *Christianity Today*, January 18, 2024, https://www.christianitytoday.com/ct/2024/january-web-only/adoption-expectations-church-theology-complexity-grief.html.

10. Russell Moore, "The American Evangelical Church Is in Crisis. There's Only One Way Out," *The Atlantic*, July 25, 2023, https://www.theatlantic.com/ideas/archive/2023/07/christian-evangelical-church-division-politics/674810/.

11. Keller, "Decline and Renewal of the American Church: Part 4."

12. Betsy Cooper, Daniel Cox, Rachel Lienesch, and Robert P. Jones, "Exodus: Why Americans are Leaving Religion—and Why They're Unlikely to Come Back," Public Religion Research Institute, September 22, 2016, https://www.prri.org/research/prri-rns-poll-nones-atheist-leaving-religion/.

13. Dean Inserra, "Will People Leave Your Church over Politics?," Lifeway Research, September 3, 2020, https://research.lifeway.com/2020/09/03/will-people-leave-your-church-over-american-politics/; Yonat Shimron, "Are White Evangelical Pastors at Odds with Their Congregants? A New Study Says No," Religion News Service, August 9, 2023, https://religionnews.com/2023/08/09/are-white-evangelical-pastors-at-odds-with-their-congregants-a-new-study-says-no/; Jim Davis and Michael Graham with Ryan Burge, *The Great Dechurching: Who's Leaving, Why Are They Going, and What Will It Take to Bring Them Back?* (Grand Rapids: Zondervan, 2023), 31–32.

14. Inserra, "Will People Leave Your Church over Politics?"

15. Yonat Shimron, "Study: Unaffiliated Americans Are the Only Growing Religious Group," Religion News Service, March 27, 2024, https://religionnews.com/2024/03/27/study-unaffiliated-americans-are-the-only-growing-religious-group/.

16. Jeff Diamant, "Though Still Conservative, Young Evangelicals Are More Liberal Than Their Elders on Some Issues," Pew Research Center, May 4, 2017, https://www.pewresearch.org/short-reads/2017/05/04/though-still-conservative-young-evangelicals-are-more-liberal-than-their-elders-on-some-issues/.

17. Tim Sansbury, personal correspondence with the author, April 9, 2024.

18. Jeffrey M. Jones, "LGBTQ+ Identification in U.S. Now at 7.6%," Gallup, March 13, 2024, https://news.gallup.com/poll/611864/lgbtq-identification.aspx?utm.

19. Jones, "LGBTQ+ Identification in U.S. Now at 7.6%"; YRBSS—United States, 2021 Supplementary Tables, "Table 4: Number and Percentage of Students, by Sexual Identity," Centers for Disease Control, last reviewed April 27, 2023, https://www.cdc.gov/healthyyouth/data/yrbs/supplemental-mmwr/students_by_sexual_identity.htm; Jim Denison, "Candace Cameron Bure Ridiculed for Biblical Morality," The Daily Article, November 17, 2022, https://www.denisonforum.org/daily-article/candace-cameron-bure-ridiculed-for-biblical-morality/.

20. Jones, "LGBTQ+ Identification in U.S. Now at 7.6%."

21. For example, the Amplify Conference hosted by Wheaton College's Billy Graham Center on October 22–23, 2024, included a presentation by Regent University professor of psychology Mark Yarhouse titled "Engaging LGBTQ Friends and Neighbors in Faith Conversations." See https://wheatonbillygraham.com/amplify/.

22. Letter to Government Officials Regarding Transgender Procedures for Minors, prepared by The Commission Appointed by the Moderator of the 50th General Assembly of the Presbyterian Church in America, January 21, 2024, https://byfaithonline.com/wp-content/uploads/2024/01/General-Letter.pdf.

Notes

23. Joe Carter, "FactChecker: Do Christian Men Watch More Pornography?," The Gospel Coalition, June 8, 2020, https://www.thegospelcoalition.org/article/factchecker-do-christian-men-watch-more-pornography/.

24. Brett McCarty, "With Drug Overdoses on the Rise, Churches Need an All-Hands-on-Deck Attitude," *Christianity Today*, May 26, 2023, https://www.christianitytoday.com/ct/2023/may-web-only/raising-lazarus-beth-macy-drug-overdose-addiction.html.

25. Anne Milgram, "Fiscal Year 2024 Request for the Drug Enforcement Administration," Department of Justice, April 27, 2023, https://www.dea.gov/sites/default/files/2023-04/HHRG-118-AP19-Wstate-MilgramA-20230427.pdf.

26. Beat It Staff, "San Francisco—Where Drug Addicts Outnumber High School Students," Beat It!, accessed February 6, 2024, https://www.beatiteap.com/san-francisco-drug-addicts-outnumber-students/.

27. Jessica Miller, "Video Game Addiction Statistics," AddictionHelp.com, January 22, 2024, https://www.addictionhelp.com/video-game-addiction/statistics/; Cam Adair, "How Many People Are Addicted to Playing Video Games?," Game Quitters, accessed April 11, 2024, https://gamequitters.com/how-many-people-are-addicted-to-playing-video-games/.

28. Adair, "How Many People Are Addicted to Playing Video Games?"

29. Cam Adair, "Video Game Addiction Statistics 2023—How Many Addicted Gamers Are There?," Game Quitters, accessed April 11, 2024, https://gamequitters.com/video-game-addiction-statistics/.

30. Jessica Miller, "Video Game Addiction Statistics."

31. Bob Smietana, "Why Faith Leaders Lost the Battle Against Online Sports Betting," Religion News Service, February 5, 2024, https://religionnews.com/2024/02/05/why-faith-leaders-lost-the-battle-against-online-sports-betting/.

32. Aaron Earls, "Super Bowl Gambling Grows, but Pastors Are on the Sidelines," *Christianity Today*, February 8, 2024, https://www.christianitytoday.com/news/2024/february/super-bowl-gambling-sports-betting-pastors-opposition.html; Leah MarieAnn Klett, "Most Evangelical Pastors Say Sports Betting Is 'Morally Wrong,' Survey Reveals Ahead of Super Bowl," *The Christian Post*, February 7, 2024, https://www.christianpost.com/news/most-evangelical-pastors-say-sports-betting-is-morally-wrong.html.

33. Oliver Staley, "An Explosion in Sports Betting Is Driving Gambling Addiction Among College Students," *Time*, December 12, 2023, https://time.com/6342504/gambling-addiction-sports-betting-college-students/.

34. Earls, "Super Bowl Gambling Grows."

35. Carrie McKean, "Panic Won't Protect the Planet Well," *Christianity Today*, April 22, 2024, https://www.christianitytoday.com/ct/2024/april-web-only/panic-protect-planet-climate-change-earth-day.html.

36. Ryan Burge, "The Concerns of Young Evangelicals Offer Political Insights for 2024," Religion & Politics, January 17, 2023, https://religionandpolitics.org/2023/01/17/the-concerns-of-young-evangelicals-offer-political-insights-for-2024/.

37. "Evangelical Views on Immigration," Lifeway Research, February 2015, https://research.lifeway.com/wp-content/uploads/2015/03/Evangelical-Views-on-Immigration-Report.pdf.

38. Burge, "Concerns of Young Evangelicals."

39. J. Baxter Oliphant and Andy Cerda, "Republicans and Democrats Have Different Top Priorities for U.S. Immigration Policy," Pew Research Center, September 8, 2022, https://www.pewresearch.org/short-reads/2022/09/08/republicans-and-democrats-have-different-top-priorities-for-u-s-immigration-policy/.

40. "The 10 Largest Refugee Crises to Know in 2024," Concern Worldwide US, December 15, 2023, https://concernusa.org/news/largest-refugee-crises/.

41. *State of the Great Commission: Report Prepared for Lausanne Global Congress Seoul 2024* (Lausanne Movement, April 2024), 73.

Notes

42. Pat Sawyer, "Framing Critical Race Theory: What Is CRT, and Should We Be Concerned?," *byFaith*, April 5, 2021, https://byfaithonline.com/what-is-crt-and-should-we-be-concerned/; Pat Sawyer, "Framing Critical Race Theory: Cautions Regarding Critical Race Theory," *byFaith*, April 13, 2021, https:// byfaithonline.com/cautions-regarding-crt/.

43. Brad East, "What Makes Critical Theory Christian?," *Comment*, June 28, 2023, https://comment.org/what-makes-critical-theory-christian/; Christopher Watkin, *Biblical Critical Theory: How the Bible's Unfolding Story Makes Sense of Modern Life and Culture* (Grand Rapids: Zondervan Academic, 2022).

44. It is probably more accurate to identify critical theory's roots in French phenomenological schools of philosophy, but these became associated with intellectuals who identified as Communists. See Paul J. Griffiths, "Christ and Critical Theory," *First Things*, August 2004, https://www.firstthings.com/article/2004/08/christ-and-critical-theory.

45. D. Clair Davis, "Friendly Battling?," distributed email correspondence, January 13, 2021.

46. John Piper, "Critical Race Theory, Part 1: The Relationships," Desiring God: Ask Pastor John, November 23, 2020, https://www.desiringgod.org/interviews/critical-race-theory-part-1; Aaron Earls, "Pastors More Reluctant to Preach on Race," *Christianity Today*, January 12, 2021, https://www.christianitytoday.com/news/2021/january/pastors-reluctant-preach-racial-reconciliation-lifeway-surv.html.

47. Burge, "Concerns of Young Evangelicals."

48. Russell Moore, "A Christian Vocabulary for an Exhausted Age," *Christianity Today*, August 25, 2023, https://www.christianitytoday.com/2023/08/culture-wars-politics-christian-vocabulary-exhausted-age/.

49. Keller, "Decline and Renewal of the American Church: Part 2."

50. Tabitha McDuffee, "Parents Today Are Kinder and Gentler. They Can Still Take Sin Seriously," *Christianity Today*, September 18, 2024, https://www.christianitytoday.com/2024/09/flourishing-family-amanda-david-erickson-parenting-neuroscience/.

51. Daniel R. Suhr, "Failure to Make the Case: Alberta's Critique of the Christian Right Largely Misfires," *World*, January 13, 2024, 31.

Chapter 6 The Zeal of Loss

1. Timothy Keller, "The Decline and Renewal of the American Church: Part 4—The Strategy for Renewal," Gospel-Changed Minds (Summer 2022), https://quarterly.gospelinlife.com/american-church-the-strategy-for-renewal/.

2. Quoted in Timothy Dalrymple, "The Splintering of the Evangelical Soul," *Christianity Today*, April 16, 2021, https://www.christianitytoday.com/ct/2021/april-web-only/splintering-of-evangelical-soul.html.

3. Aaron M. Renn, "The Three Worlds of Evangelicalism," *First Things*, February 2022, https://www.firstthings.com/article/2022/02/the-three-worlds-of-evangelicalism.

4. Stefani McDade, "New Atheism Is Dead. What's the New New Atheism?," *Christianity Today*, August 14, 2023, https://www.christianitytoday.com/ct/2023/september/new-atheism-is-dead.html.

5. I have included Mormons and Jehovah's Witnesses with other non-Christian religions in this statistic. Without Mormons and Jehovah's Witnesses, non-Christian religions are about 6 percent of the American population according to Pew Research (Gregory Smith, "About Three-in-Ten U.S. Adults Are Now Religiously Unaffiliated," December 14, 2021, https://www.pewresearch.org/religion/2021/12/14/about-three-in-ten-u-s-adults-are-now-religiously-unaffiliated/). This means that those identifying with non-Christian faiths and those identifying as LGBTQ+ are roughly in equal proportions in contemporary America (Jim Denison, "Candace Cameron Bure Ridiculed for Biblical Morality," The Daily Article, November 17, 2022, https://www.denisonforum.org/daily-article/candace-cameron-bure-ridiculed-for-biblical-morality/).

Notes

6. "2021 PRRI Census of American Religion, Updates and Trends: White Christian Decline Slows, Unaffiliated Growth Levels Off," Public Religion Research Institute, April 27, 2022, https://www.prri.org/spotlight/prri-2021-american-values-atlas-religious-affiliation-updates-and-trends-white-christian-decline-slows-unaffiliated-growth-levels-off/; Becky Sullivan, "The Proportion of White Christians in the U.S. Has Stopped Shrinking, New Study Finds," NPR Morning Edition, July 8, 2021, https://www.npr.org/2021/07/08/1014047885/americas-white-christian-plurality-has-stopped-shrinking-a-new-study-finds; David Roach, "Church Attendance Dropped Among Young People, Singles, Liberals," *Christianity Today*, January 9, 2023, https://www.christianitytoday.com/news/2023/january/pandemic-church-attendance-drop-aei-survey-young-people-eva.html; Jennifer Benz, Lindsey Witt-Swanson, and Daniel Cox, "Faith After the Pandemic: How COVID-19 Changed American Religion," Survey Center on American Life, January 2023, https://www.americansurveycenter.org/research/faith-after-the-pandemic-how-COVID-19-changed-american-religion/.

7. Quoted in Sullivan, "Proportion of White Christians in the U.S. Has Stopped Shrinking."

8. Renn, "Three Worlds of Evangelicalism."

9. Rod Dreher, *The Benedict Option: A Strategy for Christians in a Post-Christian Nation* (New York: Sentinel, 2017).

10. Jack Jenkins, "The Second Coming of Doug Wilson," Religion News Service, May 31, 2024, https://religionnews.com/2024/05/31/the-second-coming-of-doug-wilson/.

11. Kevin DeYoung, "On Culture War, Doug Wilson, and the Moscow Mood," Clearly Reformed, November 27, 2023, https://clearlyreformed.org/on-culture-war-doug-wilson-and-the-moscow-mood/.

12. Chris Brennan, "Trump's Questionable Morality Gets a Pass from Evangelical Voters. I Decided to Ask Why," *USA Today*, February 18, 2024, https://www.usatoday.com/story/opinion/columnist/2024/02/18/evangelicals-support-trump-2024-appeal-voters/72614580007/.

13. *State of the Great Commission: Report Prepared for Lausanne Global Congress Seoul 2024* (Lausanne Movement, April 2024), 41.

14. *State of the Great Commission*, 54–55.

15. Ryan Burge, "The Concerns of Young Evangelicals Offer Political Insights for 2024," *Religion and Politics*, January 17, 2023, https://religionandpolitics.org/2023/01/17/the-concerns-of-young-evangelicals-offer-political-insights-for-2024/.

16. Will Leitch, "The Young Christians Are Becoming the Bullies, Not the Bullied," Medium, October 27, 2021, https://williamfleitch.medium.com/the-young-christians-are-becoming-the-bullies-not-the-bullied-914dd4f6a164.

17. Melinda Lundquist Denton and Richard Flory, *Back Pocket God: Religion and Spirituality in the Lives of Emerging Adults* (New York: Oxford University Press, 2020), 6–7.

18. Jennifer Liu, "More Than Half of Gen Zers Think They 'Can Easily Make a Career in Influencing,' Says Branding Expert," CNBC, September 20, 2023, https://www.cnbc.com/2023/09/20/more-than-half-of-gen-zers-think-they-can-easily-make-a-career-in-influencing.html.

19. Bryan Chapell, "A Christian Journalism," in *Speaking the Truth*, ed. Kimberly Collins (New York: World Journalism Institute, 2008), 101–24.

20. Kelsey Kramer McGinnis, "Tradwife Content Offers Fundamentalism Fit for Instagram," *Christianity Today*, March 13, 2024, https://christianitytoday.com/ct/2024/march-web-only/tradwife-influencer-movement-fundamentalism-christian.html.

21. Ryan Burge, "Has Christian Nationalism Intensified or Faded? Comparing Survey Data from 2007 and 2021," Graphs About Religion, February 22, 2024, https://www.graphsaboutreligion.com/p/has-christian-nationalism-intensified; and Ryan Burge, "Who Hasn't Heard About Christian Nationalism?," Graphs About Religion, August 15, 2024, https://www.graphsaboutreligion.com/p/who-hasnt-heard-about-christian-nationalism.

22. Jack Jenkins, "New Study Finds Christian Nationalists to Be More Complex Than Media Portrayals," Religion News Service, December 18, 2023, https://religionnews.com/2023/12/18/new-study-paints-complicated-picture-of-christian-nationalists/.

Notes

23. Jenkins, "New Study Finds Christian Nationalists"; Justin Poythress, "How Evangelicals Lose Will Make All the Difference: A Critique of the Seven Mountain Mandate," The Gospel Coalition, July 10, 2023, https://www.thegospelcoalition.org/article/seven-mountain-mandate/.

24. Jenkins, "New Study Finds Christian Nationalists."

25. Ryan Burge's honest comments on the fading influence of Christian Nationalism as the nation grows more distant from the Moral Majority movements of the last century still require him to cite the recent resurgence of interest in a spate of books that include: Andrew L. Whitehead and Samuel L. Perry, *Taking Back America for God* (2020); Philip S. Gorski and Samuel L. Perry, *The Flag and the Cross* (2022); Andrew L. Whitehead, *American Idolatry* (2023); Bradley Onishi, *Preparing for War* (2023); Angela Denker, *Red State Christians* (2022); Erin L. McDaniel, Irfan Nooruddin, and Allyson F. Shortle, *The Everyday Crusade* (2022); Paul A. Djupe, Andrew R. Lewis, and Anand E. Sokhey, *The Full Armor of God* (2023).

26. Ryan Burge, "Has Christian Nationalism Intensified or Faded?"

27. David French, "Why Do They Hate Us? Race, Christian Nationalism, and White Evangelical Alienation from America," The Dispatch, December 20, 2020, https://thedispatch.com/newsletter/frenchpress/why-do-they-hate-us/.

28. Brad East, "How (Not) to Talk About 'Christian Nationalism,'" *Christianity Today*, March 13, 2024, https://www.christianitytoday.com/ct/2024/march-web-only/how-not-to-talk-about-christian-nationalism-another-gospel.html; Eric Treene, "Making Sense of 'Christian Nationalism', Part II: Should Christians Care About Nationhood?," The Washington Institute for Faith, Vocation and Culture, accessed October 11, 2023, https://washingtoninst.org/making-sense-of-christian-nationalism-part-ii/.

29. Matthew D. Taylor, "The Peril Radicalizing Some Evangelicals Goes Beyond Christian Nationalism," Religion News Service, April 4, 2024, https://religionnews.com/2024/04/04/the-peril-radicalizing-some-evangelicals-goes-beyond-christian-nationalism/.

30. Rob Pacienza, "Patriotism and the Pastor," *byFaith*, July 1, 2024, https://byfaithonline.com/patriotism-and-the-pastor/; Howard Brown, "Patriotism and the Minority Experience," *byFaith*, July 3, 2024, https://byfaithonline.com/patriotism-and-the-minority-experience/.

31. Timothy Keller, "The Decline and Renewal of the American Church: Part 2—The Decline of Evangelicalism," Gospel-Changed Minds (Winter 2022), https://quarterly.gospelinlife.com/the-decline-of-evangelicalism/; Kevin DeYoung, "The Rise of Right-Wing Wokeism: Review of 'The Case for Christian Nationalism' by Stephen Wolfe," The Gospel Coalition, November 28, 2022, https://www.thegospelcoalition.org/reviews/christian-nationalism-wolfe/.

32. Wes Bredenhof, "A Revitalized Yet Tempered Christian Reconstruction," blog post, February 6, 2023, https://bredenhof.ca/2023/02/06/a-revitalized-yet-tempered-christian-reconstruction/; Crawford Gribben, *Survival and Resistance in Evangelical America: Christian Reconstruction in the Pacific Northwest* (New York: Oxford University Press, 2021), 6–8, 82.

33. Stephen Wolfe, *The Case for Christian Nationalism* (Moscow, ID: Canon Press, 2022), 11–14.

34. Tony Reinke, "John Piper on Theocracy, Igniting Revolutions, and Patriotism in the Church," Crossway, June 29, 2024, https://www.crossway.org/articles/john-piper-on-theocracy-igniting-revolutions-and-patriotism-in-the-church/.

35. DeYoung, "Rise of Right-Wing Wokeism."

36. Katherine Stewart, "Christian Nationalism Is One of Trump's Most Powerful Weapons," *New York Times*, January 6, 2022, https://www.nytimes.com/2022/01/06/opinion/jan-6-christian-nationalism.html.

37. David Coffin, distributed email, January 25, 2024.

38. Ralph Wood, "An Evangelical's Warning to Evangelical Christian Nationalists Aims Beyond the Easy Targets," *Christianity Today*, September 25, 2024, https://www.christianitytoday.com/2024/09/joel-looper-another-gospel-christian-nationalism/.

39. Daniel Bennett, "Tim Alberta Is More Sad Than Angry at His American Evangelical Family," *Christianity Today*, January 18, 2024, https://www.christianitytoday.com/ct/2024/january-web-only/tim-alberta-kingdom-power-glory-american-evangelicals.html.

Notes

40. Ben Crenshaw, "Nietzscheans in Negative World: Response to Carl Trueman," *American Reformer*, May 18, 2024, https://americanreformer.org/2024/05/nietzscheans-in-negative-world/.

41. Wolfe, *Case for Christian Nationalism*, 436.

42. Taylor Combs, "Men Are from Right-Leaning Mars. Women Are from Lefty Venus," *Christianity Today*, September 5, 2023, https://www.christianitytoday.com/ct/2023/august-web-only/gender-politics-men-right-leaning-mars-women-lefty-venus.html.

43. David French, "A Whiff of Civil War in the Air: Malice and Misinformation Are Driving National Division," The Dispatch, October 3, 2021, https://thedispatch.com/newsletter/frenchpress/a-whiff-of-civil-war-in-the-air/.

Chapter 7 Hope for the Future

1. David O'Reilly, "What Is the Future of Religion in America?," *Trust Magazine*, February 7, 2023, https://www.pewtrusts.org/en/trust/archive/winter-2023/what-is-the-future-of-religion-in-america.

2. O'Reilly, "What Is the Future of Religion in America?"

3. David French, "The Wounds That Politics Cannot Heal," The Dispatch, December 19, 2021, https://thedispatch.com/newsletter/frenchpress/the-wounds-politics-cannot-heal/.

4. Anna Laetitia Waring, "Father, I Know That All My Life," *Hymns and Meditations* (1850), public domain.

5. Lesslie Newbigin, *The Gospel in a Pluralistic Society* (Grand Rapids: Eerdmans, 1989), 227. See also Carrie McKean, "What We Can Offer If We Uncircle the Wagons," *Christianity Today*, April 16, 2024, https://www.christianitytoday.com/ct/2024/april-web-only/what-we-can-offer-if-we-uncircle-wagons-troubled-henderson.html.

6. "The Secret to the Early Church's Explosive Growth (It's Not What You Think!)," Newbreak Church, accessed April 15, 2024, https://newbreak.church/early-church-growth/.

7. Rodney Stark, *The Rise of Christianity: How the Obscure, Marginal Jesus Movement Became the Dominant Religious Force in the Western World in a Few Centuries* (San Francisco: HarperCollins, 1997), 161.

8. Melissa S. Kearney and Phillip Levine, "US Births Are Down Again, After the COVID Baby Bust and Rebound," Brookings, May 31, 2023, https://www.brookings.edu/articles/us-births-are-down-again-after-the-COVID-baby-bust-and-rebound/; Anna North, "You Can't Even Pay People to Have More Kids," Vox, November 27, 2023, https://www.vox.com/23971366/declining-birth-rate-fertility-babies-children; Alex Fitzpatrick and Kavya Beheraj, "The Birth Rate Ticked Up in 2022. Can the Reversal Last?" Axios, October 4, 2023, https://www.axios.com/2023/10/04/birth-rate-fertility-rate-decline-data-statistics-graph-2022.

9. *State of the Great Commission: Report Prepared for Lausanne Global Congress Seoul 2024* (Lausanne Movement, April 2024), 54–56.

10. *State of the Great Commission*, 56.

11. Jennifer Benz, Lindsey Witt-Swanson, and Daniel Cox, "Faith After the Pandemic: How COVID-19 Changed American Religion," Survey Center on American Life, January 2023, https://www.americansurveycenter.org/research/faith-after-the-pandemic-how-COVID-19-changed-american-religion/.

12. Aaron Earls, "20 Vital Stats for Ministry in 2020," Lifeway Research, January 7, 2020, https://research.lifeway.com/2020/01/07/20-vital-stats-for-ministry-in-2020/.

13. Barna, "A New Chapter in Millennial Church Attendance," August 4, 2022, https://www.barna.com/research/church-attendance-2022/.

14. The Apollos Project, "Millennial Church Attendance and Trends According to Barna Research," Apollos, accessed February 10, 2024, https://www.apollos.app/insights/millennial-church-attendance-and-trends.

15. Ryan Burge, "The Religion of America's Young Adults," Graphs About Religion, September 26, 2024, https://www.graphsaboutreligion.com/p/the-religion-of-americas-young-adults.

Notes

16. Burge, "The Religion of America's Young Adults."

17. See chapter 1 of this book. See also Catherine Wilson, "Building Lasting Faith in Kids: Proven Ideas from Sticky Faith Research," Focus on the Family Canada, accessed July 31, 2024, https://www.focusonthefamily.ca/content/building-lasting-faith-in-kids-proven-ideas-from-sticky-faith-research; "What Makes Faith Stick During College?," Fuller Youth Institute, September 5, 2011, https://fulleryouthinstitute.org/blog/what-makes-faith-stick-during-college; Bob Smietana, "Young Bible Readers More Likely to Be Faithful Adults," Lifeway Research, October 17, 2017, https://research.lifeway.com/2017/10/17/young-bible-readers-more-likely-to-be-faithful-adults-study-finds/.

18. Christian Smith and Phillip Kim, "Family Religious Involvement and the Quality of Parental Relationships for Families with Early Adolescents," National Study of Youth and Religion, University of Notre Dame (2003), https://youthandreligion.nd.edu/assets/102508/family_religious_involvement_and_the_quality_of_parental_relationships_for_families_with_early_adolescents_.pdf; "The Sticky Faith Research," Fuller Youth Institute, accessed July 31, 2024, https://fulleryouthinstitute.org/stickyfaith/research; *The Spiritual Journey: How Evangelicals Come to Faith* (Grey Matter Research & Consulting, 2024), 7–12.

19. *The Spiritual Journey*, executive summary and 18.

20. Glen Stanton, "Leading Factors Leading to Lasting Faith," Focus on the Family, July 24, 2010, https://www.focusonthefamily.com/faith/leading-factors-leading-to-lasting-faith/.

21. Earls, "20 Vital Stats"; Joe Carter, "Survey: Evangelical Teens Differ from Other Christian Teens," The Gospel Coalition, October 17, 2020, https://www.thegospelcoalition.org/article/evangelical-teens-differ-from-other-christian-teens/.

22. *The Spiritual Journey*, executive summary.

23. The percent of teens identifying as Roman Catholic is roughly the same as those identifying as Evangelical, according to Pew Research, but when identifying faith specifics, Catholic teens are only about half as certain about their faith in God as their Evangelical peers and are more in keeping with trends in the general US population. See Robert Mixa, "The New Pew Findings, Catholic Teens, and the Idol of Success," The Word on Fire, September 18, 2020, https://www.wordonfire.org/articles/fellows/the-new-pew-findings-catholic-teens-and-the-idol-of-success/.

24. *The Ripple Effect: Congregations, COVID, and the Future of Church Life* (Grey Matter Research & Consulting, 2021), 6.

25. *The Ripple Effect*, 10.

26. *The Ripple Effect*, 6.

27. Benz, Witt-Swanson, and Cox, "Faith After the Pandemic."

28. Aaron Earls, "Reversing the Shrinking Share of Americans Who Regularly Attend Church," Lifeway Research, June 15, 2023, https://research.lifeway.com/2023/06/15/reversing-the-shrinking-share-of-americans-who-regularly-attend-church/.

29. David Roach, "Church Attendance Dropped Among Young People, Singles, Liberals," *Christianity Today*, January 9, 2023, https://www.christianitytoday.com/news/2023/january/pandemic-church-attendance-drop-aei-survey-young-people-eva.html.

30. Ryan Burge, "The Nones Have Hit a Ceiling," Graphs About Religion, May 20, 2024, https://www.graphsaboutreligion.com/p/the-nones-have-hit-a-ceiling.

31. Ryan Burge, "Evangelicals in America: The Stats May Surprise You," The Gospel Coalition, February 23, 2021, https://www.thegospelcoalition.org/article/evangelicals-surprise/.

32. Roach, "Church Attendance Dropped."

33. Earls, "20 Vital Stats."

34. Burge, "Evangelicals in America."

35. Aaron Earls, "Small Churches Continue Growing—but in Number, Not Size," Lifeway Research, October 20, 2021, https://research.lifeway.com/2021/10/20/small-churches-continue-growing-but-in-number-not-size/.

Notes

36. Shari Finnell, "Church Attendance Is Still Evolving in a Post-Pandemic World," Faith and Leadership, August 8, 2023, https://faithandleadership.com/church-attendance-still-evolving-post-pandemic-world.

37. Earls, "Small Churches Continue Growing"; Scott Thumma, *Twenty Years of Congregational Change: The 2020 Faith Communities Today Overview* (Faith Communities Today, 2021), https://faithcommunitiestoday.org/wp-content/uploads/2021/10/Faith-Communities-Today-2020-Summary-Report.pdf.

38. Ryan Burge, "What Predicts Church Growth or Decline?," Graphs About Religion, March 14, 2024, https://www.graphsaboutreligion.com/p/what-predicts-church-growth-or-decline.

39. Earls, "Small Churches Continue Growing."

40. Earls, "Small Churches Continue Growing."

41. Burge, "Evangelicals in America."

42. Burge, "Evangelicals in America."

43. Aaron Earls, "Church Switchers Highlight Reasons for Congregational Change," *Ministry Watch*, November 9, 2023, https://ministrywatch.com/church-switchers-highlight-reasons-for-congregational-change/.

44. Barna. "Christian Millennials Are Most Likely Generation to Lean Toward Charismatic Worship," July 23, 2020, https://www.barna.com/research/worship-preferences/; Thom S. Rainer, "What Worship Style Attracts the Millennials?," Church Answers, April 2, 2014, https://churchanswers.com/blog/worship-style-attracts-millennials/.

45. Kate Shellnut, "9 in 10 Evangelicals Don't Think Sermons Are Too Long," *Christianity Today*, January 17, 2022, https://www.christianitytoday.com/news/2022/january/evangelical-sermon-length-church-satisfaction-pandemic-surv.html.

46. Jim Davis and Michael Graham with Ryan Burge, *The Great Dechurching: Who's Leaving, Why Are They Going, and What Will It Take to Bring Them Back?* (Grand Rapids: Zondervan, 2023), 163.

47. Bryan Chapell, *Christ-Centered Worship: Letting the Gospel Shape Our Practice* (Grand Rapids: Baker Academic, 2017).

48. Bryan Chapell, *Christ-Centered Preaching: Redeeming the Expository Sermon* (Grand Rapids: Baker Academic, 2018).

49. Jerry Bridges, *Discipline of Grace* (Colorado Springs: NavPress, 2006); Bryan Chapell, *Holiness by Grace: Delighting in the Joy That Is Our Strength* (Wheaton: Crossway, 2011).

50. Kevin Brown, "What the Asbury Revival Taught Me About Gen Z," *Christianity Today*, March 1, 2024, https://www.christianitytoday.com/ct/2024/march/asbury-revival-taught-me-about-gen-z-casual-christianity.html; Kyle Richter and Emilee McEnery, "Gen Z's Biggest Obstacles May Be Their Greatest Gospel Opportunities," The Gospel Coalition, February 11, 2024, https://www.thegospelcoalition.org/article/gen-z-obstacles-opportunities/.

51. "Personalizing Jesus in an Unprecedented Cultural Moment," *Christianity Today*, February 10, 2023, https://www.christianitytoday.com/partners/he-gets-us/data-shows-that-americans-are-spiritually-open.html.

52. Ryan Burge, "How Many People Leave Their Childhood Religion?," Graphs About Religion, July 3, 2023, https://www.graphsaboutreligion.com/p/how-many-people-leave-their-childhood?utm_source=substack&utm_medium.

53. Burge, "How Many People Leave Their Childhood Religion?"

54. Yonat Shimron, "Poll: Americans Growing More Secular by the Year," Religion News Service, December 14, 2021, https://religionnews.com/2021/12/14/poll-america-growing-more-secular-by-the-year/.

55. Philip Ryken, president of Wheaton College, personal report to The Gospel Coalition Council, April 12, 2024.

56. Kevin Brown, "What the Asbury Revival Taught Me about Gen Z."

Notes

57. Jim Denison, "Thousands Attend Mass Worship Event at Mississippi State University," Denison Forum, October 21, 2024, https://www.denisonforum.org/daily-article/thousands-attend-mass-worship-event-at-mississippi-state-university/.

58. Davis and Graham, *The Great Dechurching*, 158.

59. Ryan Burge, "Are People Really Lonely and Miserable?," Graphs About Religion, September 2, 2024, https://www.graphsaboutreligion.com/p/are-people-really-lonely-and-miserable; Mark Legg, "Why Are Teens Sadder, Lonelier, and More Depressed than Ever Before?," Denison Forum, September 6, 2024, https://www.denisonforum.org/current-events/why-are-teens-sadder-lonelier-and-more-depressed-than-ever-before/.

60. Brianna Abbot, "Most Adults Should Be Screened for Anxiety, U.S. Panel Recommends," *Wall Street Journal*, September 20, 2022, https://www.wsj.com/articles/most-adults-should-be-screened-for-anxiety-u-s-panel-recommends-11663686000.

61. Jacqueline Howard, "About 15% of US Children Recently Received Mental Health Treatment, New CDC Data Shows," CNN, June 13, 2023, https://www.kcra.com/article/children-mental-health-treatment/44186947.

62. George Petras, Janet Loehrke, and Veronica Bravo, "Girls, LGBQ+ Teens at Higher Risk for Depression, CDC Mental Health Report Says," *USA Today*, December 28, 2023, https://www.usatoday.com/in-depth/graphics/2023/02/24/cdc-teen-mental-health-report-girls-lgbq-suicide-depression-risk/11262487002/.

63. Petras, Loehrke, and Bravo, "Girls, LGBQ+ Teens."

64. Aaron Earls, "Most Open to Spiritual Conversations, Few Christians Speaking," Lifeway Research, February 22, 2022, https://research.lifeway.com/2022/02/22/most-open-to-spiritual-conversations-few-christians-speaking/.

65. Earls, "Most Open to Spiritual Conversations."

66. Joe Carter, "FactChecker: Do Christian Men Watch More Pornography?," The Gospel Coalition, June 8, 2020, https://www.thegospelcoalition.org/article/factchecker-do-christian-men-watch-more-pornography/.

67. Jon Brown, "Near-Record Low of Americans 'Very Satisfied' with Lives; Married, Regular Churchgoers Among Happiest," *Christian Post*, February 11, 2024, https://www.christianpost.com/news/near-record-low-of-american-very-satisfied-with-life-gallup.html; Joseph Holmes, "The Data-Backed Case for Marriage," *Christianity Today*, February 13, 2024, https://www.christianitytoday.com/ct/2024/february-web-only/data-backed-case-for-marriage-brad-wilcox-get-married-revie.html; Jason S. Carroll and Brian J. Willoughby, "The Myth of Sexual Experience," Institute for Family Studies, April 18, 2023, https://ifstudies.org/blog/the-myth-of-sexual-experience-; Stephen Cranney, "The Influence of Religiosity/Spirituality on Sex Life Satisfaction and Sexual Frequency: Insights from the Baylor Religion Survey," *Review of Religious Research* 62 (2020): 289–314, https://doi.org/10.1007/s13644-019-00395-w; Jeffrey P. Dew, Jeremy E. Uecker, and Brian J. Willoughby, "Joint Religiosity and Married Couples' Sexual Satisfaction," *Psychology of Religion and Spirituality* 12, no. 2 (2020): 201–12, https://www.researchgate.net/publication/329958287_Joint_Religiosity_and_Married_Couples'_Sexual_Satisfaction.

68. Richter and McEnery, "Gen Z's Biggest Obstacles."

69. Barna, "New Chapter in Millennial Church Attendance."

70. Benz, Witt-Swanson, and Cox, "Faith After the Pandemic."

71. ChurchTrac, "The State of Church Attendance: Trends and Statistics [2024]," accessed February 15, 2024, https://www.churchtrac.com/articles/the-state-of-church-attendance-trends-and-statistics-2023.

72. Ryan Burge, "Have the Democrats Lost the Black Church?," Graphs About Religion, April 15, 2024, https://www.graphsaboutreligion.com/p/have-the-democrats-lost-the-black.

73. Jo Adetunji, "US Election: Why Latino and Hispanic Voters Are Shifting to Trump After a Long History of Supporting the Democrats," The Conversation, May 20, 2024, https://theconver

Notes

sation.com/us-election-why-latino-and-hispanic-voters-are-shifting-to-trump-after-a-long-history-of-supporting-the-democrats-229566.

74. Katherine Schaeffer, "Asian Voters in the U.S. Tend to Be Democratic, but Vietnamese American Voters Are an Exception," Pew Research Center, May 25, 2023, https://www.pewresearch.org/short-reads/2023/05/25/asian-voters-in-the-u-s-tend-to-be-democratic-but-vietnamese-american-voters-are-an-exception/.

75. Barna, "New Chapter in Millennial Church Attendance."

76. Ryan Burge, "The Concerns of Young Evangelicals Offer Political Insights for 2024," Religion and Politics, January 17, 2023, https://religionandpolitics.org/2023/01/17/the-concerns-of-young-evangelicals-offer-political-insights-for-2024/.

77. David Wessell, "The U.S. in 2050 Will Be Very Different Than It Is Today," Peter G. Peterson Foundation, accessed February 15, 2024, https://www.pgpf.org/us-2050/research-summary.

78. Wessell, "U.S. in 2050 Will Be Very Different."

79. Chloe-Arizona Fedor, "Nearly Half of the World's Migrants Are Christian, Pew Research Shows," *Christianity Today*, August 21, 2024, https://www.christianitytoday.com/2024/08/christian-migrant-immigration-religion-world-pew-research/.

80. Yonat Shimron, "Religious Groups with Immigrant Members Grew Fastest over Past Decade," Religion News Service, November 11, 2022, https://religionnews.com/2022/11/11/religious-groups-with-immigrant-members-grew-fastest-over-past-decade/.

81. Aleja Hertzler-McCain, "What You Might Miss in News Coverage About Latino Voters and Faith," *National Catholic Reporter*, September 17, 2024, https://www.ncronline.org/news/what-you-might-miss-news-coverage-about-latino-voters-and-faith.

82. Jeffrey M. Jones, "U.S. Church Membership Falls Below Majority for the First Time," Gallup, March 29, 2021, https://news.gallup.com/poll/341963/church-membership-falls-below-majority-first-time.aspx.

83. Hertzler-McCain, "What You Might Miss in News Coverage About Latino Voters and Faith."

84. Ryan Burge, "Hispanic Evangelicals—A Growing Force?," Graphs About Religion, April 1, 2023, https://www.graphsaboutreligion.com/p/hispanic-evangelicals-a-growing-force?utm_source=post-email-title&publication_id=1561197&post_id=142648927&utm_campaign.

85. Andrea Flores, "New Census Numbers Project over 1 in 4 Americans Will Be Latino by 2060," *Los Angeles Times*, November 9, 2023, https://www.latimes.com/delos/story/2023-11-09/new-census-numbers-project-over-1-in-4-americans-will-be-latino-by-2060.

86. Timothy Keller, "The Decline and Renewal of the American Church: Part 2—The Decline of Evangelicalism," Gospel-Changed Minds (Winter 2022), https://quarterly.gospelinlife.com/the-decline-of-evangelicalism/; Burge, "The Nones Have Hit a Ceiling."

87. Benz, Witt-Swanson, and Cox, "Faith After the Pandemic"; Barna, "New Chapter in Millennial Church Attendance"; ChurchTrac, "The State of Church Attendance."

88. Ruth Sax, "80% of Church's Newcomers Watch a Service Online Before Attending in Person," Premier Church News, March 3, 2020, https://premierchristian.news/en/news/article/80-of-church-s-newcomers-watch-a-service-online-before-attending-in-person.

89. "Online Religious Services Appeal to Many Americans, but Going in Person Remains More Popular," Pew Research Center, June 2, 2023, https://www.pewresearch.org/religion/2023/06/02/online-religious-services-appeal-to-many-americans-but-going-in-person-remains-more-popular/.

90. Ryan Burge, "Who Is Attending Online Church?," Graphs About Religion, June 20, 2024, https://www.graphsaboutreligion.com/p/who-is-attending-online-church.

91. O'Reilly, "What Is the Future of Religion in America?"

92. O'Reilly, "What Is the Future of Religion in America?"

Notes

Chapter 8 Hope for the Nations

1. *State of the Great Commission: Report Prepared for Lausanne Global Congress Seoul 2024* (Lausanne Movement, April 2024), 18.

2. Aaron Earls, "7 Encouraging Trends of Global Christianity in 2022," Lifeway Research, January 31, 2022, https://research.lifeway.com/2022/01/31/7-encouraging-trends-of-global-christianity-in-2022/; Pew Research Center, "The Changing Global Religious Landscape," April 5, 2017, https://www.pewresearch.org/religion/2017/04/05/the-changing-global-religious-landscape/.

3. Pew Research Center, "The Changing Global Religious Landscape."

4. Pew Research Center, "The Changing Global Religious Landscape."

5. *State of the Great Commission*, 41.

6. Zach Dawes Jr., "Global Christian Population Projected to Reach 3.3 Billion by 2050," Good Faith Media, February 13, 2023, https://goodfaithmedia.org/global-christian-population-projected-to-reach-3-3-billion-by-2050/.

7. Pew Research Center, "Key Findings from the Global Religious Futures Project," December 21, 2022, https://www.pewresearch.org/religion/2022/12/21/key-findings-from-the-global-religious-futures-project/.

8. *State of the Great Commission*, 66.

9. *State of the Great* Commission, 66.

10. *State of the Great Commission*, 155.

11. Jayson Casper, "Report: Iran Arrested 166 Christians in 2023, Targeting Bible Distributors," *Christianity Today*, February 22, 2024, https://www.christianitytoday.com/news/2024/february/iran-christians-persecution-religious-freedom-2023-report.html; "The World's Fastest Growing Church," Persecution.org, July 20, 2023, https://www.persecution.org/2023/07/20/the-worlds-fastest-growing-church/; Jayson Casper, "Meet the Iranian Christians Crafting an Evangelical Alliance," *Christianity Today*, February 19, 2024, https://www.christianitytoday.com/news/2024/february/iranian-christians-evangelical-alliance-leaders-forum-unity.html.

12. Sophie Drew, "Christianity Rising in Afghanistan Despite Extreme Persecution," Premier Christian News, August 13, 2022), https://premierchristian.news/en/news/article/christianity-rising-in-afghanistan-despite-extreme-persecution.

13. Michael Youssef, "A Movement of God Is Happening Among Muslims—and You're a Part of It," Leading the Way, February 2, 2019, https://www.ltw.org/read/articles/2019/02/a-movement-of-god-is-happening-among-muslims-and-youre-a-part-of-it; Josh Depenbrok, "The Miraculous Way God Is Reaching Muslims Right Now," Global Christian Relief, December 30, 2022, https://globalchristianrelief.org/christian-persecution/stories/the-miraculous-way-god-is-reaching-muslims-right-now/; Duane Alexander Miller and Patrick Johnstone, "Believers in Christ from a Muslim Background: A Global Census," *Interdisciplinary Journal of Research on Religion* 11, art. 10 (2015): 1–19, https://www.religjournal.com/pdf/ijrr11010.pdf; Daniel Pipes, "More Muslims Convert to Christianity than Ever Before," Organiser.org, July 14, 2021, https://organiser.org/2021/07/14/22715/bharat/islam/.

14. "Measuring Religion in China," Pew Research, August 20, 2023, https://www.pewresearch.org/religion/2023/08/30/christianity/; Kevin Drum (personal blog), "How Many People Really Attend Church?," July 16, 2023, https://jabberwocking.com/how-many-people-really-attend-church/.

15. Center for the Study of Global Christianity, "Status of Global Christianity, 2023, in the Context of 1900–2050," accessed July 31, 2024, https://www.gordonconwell.edu/wp-content/uploads/sites/13/2023/01/Status-of-Global-Christianity-2023.pdf.

16. Cf. Earls, "7 Encouraging Trends of Global Christianity," and Victoria S. Harrison, "Religion Statistics," https://www.gla.ac.uk/0t4/humanities/files/mindmapping/Religion1_files/docs/religionstatistics.pdf.

Notes

17. Jim Denison, "70 Million Christians in India Under Increasing Threat of Religious Persecution," Denison Forum, March 1, 2024, https://www.patheos.com/blogs/denisonforum/2024/03/70-million-christians-in-india-under-increasing-threat-of-religious-persecution/.

18. Earls, "7 Encouraging Trends."

19. *State of the Great Commission*, 30; Pew Research Center, "Key Findings from the Global Religious Futures Project"; Gina A. Zurlo, Todd M. Johnson, and Peter F. Crossing, "World Christianity and Mission 2020: Ongoing Shift to the Global South," *International Bulletin of Mission Research* 44, no. 1 (October 16, 2019), https://doi.org/10.1177/239693931988.

20. F. Liorel Young III, "Inside the 'Secret World' of Global Evangelism to Muslims," *Christianity Today*, June 6, 2024, https://www.christianitytoday.com/ct/2024/june-web-only/adriana-carranca-evangelical-mission-gospel-muslims.html.

21. Sarah Breuel, "Is Europe Post-Christian or Pre-Revival?," *Christianity Today*, December 6, 2022, https://www.christianitytoday.com/ct/2022/december-web-only/europe-revival-post-christian-continent-prayer-church-diasp.html.

22. Breuel, "Is Europe Post-Christian or Pre-Revival?"

23. Breuel, "Is Europe Post-Christian or Pre-Revival?"

24. *State of the Great Commission*, 14, 23.

25. Earls, "7 Encouraging Trends."

26. *State of the Great Commission*, 39.

27. Francis Schaeffer, *How Should We Then Live?: The Rise and Decline of Western Thought and Culture* (Grand Rapids: Revell, 1976), 246.

28. *State of the Great Commission*, 52–53.

29. Dan Kois, "The Case for Hanging Out," *Slate*, February 15, 2023, https://slate.com/culture/2023/02/hanging-out-sheila-liming-book-friendship-crisis.html.

30. Robert K. Merton, "Introduction," in Jacques Ellul, *The Technological Society* (New York: Vintage Books, 1964), "Introduction," vi, viii.

31. Merton, "Introduction," vi.

32. *State of the Great Commission*, 155.

33. "Fastest Growing Religion in Each Country Around the World," Brilliant Maps, March 3, 2023, https://brilliantmaps.com/fastest-religion/; Russ Mitchell, "The Top 20 Countries Where Christianity Is Growing the Fastest," Disciple All Nations, August 25, 2013, https://discipleallnations.wordpress.com/2013/08/25/the-top-20-countries-where-christianity-is-growing-the-fastest/; and Jayson Casper, "Middle East Muslims Are Finding Jesus. Can They Fit Within a Weakened Church?," *Christianity Today*, September 26, 2024, https://www.christianitytoday.com/2024/09/lausanne-middle-east-north-africa-evangelical-great-commission-seoul-south-korea/.

34. David Boynton and Marija Vasileva-Blazev, "Half of the World's Population Is Under 30—But They Have Little Say over the Decisions That Shape Their Future," *Fortune*, January 25, 2023, https://fortune.com/europe/2023/01/25/world-population-little-say-decisions-future-young-people-seen-and-heard-halls-of-power-boynton-vasileva-blazev/.

35. Einar H. Dyvik, "Proportion of Selected Age Groups of World Population and in Regions in 2023," Statista, January 5, 2024, https://www.statista.com/statistics/265759/world-population-by-age-and-region/.

36. *State of the Great Commission*, 64.

37. *State of the Great Commission*, 21.

38. *State of the Great Commission*, 14.

39. *State of the Great Commission*, 19.

40. Jerry Wiles, "Orality Methods and Strategy: A Growing Movement," Missio Nexus, September 13, 2017, https://missionexus.org/orality/.

BRYAN CHAPELL, PhD, is a pastor and author known for presenting the heart of the gospel of Jesus Christ around the world. He is president of Unlimited Grace Media, daily broadcasting grace-filled messages in major US cities and streaming coursework for the training of future preachers in 1,500 cities across 90+ nations at BryanChapell.com. He also leads the Administrative Committee of the Presbyterian Church in America, is Pastor Emeritus of the historic Grace Presbyterian Church in Peoria, Illinois, and is President Emeritus of Covenant Seminary in St. Louis, Missouri. Dr. Chapell's numerous books include the bestselling *Christ-Centered Preaching* and *Christ-Centered Worship*. You can join hundreds of thousands who subscribe to his daily devotions of encouragement for Christian living at UnlimitedGrace.com.

Connect with Bryan:

BryanChapell.com

UnlimitedGrace.com

ChristCenteredPreaching.com